DISCARD

TECH GENERATION

TECH GENERATION

Raising Balanced Kids in a Hyper-Connected World

Mike Brooks, Ph.D.,

AND Jon Lasser, Ph.D.

OXFORD
UNIVERSITY PRESS

OXFORD
UNIVERSITY PRESS

Oxford University Press is a department of the University of Oxford. It furthers
the University's objective of excellence in research, scholarship, and education
by publishing worldwide. Oxford is a registered trade mark of Oxford University
Press in the UK and certain other countries.

Published in the United States of America by Oxford University Press
198 Madison Avenue, New York, NY 10016, United States of America.

© Oxford University Press 2018

CIP data is on file at the Library of Congress
ISBN 978-0-19-066529-6

9 8 7 6 5 4 3 2

Printed by Sheridan Books, Inc., United States of America

Contents

Preface | vii

Acknowledgments | xi

1. Introduction | 1

2. Technology in Our Lives | 19

3. Is Our Technology Making Us Any Happier? | 35

4. The Pull of Our Screens | 57

5. The Effects of Technology on Children and Families | 81

6. Foundations of the Relationship | 103

7. Building the Relationship | 113

8. The Green Light Level: Prevention | 129

9. The Yellow Light Level: Addressing Emerging Concerns | 161

10. The Red Light Level: When Strong Intervention Is
    Necessary | 179

11. Parenting, Technology, and Schooling | 201

12. Summary | 219

APPENDIX 1: FAMILY ASSESSMENT OF SCREEN TIME (FAST) | 237
APPENDIX 2: QUICK-REFERENCE GUIDE TO STRATEGIES
                FOR A TECH HAPPY LIFE | 241
APPENDIX 3: FAQs FOR A TECH HAPPY LIFE | 249
APPENDIX 4: TECH HAPPY LIFE: RESOURCES | 269
NOTES | 271
INDEX | 307

Preface

As parents, we make decisions every day about how we should raise our kids. We put time and energy into ensuring that their needs are met. While every family is unique, we generally want our kids to be physically healthy, to do well in school, to maintain friendships, to develop interests and hobbies, and to engage with family members. If you are looking for how to best achieve these goals, there are literally thousands of parenting books on the market. Where is a busy parent to start?

Many of the published books offer solutions that are designed to be short and simple, and there's something about a quick fix that many people find appealing. After all, if a child's disobedience is disruptive at home and school, one is highly motivated to solve the problem as soon as possible. But as psychologists and parents, we know that parenting challenges rarely have simple solutions. Often, change comes from improving underlying relationships. If you are concerned about your child's use of technology in his or her daily life, then you have come to the right place. In our clinical practices and in our own homes we have observed the ways in which technology has affected the lives of children and families. There have certainly been some positive influences, such as greater capacities to communicate and to be entertained. But many parents express concern that screen time adversely affects the quality of family time and academics. While there are no quick fixes to these thorny problems in life, there is definitely hope. Just as a person can become physically fit with determination, a plan, and hard work, families can learn to achieve a more balanced use of technology. The good news is that the changes that we make now can have an immediate impact as well as benefits for years to come.

Because we know that technology is pervasive and that many parents are hungry for answers, we wrote this book to address these major concerns, emphasizing the role of prevention and providing research-based information that may be helpful in reducing excessive or unhealthy screen-time usage. While we offer guidance on issues such as when kids should get smartphones and how much screen time kids should be allowed, we offer an approach to such issues that's more flexible than the simple rules and admonitions one might get from a quick fix. Complex problems must be addressed with recognition that context and individual differences matter. A one-size-fits-all approach can't ever fit all.

This book opens with some background information about what technology has to offer, as well as the very real costs that come with it. We have much to gain in the areas of information, entertainment, and social connectivity, but many of us pay for it with sleep loss, distractibility, and diminished face-to-face interaction in real life. If these background chapters interest you less and you are more interested in taking action right away, feel free to skip ahead to Chapter 7 after reading the introductory chapter. It is there that we introduce our Tech Happy Life model, which you can put into use right away.

We've developed our approach based on our experiences as researchers, clinicians, and parents. Dr. Mike Brooks earned his doctorate in Educational Psychology and has been a gamer since the dawn of the video game era. He did his dissertation research on the effects of video game violence on children, and he worked as a usability specialist in the tech sector in the first decade of the 2000s. He has been presenting on the effects of technology for over a decade to schools, parents, students, and community groups. In his clinical practice, Dr. Brooks frequently works with kids, teens, and families to help them find a healthy screen balance. Now a father of three school-aged boys who love video games as much as their dad, he is constantly working to manage the strong pull of the screens—on his kids and on himself!

Dr. Jon Lasser earned a Ph.D. in Educational Psychology and has worked as a university professor and psychologist in the public schools, as well as a clinician in private practice, serving children and families from preschool through high school. With two daughters now in their twenties, he has had direct experience navigating the rocky terrain of screen time with his own children. In his private practice, Dr. Lasser works with children and their parents to promote social, emotional, and behavioral wellness. In many cases, Dr. Lasser works with kids and their parents to deal with the many challenges presented by screen time in family life. He is the Associate Dean for Research in the College of Education at Texas State University.

We hope you'll find that this book stands out from other resources because our approach emerges from a relationship model. In other words, how we interact with and relate to our family members guides how we spend our family time, shapes the way we communicate, and informs our decisions about boundaries, limits, and discipline. This book isn't a recipe for a six-week digital detox, but rather a blueprint from which parents and caregivers can draw both inspiration and guidance. Moreover, our approach can help with parenting in the broader sense, not merely with regard to screen use.

Most chapters have some brief vignettes that will likely resonate with you. Many of us have experienced frustrations around kids who don't want to relinquish digital devices. Some parents recognize that the adults in the house have not themselves modeled the balance that they would like to see in their kids. If the examples provided in the book seem realistic, it's because they have been adapted from examples we've observed in our own families and in our clinical practices. Some of these vignettes were also inspired by discussions with friends and colleagues. We have changed names and other details to maintain confidentiality.

We hope that you find this book helpful and that it promotes family conversations about technology. The goal is quite simple: *to help get the best out of technology to improve our lives, while taking steps to minimize its negative effects.* While we offer no instant remedies to such a challenging problem, our Tech Happy Life model can provide both strategies and guidance to help you and your family achieve the balance that you seek.

Mike Brooks, Ph.D., LSSP Licensed Psychologist and Licensed Specialist in School Psychology, Director of the Austin Psychology & Assessment Center (ApaCenter)

Jon Lasser, Ph.D., LSSP Licensed Psychologist and Licensed Specialist in School Psychology, Professor and Associate Dean, Texas State University

Acknowledgments

Dr. Brooks: I would like to acknowledge my wonderful wife, Kirsten, for her love and support over the years. I truly could not have done this without you, HB! I would also like to thank my three sons, Archer, Kai, and Torben, for the joy that they bring me, as well as for being my teachers with regard to balancing our family's use of technology. It's a moving target! To my good friend and collaborator, Jon Lasser, thanks for opening the door to this project! What a ride it's been! I want to give a special shout out to four amazing people who helped with so many aspects of this project: Caroline Phillips, Briana Brukilacchio, Dr. Laura Frame, and Dr. Kristen Beers. Ya'll rock! Many thanks go to my lovely sister, Amy McAndrew, for providing her assistance and just for being such a great sister. I also want to thank my many colleagues at the Austin Psychology & Assessment Center (ApaCenter) for supporting me through this project and providing invaluable input and feedback. To Tom Richardson, I just want to say thanks for being my best bud all of these years. Mom and Dad—thanks for the foundation that you have given me to remember what matters most in life. I know that you'd both get a real kick out of this book! To my many mentors and teachers over the years, especially Drs. Diane Schallert and Deborah Tharinger, thanks for your inspiration and support. Finally, I'd like to thank all of the creators of the video games that I've played and sci-fi/fantasy shows that I've watched throughout my lifetime. Screens can bring great joy, but they are best when they are a shared experience! May the Force be with you! Live long and prosper! The North remembers!

Dr. Lasser: Writing a book that provides research-based guidance for families around the use of technology presents unique and daunting challenges. I surely wouldn't take on the task alone and am grateful for my friend and co-author Mike Brooks. I also wish to acknowledge Illysa Foster, my best friend and wife, for taking the time to read chapters and provide valuable feedback and edits. My daughters, Jasmine and Sage, shared insight from a young adult perspective that may have otherwise eluded this middle-aged man. Much of the tedious searching for articles and citations fell to my graduate assistants, Bobbi Davenport and Michele Monserrate, and their help is greatly appreciated. Sarah Harrington has been tremendously helpful as an editor and sounding board, working with us from the initial proposal stage all the way to the finish line, and this book would not have been possible without her guidance and assistance. Finally, I wish to acknowledge the many families and teachers who shared with us their struggles and successes in trying to figure out how to sail through these choppy waters. Onward!

TECH GENERATION

1

Introduction

Diane was exasperated. Her son and daughter, age five and seven, asked incessantly for permission to play games on the iPad and would often throw a tantrum when she said no. When she did say yes, she dreaded telling them that their time was up, as they would invariably challenge her limit setting and beg for more time. She didn't object to iPad games— she even enjoyed them from time to time herself. But she also wanted her kids to have opportunities to be active outside and express themselves creatively. In her effort to establish some boundaries around screen time, she felt exhausted by the battles when her kids resisted.

Evan came home late one night from a business trip and was surprised to see the light on in his 15-year-old daughter Kelsey's room. Evan opened the door and saw his daughter on her phone, most likely using Snapchat. Evan gave Kelsey a kiss, asked her to turn off her phone and go to bed. Kelsey looked disappointed, but complied after some frantic texting. Evan looked at his watch—12:48 a.m.! He shook his head and went to bed, wondering whether his wife even knew that Kelsey had been up so late after she had gone to bed. Evan worried that Kelsey's social media use was interfering with her much-needed sleep.

Diane and Evan's stories are our stories, too. As parents, we have struggled with the challenges of raising children in a hyper-connected world. If you're reading this book, you probably share our concerns and are searching for some guidance. One of the best places to start is with a parent screen time checklist. (see Box 1.1).

BOX 1.1 Place a check next to the following
statements if they apply to you

☐ I'm concerned that my kids have too much screen time (e.g., computer, television, smartphone, video games, iPad, tablet).

☐ I want my kids to be more engaged with the world and the people around them.

☐ I worry that children's access to technology can compromise their safety.

☐ To be successful adults, children need to be comfortable with advanced technology.

☐ I give my kids access to some technologies because most of their peers already have access, and I don't want my kids to be left out.

☐ It's not clear to me at what age kids are ready for some technologies (e.g., smartphones, social media, and certain video games).

☐ It's hard to find the right balance between kids' needs for screen time and non-screen time.

If you checked any of the items in Box 1.1, then you share something with us: a belief that kids benefit from technology, but that there need to be some limits in place to avoid potential problems. Our goal with this book is to provide practical, useful solutions for parents who struggle with balancing kids' use of technology. We want to maximize the many benefits of technology while minimizing the negatives.

When we talk to parents about these issues, we hear questions such as the following:

• When should I introduce my children to electronic media?
• How much screen time should kids have?

- When should I get my child a smartphone?
- When should I allow my child/teen access to social media?
- How do I know if it's too much screen time?
- What do I do if my child is abusing or misusing technology?

Easy answers to these questions are hard to come by because each family is unique. So, a one-size-fits-all approach won't work for everyone. Within these pages you will find a resource that's easy to read, research based, and flexible enough for all kinds of families with kids of different ages. What you're reading isn't a prescription for healthy technology use, but rather a guide that will help you make informed parenting decisions around family technology usage.

As psychologists, we're sensitive to the idea of *developmentally appropriate* technology and media for children and adolescents. Video games and apps have rating systems, much like those used for movies, that help parents determine whether kids are ready for a variety of entertainment options. However, the rules are less clear when it comes to the appropriate ages for tablets, smartphones, and access to social media platforms. This book aims to eliminate some of the guesswork for parents trying to raise *balanced* kids in a hyper-connected world.

Out-of-Balance Technology Use

If they can look up from their own smartphones, tablets, and laptops long enough, what some parents see in their kids' technology use may alarm them. Many children under the age of two have access to digital media, even though the American Academy of Pediatrics reports that "for children younger than 2 years, evidence for benefits of media is still limited, adult interaction with the child during media use is crucial, and there continues to be evidence of harm from excessive digital media use."[1] Parents have seen a rapid growth in the number of apps, technologies, and television programs intended to improve skills like reading, math, problem-solving, and memory.

Yet a quick glance reveals some unsettling statistics regarding toddlers' and kids' screen time, causing parents to weigh the risks and benefits of an increasingly hyper-connected world:[2,3]

- 38% of kids under the age of two have had access to media on a mobile device
- Preschool children average around four hours of TV/video time during weekdays[4]
- 44% of elementary school children use smartphones regularly
- Kids aged eight years old and under spend only 3.6% of their screen time on homework or accessing educational content.

Adolescent and young adult use of technology looks disturbing as well. When we look around, teens can be seen clutching their smartphones, regardless of whether they are using them—as if the smartphones were part of their bodies. Even when they are socializing in groups, teens are often texting away and not even really socializing much with the friends who are standing right next to them!

Amber, age 18, was on a special European summer vacation with her parents before she was to leave for college. Amber was very active on social media and used Instagram and Snapchat to keep in almost constant contact with her friends. She hoped to share her European adventures with them as she experienced them.

Amber's parents had been saving money for quite some time to create an experience together that they hoped to cherish for years to come. While in Tuscany, Amber was frustrated about spotty cellular service. She wanted to post selfies to Instagram and Snapchat with the picturesque Tuscan landscape in the background. She became so obsessed with finding cellular service that she stopped appreciating her surroundings altogether. She got into some heated arguments with her parents about this. In exasperation, she screamed at them, "You don't understand! If I can't share all this with my friends, what's the point?!" Her parents were both hurt and frustrated by their daughter's behavior. They felt particularly sad that they had paid so much money for what was supposed to be a magical, bonding trip with their daughter who was about to leave home.

Some of the unsettling statistics regarding teens' technology use include the following:[5,6,7,8,9]

- Teens aged 13–18 average nine hours of entertainment media use per day, excluding screen use for school or homework
- 24% of teens report using the Internet "almost constantly"
- 50% of teens report "feeling addicted" to their phones, and 59% of parents report that they feel that their teens are addicted to their phones
- 32% of youth (aged 10–23) have posted personal information (e.g., Social Security number) online, 32% have posted their phone number, and 11% have posted their home address
- 23% of youth (aged 10–23) have witnessed cruelty online and 13% report being a victim of it
- Between 8% and 38% of girls and boys report viewing images of sexual violence or child pornography online before age 18
- Over 90% of boys in the United States report that they have viewed pornography online before age 18.

Given the amount of time that kids and teens are viewing various screens, there are good reasons to be concerned that their screen time is out of balance and that the content available to them may present significant health and safety risks.

What Do We Mean by *Balanced*?

A balanced approach to the use of technology aims to reap the advantages of screen time and to reduce its negative aspects. We like technology and think that it serves many useful purposes in our professional and personal lives. These benefits include increased productivity and creativity, enhanced communication, and easy access to multiple forms of entertainment. However, we also know that too much of a good thing can be detrimental, so by *balance* we don't mean that technology should be eliminated. Rather, we think that parents can be thoughtful and considerate about setting limits and monitoring technology use. This helps children and families gain the many positives of technology while minimizing its adverse effects.

Ultimately, one of the goals of parenting is to help children learn self-regulation. After all, they will eventually leave our active care, and we want them to go with the values and skills to manage their lives effectively. We keep this goal of the balanced use of technology in mind throughout this book.

Technology as the Double-Edged Sword

There remains little doubt that technology has enhanced our lives and has brought great happiness and productivity to children and adults alike. Microprocessors, broadband Internet, and wireless technologies have enhanced our capacities to connect with one another, create, collaborate, play, and share with greater ease, freedom, and efficiency. To be clear, this book is not about demonizing screens, but rather acknowledging some of the concerns associated with too much screen time and promoting solutions to those problems.

Ironically, aspects of our lives that have been enhanced the most by technological change have also become the most vulnerable. French cultural theorist Paul Virilio observed, "The invention of the ship was also the invention of the shipwreck" (Dumoucel, 2010). One can say the same about social media platforms, such as Facebook and Instagram, which facilitate communication and social connection. The ease of connection afforded by these platforms also opens the door to cyberbullying, sexual predation, distracted driving, and sexting.

Curiously, in an effort to enhance relationships through social media, often teens (and adults) experience fewer meaningful relationships.

What does it look like when we're out of balance with technology?

- Decreased face-to-face social interaction
- Reduced or disrupted sleep
- Decreases in focused, uninterrupted attention
- Decreased productivity
- Limited physical activity
- Previous interests and recreational activities replaced almost exclusively by technology
- Decreased sense of well-being.

So what does balance look like? Since each family is unique, balance will look different for everyone. Ideally, families that achieve balance feel good about the amount of technology in their lives. Each family member is relatively comfortable with how other family members use their technology. Also, a balanced use of technology means that individuals are able to effectively meet their own physical, educational, social, and psychological needs so that they are, in a sense, happy and productive. But we also recognize that balance is a moving target. As children mature and the available technologies change, parents will continue to re-evaluate, monitor, and have conversations with their family members about how they can best obtain the positives that technology has to offer without letting it interfere with overall happiness. In this sense, *balance* can be considered an ongoing process that requires monitoring and adjustments.

It's Not Just the Kids!

Brittany, age 15, expressed ongoing frustration to her therapist about her mother's cell phone use. "When she picks me up from school, she won't get off of her cell phone! She doesn't even stop to ask me how my day went. She keeps talking on it all the way home." True to form, when her mother picked her up from sessions, Ms. Jones was on her cell phone from the moment she walked into the office until the moment she left. The therapist attempted to address these issues with the mother, but she was not receptive to changing her own behavior.

Parents can be out of balance as well, particularly if they are spending too much time on their devices at the expense of meaningful interactions with their children. We serve as models for our kids and must think about the examples we set when we spend too much time on our computers and phones. As parents, we don't get a free pass just because we are engaging in work. From our kids' perspectives, we are disengaging from the family and our relationships to check texts and email, get news updates, and post to Facebook. In a 2016 survey conducted by the nonprofit organization Common Sense Media, 28% of teens reported that they felt like their parents were addicted to their phones, and 27% of parents reported that they felt addicted to their phones.[10] Like the old anti-drug public service announcement on TV, many of our kids might rightly claim, "I learned it from watching you!"[11,12]

Technology as "Death by a Thousand Cuts"

While screen time poses many dangers (e.g., sexting, cyberbullying, texting while driving), perhaps there is one subtler danger that supersedes all the rest. It is the insidious way that screen time has infiltrated all of our lives. Technology has become so much a part of our lives that we cannot imagine being without it. Not only kids, but also parents, seem tethered to cell phones. These cell phones capture all of the promises and challenges of technology in one small but immensely powerful device that fits into the palm of our hands. We have gone beyond being "connected" to often being "hyper-connected"—to our detriment and that of those around us as well.

The allure of technology is like the seductive nature of the Dark Side of The Force in the *Star Wars* mythology. Our original intentions are good, but then the technology begins to have a power over us. We are no longer using it to serve our wants or needs. Instead, we become beholden to it, like servants who must constantly respond to its bidding.

Our kids and teens are particularly vulnerable to the siren's call of technology. Indeed, there is some evidence to suggest that young brains are susceptible to becoming "wired" for and dependent upon technology to get periodic "fixes." It appears that the same reward system in the brain that is involved in drug addiction is also involved in behavioral addictions such as gambling and, possibly, use of digital technologies.[13,14,15,16]

Moreover, it may be that we have all become conditioned to respond to the sounds of our phones—much like Pavlov's dogs, who were trained to salivate upon hearing the sound of a metronome that was repeatedly paired with food. According to University of Michigan neuroscientist Dr. Kent Berridge, the "ding" of our phones likely cues us to respond the same way that Pavlov's metronome cued his dogs to salivate.[17] Essentially, technologies such as texting and social media appear to create an itch that must be scratched. The constant pull of technology that causes us to be tethered to our screens is leading to the proverbial "death by a thousand cuts."

Our Happiness Can Be Undermined by Technology

It can be argued that our primary goal in life is to seek happiness and minimize suffering. We are not talking about happiness through stimulating our nerve endings, which is more accurately referred to as *pleasure*. That has its place in life, but we all know that seeking too much pleasure can lead to *a lot* of unhappiness. We are talking about a deep-rooted contentment in life. In a sense, every goal we have in life, such as attending a competitive college and getting a "good" job, ultimately is aimed at increasing our sense of happiness or well-being. As parents, our long-term goal is to raise happy kids who grow into well-adjusted adults.

Our incessant use of technology poses a formidable and insidious threat to our happiness. We are happiest in life when we are engaged in it. This is particularly true of our relationships, with which much of our happiness is inextricably linked.[18] When we are engaged in meaningful, positive, need-satisfying relationships, we tend to feel happy. On the other hand, when we are feeling alienated, isolated, rejected, or in conflict, we tend to feel quite unhappy.

The grip that our screens have on our kids—*and on us*—results in us constantly checking our devices, and our attention is being subverted at chronic and fundamental levels. Linda Stone, a former Apple and Microsoft executive, refers to the current era as the Age of Interruption, defined by "continuous partial attention." In this state, our attention is nearly always fragmented and distributed across various platforms, motivated by a desire for connectedness (to social media, email, news) rather than productivity and relationships.[19] To paraphrase lyrics from a Pink Floyd song, "We have become . . . comfortably distracted." Yet our engagement in life and relationships is *dependent upon* our sustained attention. If we do not learn to regulate our screen time, our kids' well-being, as well as our own, might be significantly impaired.

There is considerable evidence that rates of clinical and subclinical mental health problems are growing in adolescents and young adults. In the case of depression alone, there has been a 37% increase in major depressive episodes from 2005 to 2014.[20] Alarmingly, 49.5% of kids and teens are estimated to have a diagnosable mental health issue, while only 7.4% receive any mental health care within a given year. Even these distressing statistics are likely to underestimate the true scope of the mental health issues our children currently face.[21]

It is very possible that teens' and young adults' compulsive use of devices is contributing to the rise in mental health issues during adolescence. For example, research has shown that the *mere presence* of cell phones (i.e., the cell phone is not actually even being used, it is just visible) diminishes the quality of face-to-face communication.[22,23] Cornell University developmental psychologist Dr. Janis Whitlock, a leading expert in youth mental health, suspects that the primary cause of modern teens' unhappiness is the "cauldron of stimulus that they can't get away from, or don't want to get away from, or don't know how to get away from."[24]

It is likely that many factors contribute to the burgeoning problem of mental health issues in youths. A mindful use of technology has the potential to improve our health, productivity, and well-being. It might be a case, given the double-edged sword that technology represents, that we are not particularly adept at maximizing the positives of technology and minimizing the negatives. Regardless, alleviating mental health issues such as anxiety and depression requires one's attention. One must recognize them as problems to be addressed and must seek out various supports and resources. If an individual who is suffering from mental health issues is constantly distracted by technology, then he or she will not likely be able to make the changes necessary to improve well-being effectively.

Our Approach

A Holy Grail of parenting is that our kids become adept at self-regulation, including with regard to technology use. As much as we feel compelled to guide, manage, and control their lives, our kids must learn to make their own healthy decisions to become successful adults. Again, we want our kids to be able to have the numerous pros of technology while minimizing the often subtle cons of technology. Our approach to technology balance is based on a few basic principles:

- *Parenting style matters.* We support the use of a research-based parenting style (called *authoritative parenting*), characterized by a combination of warmth and limit-setting, that applies well to managing screen-time challenges at home. The challenges of screen time are addressed within an authoritative parenting framework.

- *We influence our children through our relationship.* When we are trying to guide our children into having healthy relationships with technology, we must first step back and examine our relationships with them. This is where the influence that we have with our children regarding technology use is nested. The stronger and more positive the relationship with our kids, the more likely we are to influence them in positive ways concerning technology.[25,26,27] However, if our relationships with our children are conflictual or adversarial, it is unlikely that they will be receptive to our efforts to guide their technology use. In fact, in such cases, they might do the opposite of what we are suggesting just to spite us!

- *We are their role models.* Just as it is important to model healthy exercise and eating habits for our children, it is essential that we use our own technologies in healthy ways.[28] Otherwise, we might end up modeling the unhealthy habits that we are trying to prevent!

- *Support rather than control.* If we want to make good family decisions around technology and set and maintain appropriate limits, then we need to work *with* our children (rather than against them) to establish a healthy balance. To support the skill development of self-regulation, it's critical that we do not try to completely control all of our children's screen time. While we can (and should) have greater control over our kids when they are very young, we must allow them more autonomy as they get older.[29] Otherwise, they do not get to practice the important skill of self-regulation.

- *Prevention works best.* It's much easier to invest a little time on the front end to prevent technological imbalance than to try to restore balance once things get out of control. Our Tech Happy Life model is based on a three-tiered public health approach (preventing, addressing, and intervening), but these three tiers rest upon an important foundation: *the relationship between you and your child.* That relationship determines the effectiveness of your role as a guide and teacher. We also recognize that some readers may feel like they missed the opportunity for prevention, so we provide resources for families at all three tiers.
- *It's never too late.* Some parents tell us that they feel as if technology has sucked their kids into a black hole, with no chance of them ever emerging. They might also say things like, "Oh, no! We should never have let our son get a smartphone so young! We already blew it!" To that we say that it's never too late to take inventory, set some realistic goals, and begin to restore balance.

A Starting Point

In order to make healthy decisions about technology use, family members need to communicate about their values and expectations. One starting point for this ongoing conversation is a discussion about current practices. Do we have too much "screen time" in our lives, not enough, or is it just about right? *Screen time* may include use of smartphones, computers (desktop or laptop), tablets, video games, iPad, TVs, and so on. Take a moment to sit down with your family and have each family member who is old enough to participate read and complete the survey, the Family Assessment of Screen Time (FAST), found in Appendix 1. Each member of the family should think about whether he or she currently doesn't have enough screen time, uses too much screen time, or falls at some point between the extremes.

After all family members have rated their own screen time, they should then rate their views of other family members' screen time. Next, after everyone has completed the ratings independently, ask the following questions, allowing everyone an opportunity to answer. A few ground rules:

1. Each perspective is valuable, so avoid criticizing or judging. The opinions of your family members matter!
2. Everyone gets a turn, so listen carefully to others when it's their turn.
3. The focus is on what we think and feel right now, not on the past or the future.

Discussion Questions

1. What made you choose that spot on the line?
2. What do we gain from screen time? How does it help us?
3. What do we lose from screen time? How does it hurt us?
4. How do we know when it is out of balance? What does too much screen time even look like?
5. This book is about finding the right balance between screen time and other activities. What would a good balance look like to you?

Now that you've had a chance to discuss this as a family, take some time to think about each family member's point of view. Honestly assessing the role of technology in your family requires that every member's perspective be taken into consideration.

The Tech Happy Life Model

As parents, we are motivated to find ways to raise healthy, well-adjusted kids using efficient strategies that are in harmony with our values. As such, we're always looking for ways to prevent problems, rather than solve them, whenever possible. Why? Because it saves time, energy, and ultimately makes for happier kids and parents. There is powerful wisdom in the old adage, "an ounce of prevention is worth a pound of cure." This is particularly useful in our management of technology in the family. We would much rather prevent battles over screen time than fight those battles. As realists, we know that we can't prevent all problems, so we try to tailor our approach to match the magnitude of the concern. We call this our Tech Happy Life model, and in the following we explain how it works. The basic idea is that there are three levels at which we can tackle screen-time problems, and we should be able to address specific concerns at one of those levels, depending on the situation (Figure 1.1). Using the Tech Happy Life model, we can achieve a healthy balance of electronic media in our family lives and effectively manage concerns as

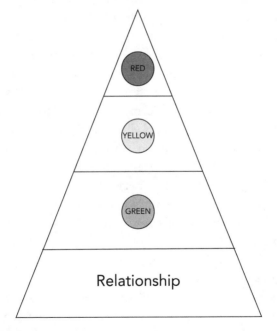

FIGURE 1.1

The Tech Happy Life Model

they arise. (By the way, we didn't invent this approach. It comes from the field of public health.[30] We've applied it to families and technology because the principles have been demonstrated to work in other areas, and they fit squarely with our own ideas.)

The *Green Light Level* is all about prevention. If technology overuse were a medical condition like obesity, strategies within the Green Light Level would include things like regular exercise and healthy food choices. The idea is that, since obesity hasn't set in yet, we take steps to prevent it entirely. The costs of strategies used within the Green Light Level are relatively small when compared to the enormous expenditures associated with treating disease. So, when we spend a little time and effort now nurturing and reinforcing our relationships with our kids, we save a lot later by not having to tackle screen-time problems after they have developed.

Continuing with obesity as our example, let's say we go to the doctor for an annual checkup and she tells us we've gained some weight and have high blood pressure. Now more active measures are needed to get back to a healthier state. We address those concerns with *Yellow Light Level* approaches. We may have to exercise more, or go on a diet. When it comes to screen time, this might involve something like requiring homework to be completed before kids are allowed to have recreational screen time, as well as strictly enforcing time limits.

Many (if not most) people who follow *Yellow Light Level* recommendations will be able to reduce or eliminate the concerns that raised red flags in the first place. We get our weight back down, or technology overuse improves. Most important, the behavioral changes introduced at the *Yellow Light Level* often become lifestyle changes that are maintained over time for long-term benefit. In a sense, we find ourselves "returned" to *the Green Light Level* (Table 1.1).

Some of us may need more intensive intervention after *Yellow Light Level* efforts have been tried and proven unsuccessful. So, let's imagine that following changes in diet and exercise, one is still overweight, and now has certain health problems (e.g., extremely high cholesterol levels, partially blocked arteries). *Red Light Level*

TABLE 1.1 The Tech Happy Life Model Level Descriptions

Level	Level Name	Focus of the Level
Level 3	Red Light	*Intervening* to fix serious problems
Level 2	Yellow Light	*Addressing* minor issues
Level 1	Green Light	*Preventing* concerns
Foundation	The Relationship	*Building a strong bond* with our children

intervention might involve medication, or possibly even surgical intervention. In the case of screen time, *Red Light Level* might mean, for instance, removal of a video game system or replacement of a smartphone with a flip phone.

As you learn more about the model later in the book, you'll note that there appears to be considerable overlap between the parenting strategies at various levels. This is deliberate and consistent with our model. In the public health area, professionals advise us to wash hands to prevent illness and then seek medical attention when we become ill, but that doesn't mean we discontinue hand washing. In our Tech Happy Life model, parents utilize multiple strategies to varying degrees, but the intensity of the interventions is adjusted to match the severity of their concerns.

We have added another component to this public health model approach to the balanced use of technology that we believe is essential for the effectiveness of the model. We think that strong relationships with our kids are crucial for the three levels of the model to be successful. We influence our children through our relationships with them, and the stronger the relationship, the more likely it will be that we can influence them in positive ways. So, it is critical that we take great care as parents to invest the time, energy, and attention necessary to build this positive bond with our kids. Our own media use can undermine this goal!

Our focus is on the application of the public health model to technology use in our families. The promises and challenges of technology are here to stay and will only grow in orders of magnitude in the years to come. We are only at the tip of this very formidable iceberg. While there is no way to put this genie back into the bottle, there are powerful ways to capitalize on the benefits of screens while reducing the downsides.

As parents, it is our responsibility to help our children learn to find and maintain a healthy life balance in this challenging hyperconnected world. While there aren't any simple solutions to this increasingly difficult problem, there are powerful and effective ways that we as parents can make a difference. In the chapters that follow, we will describe the challenges of technology in more detail, as well as how to use the Tech Happy Life approach to help you and your children find greater balance.

2

Technology in Our Lives

Blake and Jack, both age 11, are neighborhood friends who have been gaming in one form or another since they were toddlers. If their respective parents left it up to them, the boys would play video games until they passed out from exhaustion . . . and that's only a very slight exaggeration. Their parents try to limit them to about two hours of recreational screen time per day, but in the summer it is a struggle to keep to that limit. Although they enjoy gaming together, Blake and Jack complain that they are "bored" and that "there's nothing to do" if they aren't allowed to play video games or watch videos. Both Blake and Jack are fairly sedentary, and their parents worry about their lack of fitness, weight gain, and limited in-person socialization.

Despite their best efforts, their parents have been unable to get Blake and Jack to be more active and to spend more time outdoors during the summer. However, Blake and Jack are longtime Pokémon fans, and in the summer of 2016 they both became enthralled with the alternate reality game Pokémon Go. In the game, players use the GPS on their smartphones to locate, capture, and collect Pokémon, the name of which is an abbreviation for "pocket monsters." Players then power up their Pokémon, evolve them into stronger versions, and use them in battles against other Pokémon. Since downloading the game to their smartphones, Blake and Jack have been roaming the neighborhood for hours collecting Pokémon and socializing with other neighborhood kids who are also players. Their circle of friends and physical activity have expanded since playing Pokémon Go. Their parents are pleased and have backed off some on their screen-time limits for them. On the downside, everywhere they travel, whether to the lake, hiking, or out to eat, Blake and Jack want to pull out their smartphones and look for more Pokémon. This has resulted in chronic struggles over the boys' access to the game.

What do you think of Blake and Jack? Should their parents allow them to have extra screen time? What should they do about limiting their access to the game? Should they even have smartphones to begin with? What has been lost? What has been gained? Do the pros of *Pokémon Go* outweigh the cons?

We live in a rapidly changing technological world that is filled with Facebook, Instagram, Twitter, PlayStations, iPhones, tablets, Fitbits, YouTube, Netflix, and, more recently, virtual reality headsets. By the time you read this, some of these technologies will likely have evolved. These advances aren't going to slow down. Google, Facebook, Apple, Amazon, and other companies are constantly trying to innovate and to offer technological advances to keep ahead of one another and the upstart competitors that try to establish themselves.

Andy, age eight, has many sets of Legos and Bionicles that he has received over the years for birthdays and Christmases. While he enjoys putting together the boxed sets that usually take him from 10 minutes to a couple of hours, he doesn't play with them afterward. Some go on shelves for display, but most of them go into one of his many toy bins and fall apart over time. He doesn't really notice or care to fix them. He doesn't take them out and use his imagination to create his own houses, buildings, new creatures, or epic battles.

His Buzz Lightyear, Woody, and other Toy Story figures are grouped into one very large toy bin that is gathering dust. But he spends almost two hours daily, and more on weekends and when allowed, building his worlds in Minecraft. He often gathers with a few of his neighborhood friends to play it on an iPad. Several of them are a few years older than him, but they all seem to enjoy the experience. They share tips, strategies, and show off their latest creations. He has another group of online friends with whom he plays the PC version of Minecraft. *Even when he isn't playing it, he and his friends talk incessantly about it. Andy doesn't really like playing with his toys, but he still loves to play.*

We have come so far in relatively little time. The first home computers of the 1980s seem laughably weak in comparison to the technologies we use today. From 1956 to 2015, experts calculate that the total processing power of computers and other devices has undergone a 1 trillion-fold increase.[1] While it is not easy to compare performance of old technologies to that of new ones, based upon CPU speeds, the iPhone X, which contains 6 CPU cores that work together, runs about 10,000 times faster than the Apollo guidance computer that landed men on the moon in 1969.[2,3]

The rate of technological development has far outpaced that of human evolution. The oldest known fossil records of *Homo sapiens* are about 300,000 years old.[4] Since life on earth first emerged about 3.8 billion years ago, one can estimate that it took evolution over 3.799 billion years for humans to evolve from the most primitive living organisms. Yet it has only taken around 80 years to go from early computing machines (ENIAC, Colossus, Turing Machine, etc.) to today's supercomputers.[5]

This begs the question: What are things going to look like 80 years from now? In 800 years? In 8,000 years? It's almost unfathomable, especially if we keep up the pace defined by Moore's Law (i.e., that the number of transistors in a dense, integrated circuit doubles about every two years). Computer power and capabilities are going to keep advancing until— what? Some visionaries and futurists have predicted a utopian future in which technology has enabled us to solve all of the world's problems. Even President Ronald Reagan proclaimed in 1989, "The Goliath of totalitarianism will be brought down by the David of the microchip."[6]

In contrast, a dystopian view of the future popularized in many books and movies portrays a much bleaker outlook. Consider these scenarios:

- We are all jacked into *The Matrix* and live our entire existence in a virtual world that was created by artificial intelligence run amok.
- We live out our social lives as our avatars in the virtual worlds within the OASIS in Ernest Cline's bestseller, *Ready Player One*.
- Supercomputers take over the world and view us as pests to be exterminated, as in *The Terminator*.
- We release artificial superintelligence into the world that causes us to become emotionally attached to our creations, as in the movies *Her* and *Ex Machina*.
- We create synthetic humans to be used for our amusement, as in the HBO series *Westworld*.

Scary future scenarios aren't merely the realm of science fiction either. There are a number of prominent thinkers and technologists, such as Tesla and SpaceX CEO Elon Musk, who voice grave concerns about the rise of artificial intelligence.[7] Regardless of how technology changes our future, going back to simpler times is not an option. This train is only moving forward.

The Good Old Days

Sometimes the breakneck pace of change has us longing for simpler times, before cell phones and the Internet altered our cultural landscape. For many of you reading this book, simpler times means the years before the internet age. Kids would spend hours playing with Star Wars figures and Barbie dolls, using dramatic and imaginative play to recreate familiar storylines and invent new ones. Packs of neighborhood kids would play outdoor games such as hide-and-go-seek, freeze tag, capture the flag, and football. Groups of children would comb the neighborhoods or nearby woods and bayous, collecting insects and rocks, and catching critters. During the summer, kids might spend endless hours at the neighborhood pool playing games such as Marco Polo and shark. They would fly kites and ride bikes through the neighborhood and wooded trails (sans helmets, yikes!). Many kids spent hours playing board games such as Monopoly and Risk. Or they spent time jumping rope, playing pickup basketball games at the neighborhood court, and listening to music from "boom boxes." Countless hours were spent just in each other's company, forging friendships and having fun.

Kids in those days didn't need a Fitbit to tell them whether they achieved their 10,000 steps per day because they hardly sat still. Sure, these kids would watch some TV and play video games on their Atari 2600s, but neither would hold their attention for long. The screen options were very limited. Soon, they were out the door to find one another and create fun times and memories to be cherished.

It's not that kids these days no longer participate in these activities. It's rather that the time they spend in play activities and outdoors has diminished. For example, by one estimation, today's kids spend less time outdoors than prison inmates.[8,9] Indeed, according to data compiled by the data-streaming site CordCutting.com, the majority of Americans spend more time watching shows on Netflix than they do exercising, reading, and socializing with friends—combined! [10] While exact figures are difficult to come by, the time that kids spend on screens *has* to mean that such involvement has displaced other activities, such as time outdoors and unstructured play time.

Tyrell, age five, is waiting at the pediatric dentist with his mother for his checkup. His mother, Tanya, points out that there are a number of toys that he could play with in a special area of the waiting room. Tyrell gives the toys a quick glance. "I'm too old to play with toys. Toys are for babies," he proclaims. Then he looks at his mother's smartphone. He smiles as he asks, "Can I play a game on your phone?"

Importantly, there is a body of research indicating that unstructured, creative play is critical to children's development. Such activity helps children develop valuable cognitive skills such as self-regulation.[11] *Self-regulation* refers to the ways in which we control our emotions and behaviors to meet situational demands. For example, though we may have a desire to eat from a plate of delicious food set in front of us at a restaurant, we may choose to delay gratification until everyone else at the table has been served. Without self-regulation, behavior may be impulsive and maladaptive. The importance of self-regulation cannot be overstated, and it has been said that "nearly every major personal and social problem affecting a large number of modern citizens [such as alcoholism, drug addiction, obesity, excessive spending, and violence] involves some kind of failure of self-regulation."[12]

Given the importance of both play and self-regulation, it's concerning that research published in 2000 suggests that today's children are engaged in less play and have poorer self-regulation compared to children 60 years ago.[13,14] It's worth noting that this finding *preceded* the use of smartphones, tablets, and apps. Some researchers attribute these findings to changes in the nature of play. In modern play, the toys and video games have greater prescribed qualities. This determines how they are to be used and structures play, which limits the opportunities for children to create rules, improvise novel scenes, and manage their own play. When children engage in imaginative play, they talk about the activities of their imagined characters, develop backstories, and create motivations and dialogue. This private speech allows children to work through the challenges and narratives of their play. Many researchers believe that modern toys and video games lend themselves to less imaginative play and therefore elicit less private speech. In turn, this may hinder the development of self-regulation because self-regulation depends, at least in part, on private speech.[15] Dr. Peter Gray, a research professor of psychology at Boston College, not only provides evidence that children's free play has declined significantly over the past several decades, but also argues that this decline is partly to blame for the rise in psychopathology among children and adolescents.[16]

That being said, some of the play that kids have nowadays is just different. For example, they may do the following:

- Create worlds in *Minecraft*
- Fight epic space battles in *Star Wars Battlefront*
- Work together as a band of adventurers to defeat fantastical creatures in *World of Warcraft*
- Engage in cooperative and competitive battles in *Clash of Clans*
- Go on expeditions in the real world collecting Pokémon in the game-changing magic of *Pokémon Go*.

As parents, it is important that we not automatically dismiss such forms of play as inferior to what many of us did when we were young. Video games are a different format of play than more traditional play, but different doesn't always mean bad. Some of these video games have been shown to offer benefits, such as enhanced cooperative and helping behaviors, engagement, goal-setting behavior, and persever-ance.[17] However, it is critical that free play not be displaced altogether, for children will then miss out on its numerous advantages. Our approach is not that one must choose *either* technology *or* in-person experiences, but rather that *both* can be part of our children's lives and our own.

Beware of Technojudgment

As parents, we can all get caught up in the tendency to judge and finger-wag with regard to how our children are growing up these days, especially when it comes to technology. We are tempted to admonish our children with statements like, "Back in *my* day, our cell phones were two Dixie cups and a string!" or "When I was a kid, we didn't catch Pokémon! We caught *real* creatures! We waded in bayous barefoot, miles from home, catching snakes, turtles, and crawfish with our bare hands!"

We need to avoid this kind of "technojudgment." If we can take a step back, we know that we didn't take kindly to judgmental statements when we were kids. Rest assured, our kids don't like hearing that sort of thing from us either. All of us are, at least in part, products of our environments, culture, and time. These factors shape our view of the world and of each other. Most of us probably grew up watching more than our share of mindless television. If we were growing up now, we would be doing the same sorts of things our kids are doing. Here's the reality that we all know to be true: *The only reason we didn't use smartphones and tablets when we were kids is that they did not exist back then.*

Kids Technojudging Parents

On the other side of the coin, kids and teens growing up today sometimes "technojudge" their parents by accusing them of being "out of the loop" or "narrow-minded." One day—*far* in the future—our kids may very well be parents of teens. And, should this happen, it is a certainty that *their* teens will be using technologies that drive them absolutely bananas. Kids and teens will always be the adopters of new technologies that push the envelope in ways to connect socially, create, explore, gain status, and have fun. Parents need to understand the source of their children's frustration. They should acknowledge that this difference between how the older and younger generations use technology can feel judgmental, and we have to find ways to explain that to our children instead of becoming offended.

Technojudging Other Adults and Parents

Since you are reading this, you are probably trying to make some effort as an adult and/or a parent to manage technology in a more balanced way. Even as you try to set some healthy limits for yourself and your family, you will see other adults and parents with a much "looser" approach to technology. Some kids and teens seem to receive few limits or restrictions on their screen use. They are exposed to content that is inappropriate to their developmental level, and their quantity of screen time is off the charts. On the other hand, some parents might be much more restrictive with their kids and teens regarding technology use. You might view them as being unfair or overly protective.

What should you do as a parent? Step in and say something? Let's use an analogy involving diet. Many parents do not enforce healthy guidelines for their children's eating habits, or at least not with much success. It is not an option to try lecturing other parents on how they are feeding their kids, whether you view them as too loose or too restrictive. There is no way to do that effectively without it backfiring. Do you like adults commenting on what you are feeding your kids? Similarly, other parents will not take kindly to unsolicited advice on their kids' technology use.

We recommend that you focus on yourself and your own family. All we can do is set what we believe to be healthy limits for ourselves and our kids. If other parents ask us, then we can calmly explain our approach, reasoning, and strategies. In the meantime, it's best to focus on ourselves and our family rather than on judging other parents for their approach to screen use. It should be noted that when a child is visiting a friend's house, it is usually a good idea to have a discussion with the other parent(s) regarding what media types or content your child is allowed to access. We will cover this topic more in later chapters.

Technojudging Ourselves

Finally, we might notice that some parents are more actively involved in their children's screen time. There is so much pressure today to be a "good" parent. We might feel like we have allowed our kids too much access to screens too soon. We also might be judging ourselves harshly at times for our own screen time. We encourage you to question and examine, but to refrain from making categorical judgments about yourself such as, "I'm a bad parent" or "I've failed as a parent." Being self-compassionate leads to improved well-being when compared to self-criticism.[18] Moreover, self-criticism can lead to more willpower failures instead of greater self-restraint.[19] We can judge the behavior (e.g., "I need to stop checking my cell phone during meals"), but it's healthier to refrain from judging the self (e.g., "I'm a bad parent for checking my cell phone during meals").

Digital Immigrants and Digital Natives

Technojudgment often seems to be the product of a generation gap. Parents in the 1950s flipped their collective lids about Elvis and throngs of teens shaking their hips to scandalous "rock & roll" music. We now look back at those times and think, "Geez! Why couldn't those parents have just chilled out?" Are today's frustrated parents, who see their kids constantly checking their phones, gaming, using social media, and taking selfies, just like the parents of the first generation of kids raised on rock music? Are many of today's parents, educators, social scientists, and media pundits making mountains out of molehills?

Parents who grew up as we did, without the Internet, smartphones, tablets, and the like, are sometimes referred to as *digital immigrants*. In contrast, *digital natives* are those who have had those technologies available to them since infancy or early childhood. For the digital native, there wasn't a time without the Internet. Many digital immigrants fall into the trap of criticizing kids, teens, and young adults who have become attached to their technology. Every new form of media, from books, to newspapers, to the radio, and television, had naysayers and social critics predict the demise of society. "We will soon be nothing but transparent heaps of jelly to each other,"[20,21] lamented a London writer in 1897 in his critique of the advent of the telephone. This seems laughably absurd today, yet many people express similar fears about current technologies. By now, most of us have seen those headlines and have read alarmist articles, such as Dr. Nicholas Kardaras's *New York Post* article entitled, "It's Digital Heroin: How Screens Turn Our Kids into Psychotic Junkies."[22] Are concerns about cell phones and other technologies, and how younger people use them, just another manifestation of self-righteous, generation-gap, finger-wagging or catastrophizing?

Annabel, age 14, is in the ninth grade at an affluent, competitive public high school. With blonde hair, blue eyes, and an All-American smile, she has joined the cheerleading squad. She wears the latest fashions, which she often learns about through various beauty YouTube channels to which she subscribes. She lives for the "Friday Night Lights" atmosphere of the football games. She has started attending parties with older high school students whenever she can. She has a gaggle of friends and acquaintances from school and other circles with whom she keeps up through social media such as Instagram and Snapchat.

Not only is Annabel never without her phone, it is almost always in her hand. She is a big fan of Kim Kardashian, and posts many selfies throughout the day. She has started to dress more provocatively for these selfies because she gets more "likes" that way. She goes to great lengths to dress and pose for the "perfect" selfie. She often uses apps to edit her photos so that she appears super thin with a flawless complexion. She feels an overwhelming need to see what her friends are posting and often becomes quite distressed when her posts don't get as many likes as her friends' posts. Boys often flirt with her through social media, with some making very suggestive comments and outright requests for nude pictures.

Annabel's parents, Steve and Kelly, don't know the extent of what Annabel is up to, but have noticed the changes in her appearance and preoccupation with her phone and social media. When confronted by her parents with their concerns, Annabel is dismissive. She says, "I'm doing the same things that everyone else is doing at my age. It's normal. It's nothing to worry about." But her parents still worry.

Are Steve and Kelly's concerns just a form of technojudgment and representative of the digital divide? Are they just overly concerned parents who don't understand what is "normal" these days? As parents, it would be a cliché to say, "Yes, this *is* different!" since that's what parents of every generation think as well. How do we know whether some of the concerns around technology use are legitimate? Let's take a closer look at the pros and cons of technology to see whether there are valid reasons for concern here.

The Pros and Cons of Technology

It's safe to say that we should avoid technojudgment, generational finger-wagging, and catastrophizing. Such judgment and alarmism can cause a lot of family tension and division. It's generally not welcome (who likes to be judged?), nor is it an effective way to change behavior. Instead, let's take a quick look at some points on which just about everyone can agree:

- Technology is here to stay.
- It is evolving rapidly.
- It is increasingly becoming more integrated into our daily lives.
- There are many pros and cons of technology.

When we talk of the "pros" or benefits of technology, some of the broad categories include the following:

- Increased knowledge
- Increased productivity

- Greater access to entertainment
- Greater tools and opportunities for creativity
- Improved social connection.

Some of the broad categories of "cons" include the following:

- Decreased attention
- Decreased social connection
- Decreased sleep
- Decreased physical activity
- Decreased productivity.

It is easy to see how the double-edged sword of technology cuts both ways. For instance, Annabel might be connecting frequently with friends via social media and texting. These interactions might be mostly harmless or even beneficial, such as talking about dating, fashion, and making social plans. However, she is occasionally disconnecting from the friends in her physical presence while doing so. The writer who relishes the productivity power of her word processor and research tools also gets distracted by Facebook, checking newsfeeds, receiving push notifications, and going down the YouTube wormhole.

In essence, technology seems to enhance, or detract from, just about every aspect of the human experience. Advances can be for good *and* ill. Notice how it is better to use "and" here instead of "or." The word "or" implies that technology has a dichotomous, or black or white, influence on us. However, *technology is often providing the pros and the cons, such as connection and disconnection, simultaneously.*

What Are We Judging Against?

When we talk of the various pros and cons of technology, it may make us ask, what criteria are we judging technology against? Even when we speak of "technological advances," what exactly do we mean? Is it just that the technology is faster or more sophisticated, or does it mean that it enhances our lives or work production? When we say that texting or social media improves communication, what makes that good? When our technology use contributes to sleep loss, why is that bad? If parents make a family rule prohibiting electronics at the dinner table, why do they choose to make such a rule in the first place?

Although we want to avoid judging others for their technology use, at the same time, we do want to use technology in such a way as to reap the positives while minimizing the negatives. In this sense, we are not judging people, but we are evaluating the effects of technology in our own lives and those of our children. As parents, it is our responsibility to guide our children in their use of technology. In order to do this, we have to use some standard, some criterion, to guide our decision-making. If we are asking this as parents, the question becomes *what do we want for our kids?*

What Do We Want for Our Kids?

The ways in which technology affects our children, both positively and negatively, are critically important to us as parents. We all want what is best for our children. We want them to be successful in life. What do we even mean by "successful?" Many parents may dream of (or be obsessed by) Ivy League educations and prestigious jobs in fields such as law, medicine, finance, or the tech industry for their children. However, we think most parents, when pressed, will define true success differently. In our presentations, we ask parents, "What do you ultimately want for your children? What would you want to see in your adult children that would help you feel like you raised your child successfully?" We get answers like these:

- Is not financially dependent upon us as parents
- Has a network of friends/positive relationships
- Becomes a good partner/spouse/parent
- Contributes positively to society (or at least not negatively!)

- Develops self-discipline
- Makes healthy life choices (e.g., sleep, exercise, nutrition)
- Is able to love others and be loved by others
- Is happy.

Arguably, happiness is the underlying goal that we all seek in life. As mentioned in Chapter 1, we are talking about a deep-rooted contentment in life, not the more superficial pleasures. Certain sources of pleasure, such as food, drugs, and sex, can provide us with temporary positive feelings, but ultimately contribute to high levels of unhappiness if pursued to excess. In a way, all other goals circle back to this master goal of happiness in the deeper sense of the word.

Importantly, there is a good deal of research, along with our own personal experiences, that tell us that most of our happiness is nested within positive relationships.[23] We will return to this theme because, if we are to be truly happy, we are most likely to find that in close, healthy social relationships. Technology has the capacity to both facilitate *and* undermine our social connectedness.

A Quick Thought Experiment

Let's take an example that most parents can relate to: our desire for our children to do "well" in school. In this hypothetical conversation with Susan regarding her 10-year-old daughter, Briana, it would look like this:

QUESTION: Why is it important for Briana to get good grades in school?
SUSAN: So she can get into a good college.
QUESTION: Why is it important for her to get into a good college?
SUSAN: So she can have a good career track and a high-paying job.

QUESTION: Why is it important for her to have a good career track and a high-paying job?

SUSAN: So she meets her material needs and gets everything that she needs and wants.

QUESTION: Why do you want those things for Briana?

SUSAN: So—so she will be happy!

One can argue that the ultimate criterion by which we judge technology, for ourselves and our children, is whether it results in increased happiness. Certainly, this is debatable and can become quite philosophical, but we must have some criterion upon which to evaluate whether our, and our children's, technology use is beneficial or harmful. So, is our use of technology making us happier as a society? We'll tackle this important question in the next chapter.

3

Is Our Technology Making Us Any Happier?

We all experience the many benefits of technology on a daily basis. We connect with friends, increase productivity, access information, play incredibly engaging games, and have easy access to virtually all media forms. Just think for a moment of all the hilarious YouTube videos and Facebook posts you've seen. Many of us have laughed until we cried at "Charlie Bit My Finger," "The NFL: A Bad Lip Reading," and "David After Dentist," as well as the endless parodies of these and other videos. Consider all of the enjoyable exchanges that you've had with friends and acquaintances through texting and social media over the years. They are countless, and we keep coming back for more.

Curiously, although technology is extremely powerful and allows us to do a great many things better than we could in the past, it seems we are not any happier as a society. Measuring societal happiness isn't easy to do, and we only have data from several decades. That being said, research suggests that levels of happiness in the United States have been flat for decades and might even be dipping over the past few years.[1] Some research suggests that depression and anxiety in teens and young adults are on the rise.[2] The number of prescriptions for antidepressant medication has nearly doubled from 1999 to 2012, going from 6.8% to 13%.[3] More than 1 in 10 Americans take antidepressant medication. Increases in the awareness of and access to antidepressants are likely to at least partially explain this rise. However, there is still compelling evidence that societal happiness in the

United States is decreasing. For example, the suicide rate in the United States has been trending upward for every age group under 75 since 1999.[4] In a Harris poll, the percentage of Americans who rate themselves as "very happy" was down slightly in 2016, going from 35% in 2008 to 31%.[5] Similarly, data from the 2017 World Happiness Report indicate that US happiness has declined from 2006 to 2016. In his examination of the variables that could be associated with this decline in happiness, noted researcher and economist Dr. Jeffrey Sachs concludes, "America's crisis is, in short, a social crisis, not an economic crisis."[6]

The younger generation also seems to be struggling in terms of well-being. According to data from the Department of Health and Human Services, the percentage of adolescents aged 12–17 who have experienced a major depressive episode has gone up from 7.9% in 2006 to 12.5% in 2015. Data from the National Institute of Mental Health indicate that there were 6.3 million teens aged 13–18 with an anxiety disorder in 2015. This represents a whopping 25% of that age group. The overall teen suicide rate has also been increasing in recent years, particularly for girls aged 10–14.[7]

Dr. Jean Twenge, a professor of psychology at San Diego State University and author of *iGen* and *Generation Me,* believes that technology is partially responsible for declining levels of happiness in young Americans. Of the younger generation, she says, "Our current culture of pervasive technology, attention-seeking, and fleeting relationships is exciting and stimulating," but she also points out that it "may not provide the stability and sense of community that mature adults require."[8]

Why Doesn't Technology Make Us Happier Overall?

The positives of technology are indisputable. Yet, we still aren't any happier. If you are a parent reading this book, you are likely to remember a time when you didn't have unlimited access to music, movies, TV shows, video games, creativity tools, and friends via texting and social media. One doesn't need empirical data to point to the truth. We can look within ourselves. *How happy am I, on a daily basis, because I have access to these things now?* If you are like us and most people, having access to all of these sources of entertainment and social connection doesn't actually move your happiness needle.

Importantly, we can't necessarily say that our technology use is *the cause* of decreased (or flat) levels of happiness over time. As they say in the sciences, correlation doesn't equal causation; that is, just because two events co-occur does not necessarily mean that one *causes* the other. Aggregate societal happiness is influenced by countless variables. It's just that with all of the continuously increasing power, freedom, social connections, and fun that technology affords us, we don't see that translate into large, societal increases in daily happiness. *The benefits of technology are not a cure-all for the struggles in our society.*

At first glance, this seems a bit counterintuitive. How could it be possible that technology doesn't make us a lot happier? There are a number of reasons why, even with all of the power and possibilities that technology affords us, we aren't really any happier on the whole. Let's take a look at some of these possible reasons.

Hedonic Adaptation

We are adaptive creatures, and that means we adapt to things that make us happy relatively quickly. In the social sciences, psychologists have coined the term *hedonic adaptation* or the *hedonic treadmill* to describe this phenomenon.[9] So, whether we get a new car, ultra high-definition TV, new smartphone, designer handbag, or win the lottery, our level of happiness tends to return to our baseline (standard or default) level of happiness fairly quickly.

Although there is much research to indicate that hedonic adaption does occur, we also can reflect on our own experiences to see the evidence of it.[10] How long did that new TV, couch, or car really make us happy? Or the new smartphone? Perhaps we get a happiness bump for a few days, but it dissipates rapidly. If these material items provided lasting happiness, then we wouldn't need to keep buying more!

Although technology offers innumerable ways to increase our happiness, we seem to have adapted to those such that we don't actually feel happier overall than we did prior to having the technological advances. The irony is that we are constantly fooled by the seductive idea that "*I will be happier when I get this_____.*" The advertising industry is well aware of this human tendency, and exploits it to great profit.

The Pros and Cons Even Out

Since technology affords us greater levels of power, freedom, social connection, and fun, potential dangers and pitfalls are also inherent in this technology. We cannot have the pros without the cons. They come bundled together. Thus, to some extent, the positives and negatives cancel each other out to leave our happiness level back where it started. For example, texting and social media can be used to enhance social connections, and they also lead us away from our in-person relationships. Just look at groups of teens and young people out together at a restaurant, staring at their individual devices. Dr. Kenneth Gergen, a psychologist and professor at Swarthmore College, wrote about this challenge in 2002 and referred to this as "absent presence."[11] He defined this as when "[o]ne is physically present, but absorbed by a technologically mediated world of elsewhere." Similarly, MIT professor and renowned researcher Dr. Sherry Turkle describes this as a problem of being "alone together" in her book by that name.[12]

Not Meeting Our Physical Needs

All of this technology is causing many of us to lose sleep and become too sedentary. Children need about 9–11 hours per night, teens need about 8–10, and adults need 7–9 hours per night.[13] The 2014 Sleep in America Poll from the National Sleep Foundation found that 90% of 15–17-year-olds reported getting 8 hours or less of sleep per night, with 56% reporting less than 7 hours per night.[14] Undoubtedly, many young people's sleep is being negatively affected by technology. For example, in a literature review of 67 studies on the relationship between children and adolescents' sleep and screen use, the authors found that both sleep onset and duration were adversely affected by screen use in 90% of the studies.[15] Despite our rapid adoption of technologies that can negatively impact our sleep, our need for sleep hasn't diminished in thousands of years. Sleep deprivation is well documented as a contributing factor to numerous physical and psychological problems, including obesity and depression.[16]

Screen use can negatively affect sleep in several ways. For instance, tech screens, including smartphones and tablets, emit a blue light that decreases melatonin production, which is a hormone that helps regulate the sleep-wake cycle.[17,18] Video game players' sleep can be disrupted by increased central nervous system activity when they play prior to bedtime.[19] Also, the appeal of screens can entice people to use them (e.g., gaming, binge watching, social media, responding to texts) instead of going to bed on time.[20] Moreover, a wealth of research indicates that our physical activity is inextricably linked to our physical health and emotional well-being.[21] Our screen use is likely contributing to a more sedentary, sleep-deprived lifestyle that, in turn, is having a negative impact on our happiness.

Delayed Gratification

Sometimes it pays to wait, and one's ability to do so has been the focus of much research. Psychologist Dr. Walter Mischel conducted his famous "Marshmallow Test" studies while at Stanford University.[22] In short, he found that children who were able to delay gratification (i.e., wait several minutes to earn two treats rather than having one right away) also experienced positive outcomes later in life. These positive outcomes included higher grades, fewer behavior problems, higher SAT scores, higher rates of college attendance, and higher incomes as adults.

In essence, willpower or self-control, which includes delaying gratification, is an important skill.[23] If we aren't able to restrain ourselves from immediate pleasures, then we can end up paying long-term consequences. For example, if we can't inhibit ourselves from eating junk food, then our health is likely to suffer over time. Researchers also refer to this as "temporal discounting," which is the tendency to make short-term, unhealthy choices that are gratifying in the moment, while devaluing greater, long-term rewards because they are distant in time.[24]

Researchers have found that willpower or self-control is like a muscle that can be exercised. It gets stronger with use. Likewise, one might also argue that we get more skilled at seeking immediate gratification with practice. In a manner of speaking, we are practicing immediate gratification almost constantly with our screens. Our finely tuned skills at seeking immediate gratification may cause us to miss out on long-term rewards. For instance, frequently accessing our smartphones and screens (e.g., for newsfeeds, social media, texting) might contribute to negative physical and mental health outcomes over time.[25,26]

The Paradox of Choice

Dr. Barry Schwartz describes in both his book, *The Paradox of Choice*, and in his TED talk that having too many options can, ironically, make us *less* happy.[27,28] When we are faced with numerous choices, it becomes too challenging for our brains to select the "best" choice because there are too many variables that weigh into the decision-making process. Thus, when we make a choice among many options, we can always imagine that we could have made a "better" choice. In an ironic twist, our happiness suffers when we believe we would have been happier making a different choice.[29]

With regard to technology, it affords us practically infinite possibilities. In any given moment, we must decide which is the "best" choice. Play a game? Which one? Text a friend? Watch our favorite YouTube channel? Post to Instagram? Make a music playlist? Check the news? Answer email? You can see that this list goes on and on. Those endless options lead us right into the paradox of choice. No matter what we end up doing with technology, we must digest the regret that we might have selected something better than we did. This paradox of choice may be related to "FoMO" (or the fear of missing out). FoMO can be more technically defined as "a pervasive apprehension that others might be having rewarding experiences from which one is absent."[30] Indeed, researchers have found that FoMO is associated with a more negative mood and lower life satisfaction. Furthermore, FoMO, and the decreased happiness associated with it, might be stemming from not meeting our psychological needs for relatedness, competence, and autonomy.[31] We will come back to this theme in later chapters.

Despite the negative consequences associated with having too many options, we prefer having more choices than having fewer or no choices.[32] Social psychologists Drs. Dan Gilbert and Tim Wilson have termed this *miswanting*. Miswanting occurs when we incorrectly predict what will make us happy.[33] When it comes to our screens, we desire all the choices that they provide, yet we seem to incorrectly predict how much happiness that they bring.

Decision Fatigue

A concept related to the paradox of choice that might be causing us problems is called *decision fatigue*.[34] Our brains are like a muscle that can become fatigued with exertion. In particular, the day-to-day decisions that we make tax our cognitive resources such that we become more mentally fatigued the more decisions that we make. This fatigue, in turn, causes us to have more failures of self-control or willpower (e.g., we fail to refrain from eating unhealthy foods). We also tend to make poorer decisions because we lack the energy to carefully sort through various options. With our screens, we now make an almost incalculable number of "microdecisions" throughout the day (e.g., whom to contact, what to post, what to like, which links to follow while on the web). While many of these decisions are made below conscious awareness, decisions are being made nonetheless. Some studies show that making choices can lead to reductions in self-control.[35] It's possible that many of us end up making poorer choices due to decision fatigue and this, in turn, leads to decreased happiness. As Dr. Kathleen Vohs, distinguished professor at the University of Minnesota, notes, "Self-control and decision-making are central, vital skills for functioning in human culture."[36] Thus, the seemingly endless choices that our technologies afford us might be, in essence, depleting a limited resource (self-control) that is essential for our effective functioning in society.

Social Comparison

There is a large body of literature indicating that social comparison affects our level of happiness.[37] That is why an NBA star making $10 million a year can be quite upset if a player with inferior stats joins the team but is making $15 million per year. We might look at the first NBA player and call him a crybaby for complaining about earning $10 million per year playing a sport he loves. However, while we are comparing our income to his, he is comparing himself to the player making $5 million more a year with inferior stats.

All the world's indeed a stage due to technology, the media, and advertising. Our sense of adequacy and perspective is compared to essentially the entire world. Thus, a teen girl posting a selfie on Instagram is not only comparing herself to her closest friends, but to a myriad of tangentially related acquaintances, teen idols, pop stars, movie stars, and social media celebrities. She is also comparing herself to other teen girls who have curated their photos using various filters and photo editing apps to get that elusive "perfect" selfie. Adults as well see all of the Facebook posts of friends and acquaintances who are sharing about their adventures, wonderful vacations, adorable children, and various forms of success. In support of this idea, a group of researchers found that Facebook use among college students increased feelings of depression, but only when it triggered feelings of envy.[38,39]

Diminished Attention

Our focused attention is the foundation for everything great in life: our relationships, our productivity, and, ultimately, our happiness. There is a growing body of research indicating that mindful attention can decrease stress and increase well-being.[40,41] In contrast, the frequent attention-jumping we do these days with our technologies, such as texting and social media, means that we don't sustain focused attention for long. "Multitasking," which involves rapidly toggling attention among two or more tasks, appears to have a negative impact on productivity and well-being.[42,43,44] Also, researchers have found that one's enjoyment of an activity is reduced when it is disrupted, such as by a cell phone, and this reduction in enjoyment is due to the shift in attention.[45] Interestingly, in one study of multitasking, those who perceived themselves to be good at multitasking tended to do the worst at tests of multitasking in laboratory tests.[46]

In a recent study, University of Texas at Austin researcher Dr. Adrian Ward and colleagues found a "brain drain" effect for the mere presence of a smartphone. That is, the presence of a smartphone, even when silenced, appears to reduce cognitive capacity. The researchers found that those individuals with the highest smartphone dependence were more adversely affected by the presence of their smartphones than those who are less dependent.[47] Study participants overwhelmingly rated that the presence of the smartphone did not interfere with their cognitive performance when, in fact, it was adversely affected—consistent with the study finding that people who rate themselves as adept multitaskers are actually poor at it.[48] A key insight from this study is that we may not be very aware of how our functioning is being impaired by our devices.

Disruption of Flow States

Through decades of research, Dr. Mihaly Csikszentmihalyi, Distinguished Professor in Psychology and Management at Claremont Graduate University and cofounder of the positive psychology movement, identified states of "flow" as being critical to our well-being and happiness.[49] Flow is described as being fully attentive to and immersed in an activitiy such that one often loses a sense of space, time, and self. In everyday terms, it is often referred to "being in the zone." A deep state of absorption in an activity, whether it is work or a hobby, is essential for flow experiences. With the frequent disruptions to our attention that occur because of our screens, flow experiences and the positive feelings that can be generated from them can be undermined.[50]

Decreased Social Connectedness

There is a mountain of research indicating that our happiness is inextricably tied to our social relationships.[51] One of the challenges of the digital age is that a sizable percentage of kids, teens, and adults across the world are spending more time with technology instead of with each other or in other need-satisfying, face-to-face relationships. As acclaimed MIT professor and psychologist Dr. Sherry Turkle observes, we seem to be expecting more from technology and less from each other.[52]

Some of the original research showing the importance of social connectedness to well-being comes from the rhesus monkey studies of Dr. Harry Harlow.[53] One of the main findings from Harlow's research (which, by the way, seems quite cruel by today's standards) is that infant monkeys, removed from their mothers and their group, ultimately showed profound symptoms of depression, anxiety, and even psychosis despite having their physical needs met (e.g., food, water). They could not successfully be reintegrated to the group because they were unable to emotionally bond with other group members in a healthy way.

Sadly, studies of children neglected from infancy within Russian and Romanian orphanages also found that these children suffered from cognitive, social, and emotional deficits even after finally receiving compassionate care.[54] Nurturing care could not completely undo the damage done by the neglect that these children experienced during critical developmental windows. Generally, the earlier in infancy that the neglect occurred and the longer it lasted, the worse the damage.

We are social creatures by nature. In fact, in order for our brains to develop fully, we need in-person social connectedness. This begins with parents and caregivers holding and feeding their newborns and providing comforting cuddles and hugs. Both touch and eye contact are critical for the formation of healthy relational bonds.[55,56,57] The heart of this healthy attachment is warm, focused, in-person attention to our kids.

When our attachment and social needs are unmet, this can result in symptoms such as anxiety and depression.[58] Conversely, most of our happiness is related to our social connectedness. When we have a number of warm, connected, healthy relationships, we tend to feel happy. Studies show that in-person friendships decrease cortisol, the stress hormone, while increasing oxytocin, a hormone associated with bonding and pleasure.[59,60] When we feel disconnected, alienated, ostracized, alone, or in conflict, we tend to be fairly unhappy. Indeed, social rejection has been found to activate some of the same centers of the brain that physical pain does.[61] Thus, rejection is quite literally painful.

The technologies that we use, such as texting and social media, often keep us jumping around and consequently less engaged in deep, meaningful, in-person conversations.[62] We need uninterrupted time to develop a coherent sense of self and the skill of empathy. Our relationships need nurturance in the form of un-divided attention and empathic connection in order to grow and thrive. There is evidence that our ability to empathize with others is weakened when we are cognitively occupied or distracted.[63] Moreover, frequent use of social media appears to have a negative impact on well-being, whereas frequent face-to-face interactions have a positive effect.[64] Again, the irony is that the drive, the need to connect with others, is what leads us to text and use social media in the first place. Yet, we end up taking our sustained attention away from the in-person relationships that are the ultimate source of much of our happiness.

What's the Return on Investment?

We know that technology provides many positives and is not inherently bad. It can enhance our happiness in so many ways, but doesn't increase our well-being overall. Perhaps part of the problem is that we aren't particularly effective at maximizing the pros of our screen use while minimizing the cons. There's a wonderful term from economics that we can borrow here: *return on investment* (ROI). Do the benefits returned outweigh the costs invested? Does this pay off?

When applied to our lives and technology, we can ask ourselves: "Does the money, time, and energy that I invest in this screen use yield a positive return in terms of happiness?" Yes, sometimes we suck up short-term happiness "losses" for long-term gains (e.g., rigorous studies to open college/career opportunities). But at some point, we should receive a positive ROI from our screen use. When we and/or our kids are not, we really have to take a hard look at our screen time. To be clear, this is not black or white. Sometimes our tech use, and that of our children, does yield a positive ROI. Sometimes it does not. The challenge is separating the wheat from the chaff.

Consider David's situation:

David is a 17-year-old teen from an upper middle-class family. He goes to a fairly affluent public high school. While very bright, he underperforms in most of his classes and is generally a B–C student. He doesn't have an after-school job or any organized extracurricular activities. Although he used to be involved in sports such as cross-country running, he has become more immersed in his world of gaming. He is an avid League of Legends *player. He spends three to four hours per day playing and up to twice that on weekends, holidays, and throughout the summer. He has a very high-end computer that he built himself. Although extremely tech-savvy, most of this energy is directed to gaming. He avoids spending time with his parents and his 13-year-old sister. He declines invitations to play family games. Even when he goes on family trips or out to eat with them, he is on his cell phone either texting, using social media, or playing games. He rarely engages in activities with friends in real life. When not on a screen, he seems nervous, fidgety, distracted, and unhappy. He has aspirations to become a professional* League of Legends *player on the tournament circuit. He says he is happy overall, but only when allowed to game as much as he wants.*

What do you think of David? Clearly, he is capitalizing on some of the benefits of "advanced" technology. He claims to be quite happy when allowed to play *League of Legends* to his heart's content. Yet, he is not particularly happy when not playing his game. The positives that he's receiving from his screen use don't seem to provide much in terms of overall life satisfaction. What if David is allowed to pursue his dream of becoming a professional gamer, and this doesn't pan out? He might end up suffering in the long term for his choice to focus on gaming over his studies, physical activities, and in-person relationships.

Interestingly, some of the same parents who would be concerned about the amount of time David was spending on *League of Legends* might be less concerned if he were playing chess, tennis, or the violin. One might consider this a form of "technojudgment." It would be quite challenging, if not impossible, to prove that playing chess or violin is somehow inherently superior to playing *League of Legends*. However, one could make a strong case that doing too much of any single activity can ultimately become detrimental, whether it involves a sport, a musical instrument, or a video game. This can be, at least in part, because of what is known as the *displacement effect* or the *displacement hypothesis*. At a certain point, the focused time spent on one activity begins to displace time that could be spent in more beneficial or need-satisfying activities, such as sleep, outdoor activities, academics, or social time with friends. No matter how beneficial it is to play *League of Legends* or the violin, if a teen is only getting five hours of sleep per night because of this activity, then he or she will suffer the effects of chronic sleep deprivation. With regard to technology, a number of researchers have found evidence in support of the displacement hypothesis.[65,66]

Next, consider Elizabeth:

Elizabeth is a 14-year-old girl in a working-class family. She received a smartphone for her thirteenth birthday. She said she really "needed" a smartphone because all of her friends had one, and she was being left out of her social group by not having one. As soon as she received her cell phone, she joined the same social networking platforms that her friends were using. Now she checks her phone and is texting or posting over a hundred times per day.

Elizabeth's parents worried about the amount of time that she was spending on her phone. When she was with them, she always had it in hand and would disengage from conversations to check it, text, or post. Her phone use stretched out the time she needed to complete her homework because she kept checking it as she worked. Her grades dropped. She kept her phone in her room at night against her parents' wishes. She became more moody and irritable. Elizabeth and her parents experienced ongoing battles over her phone use that often spilled into heated arguments. Mostly, her parents felt sad and frustrated that she was so disengaged from them.

Elizabeth is spending a lot of time on her phone, but it doesn't appear that this time is actually improving her well-being. She seems so absorbed with her phone that it is having negative effects on her sleep, grades, mood, and relationship with her parents. While we can see that asking about the "return on investment" doesn't always yield clear-cut answers, it is worth asking. It is critical that we help our kids learn to ask themselves this question about the ROI of their own screen time. Ultimately, if they can internalize this strategy, it can serve them well throughout their lives.

What's the Opportunity Cost?

When we explore why our screen use doesn't appear to be making us any happier overall, another concept from the field of economics is relevant: *opportunity cost.* It is defined as the loss of potential gain from alternatives when a single option is chosen. In terms of our screen use, this would mean that, even when our use does yield positives, we should ask, *Is my screen use displacing other activities that might have been even more beneficial?* In the case of David and his *League of Legends* gaming that he enjoys, we don't have to argue about whether he is actually enjoying it. He is! However, *what is he not doing* because he is gaming? Is it displacing other, possibly more beneficial, activities? What is he missing out on that might yield a better return on investment? Given the paradox of choice, as described previously, this can be a challenge to do! Still, it is an important question to ask. Also, it is another concept that we hope that our kids can internalize and put to good use.

Our Struggles with the Pros and Cons of Screens

A strong case can be made that our screens don't seem to be making us happier. At present, it doesn't appear that most of us are very adept at weighing the opportunity costs of our screen use, or utilizing self-control to ensure that we are getting a good return on investment. Why is this so? We believe some of the answers are in our evolutionary history.

Throughout much of our existence as hunters and gathers, we lived in small groups up to about 100–150 people. [67,68] The figure of 150 is known as "Dunbar's number," after anthropologist Dr. Robin Dunbar. It refers to the maximum number of stable social relationships that humans can maintain given the cognitive load that is required to do so. In these hunter-gatherer tribes, we were concerned only with the survival of ourselves, our offspring, our extended family, and our fellow tribe members. We evolved to focus on specific, immediate threats versus uncertain, vague, long-term threats. We focused on immediate concerns because this had survival value. Thus, we had absolutely no notion of how the animals that we hunted or the fires we lit might affect others on the other side of the globe. In evolutionary terms, this sort of thinking has little utility.

Consider climate change as an example. It has been well documented that climate change is real and that humans are contributing to this problem.[69] Despite the consensus among the scientific community, a large percentage of Americans do not believe that climate change is real and that humans are to blame.[70] While there are many reasons for this, at least in part, it is because it is difficult for us humans to envision how current behaviors relate to long-term, distant, consequences. Even for the many who do believe that climate change is real, it is extremely difficult for us to give up the immediate, short-term benefits of using fossil fuels, such as driving little Johnny to soccer practice, because this *will* contribute to global warming in such a way that, when combined with similar actions of billions of other humans over decades, *might* lead to the disappearance of the island nation of Micronesia in 100 years. Sound a bit confusing? That's exactly because our brains have not evolved to think in this way. It seems so distant, vague, and remote that we tend not to alter our behavior over concern for such possibilities.[71,72] As cognitive psychologists Drs. Steven Sloman and Philip Fernbach argue in *The Knowledge Illusion: Why We Never Think Alone*, we evolved to live in a world in which shallow, causal reasoning was all that was necessary for our immediate survival.

Similarly, when it comes to food, our brains did not evolve to think about how eating cheeseburgers, French fries, and soft drinks will, over the years, increase our chances of becoming obese and suffering physical ailments. The tech revolution brings us the Internet, smartphones, and social media, but our species did not evolve under conditions in which thinking in terms of *possible, vague, distant* consequences such as diminished attention and impaired relationships would affect survival. Our daily lives are rapidly changing because of advances in technology, and it is likely that it is beyond our capacity to rationally or accurately evaluate the long-term potential effects of technology on our lives. We really have no idea how technology will advance in the coming decades, how we will be using it, or the effects that it will have on us. It's just too complicated, vague, and distant to motivate us to alter our current behavior. In a manner similar to the way in which we avoid tackling global climate change or avoiding junk food, we tend to push any of those concerns to the back burner. They just don't register as relevant threats to our day-to-day well-being.

Out of Sync with Our Evolutionary Heritage

A better understanding of our evolution can help illuminate why our screen use can negatively affect our well-being. Arguably, the problem is that our screen use can lead us to live in a manner very different from the environment in which we evolved. Humans evolved, over the course of millions of years, to interact in certain ways with our environment. From an evolutionary perspective, our brains and bodies evolved to interact with the world around us and with each other in ways that would ensure our genes would be passed to the next generation (in other words, reproduction). Thus, for most of our existence as sapiens, we evolved to eat certain foods, have a certain amount of stimulation within our environments, and create small, social groups that were *always* in person. We also evolved to require a certain amount of sleep per night and to be relatively active.

We might even say that the "ideal" ways to meet our physical and psychological needs are not unlike the ideal ways in which our hunter-gatherer ancestors met theirs. Screen usage often results in us living incongruously with our evolutionary heritage. For example, perhaps we don't get enough sleep and exercise, or infrequently meet with people face-to-face. To the extent that our screen use interferes with, or at least limits, our ability to meet our evolutionary needs, we may pay a price in terms of our physical and emotional well-being.

The Ideal Way to Be Active

As an example of how we appear to be living out of sync with our evolutionary heritage, let's take a closer look at our physical activity. In a problem related to the obesity epidemic, Americans are generally far too sedentary. *Sedentary* is generally defined as taking less than 5,000 steps per day.[73] Our bodies evolved to hunt, gather, build, and move. As hunter-gatherers, historically we spent a great deal of time searching for food.[74] The hunter-gatherers' daily energy expenditures for physical activity typically were about three to five times that of modern sedentary individuals.[75]

In contrast to our ancestors, most of us are very inactive for the majority of our days. The average American sits approximately 13 hours per day.[76] We sit in our cars during commutes, at our desks while on the computer, and we sit to watch TV, stream content, or play video games. Combined with a recommended 8 hours of sleeping, that means that Americans are sedentary 21 out of 24 hours per day. Moreover, recent research indicates that one hour at the gym per day does not make up for a sedentary lifestyle.[77,78] As acclaimed cardiologist and researcher Dr. James O'Keefe and colleagues noted regarding our increasingly sedentary lifestyles, ". . . our innate exercise capabilities and requirements that evolved via natural selection over thousands of millennia remain essentially the same as for our Stone Age ancestors. Marked deviation from those indigenous exercise patterns predictably results in physical disability and disease."[79]

As we are lured to spend more time on our screens, this has the potential to make us much more sedentary than our ancestors. Remember the dystopian future depicted in the Pixar film *Wall-E*? Humans spent their time on screens, not interacting in person, and zipping around in hover chairs because they were too obese to walk. And we watched this and laughed uncomfortably as we sat in our movie theater seats, eyes glued to the screen and not each other, with tubs of hot, buttery popcorn, some candy, and a soda. Yikes! Did we get the message?

The Consequences of Living Out of Sync with Our Evolutionary Heritage

A number of prominent researchers have warned of the consequences of our tendency to live in a way inconsistent with our evolutionary heritage. Dr. James O'Keefe and his colleagues explain that "the systematic displacement from a very physically active lifestyle in our natural outdoor environment to a sedentary, indoor lifestyle is at the root of many of the ubiquitous chronic diseases that are endemic in our culture."[80] Similarly, Dr. Daniel Lieberman, a paleoanthropologist at Harvard University, describes how there are a number of common "mismatch diseases" in our society, such as type II diabetes, back pain, and asthma, that occur, at least in part, because our Paleolithic bodies are not well-suited to modern conditions.[81] Extending these observations, Dr. Colin Shaw, a researcher with the University of Cambridge's Phenotypic Adaptability, Variation, and Evolution research group, noted that "[c]ontemporary humans live in a cultural and technological milieu incompatible with our evolutionary adaptations."[82] Taken together, it would appear that our screen use may contribute to (or at least is not freeing us from) a lifestyle that is in disharmony with our evolutionary heritage. While there is room for debate about some of the particulars, a strong case can be made that it is this fundamental disharmony that is at the root of why our screens don't seem to be making us any happier overall.

From this evolutionary standpoint, we are all digital immigrants. *Our bodies and brains did not evolve to live in the world in which we now live.*[83] As neuroscientist Dr. Adam Gazzaley and psychologist Dr. Larry Rosen detail in their book *The Distracted Mind: Ancient Brains in a High-Tech World*, many of the problems that arise from our technology use are because our brains evolved to live in a very different world from this digitally hyper-connected one.[84] While we truly are adaptive creatures, the fast pace at which technology and society are changing is not something with which evolution can keep pace. Technological evolution zooms past biological evolution.

We *are not* advocating that we need to live just like our Stone Age ancestors to be happy. Just as we all must eat to live in this world, we all need to use technology. It's not realistic for us to become luddites and opt out of technology completely. However, we can see that we pay a steep price for living in a manner that is disharmonious with our evolutionary heritage. Our physiological and psychological needs, which have evolved over millions of years, have not really changed. Yet the world that we live in today is very different from that of our ancestors.

We are stuck with the challenge of meeting old needs in a different world. We must meet these needs to be healthy and happy. In a sense, our physical health and happiness are the "payoffs" for meeting these needs effectively. On the other hand, there is a consequence for not meeting these needs well. This often comes in the form of various manifestations of physical and mental health problems. In turn, these physical and mental health problems can negatively affect our overall happiness.

The Takeaway?

We all want to be happy in life, and we want this for our children as well. Technology offers many benefits that have the potential to improve our well-being. Yet, this doesn't seem to be happening. In general, societal happiness levels are flat or dropping. This seems to be particularly true of young people. How can this be? Among many other factors, perhaps we are struggling to capitalize on the advantages of our screens while limiting the downsides. When we examine this puzzle more closely, it seems that the underlying problem is that our screen use results in us interacting with our environment and each other in ways that are disharmonious with our evolutionary ancestry. If we are not mindful of these disharmonies, as individuals and as parents, we and our children can end up paying a steep price in terms of our physical and psychological well-being.

Ultimately, our tendency to seek engagement, connection, and happiness in the short term causes us to experience some very real consequences in the long-term. Concerns about these consequences are valid and not just a form of alarmism or technojudgment. Our goal and responsibility as parents is to help provide our children with the environment and tools to be truly happy in life. We want them to thrive. So it is critical that we find ways to capitalize on the positives of technology and minimize the negatives.

However, we face a very challenging task. Our brains and bodies evolved to live in a world very different from the world in which we now live. Adaptive drives that evolved during the long hunter-gatherer phase of our existence make it hard to resist the allure of the technologies that we have created. Like unhealthy foods, these technologies are almost impossible to resist. In order to more effectively manage our technology use, and that of our children, it can be helpful to better understand the pull of our screens. That is the topic of Chapter 4.

4

The Pull of Our Screens

Jenny, a high school freshman, keeps her phone in her room at night. She often is texting and using social media well past when she should go to sleep. When she wakes up in the morning, she checks her cell before rolling out of bed. While getting ready for school one morning, she misplaced her phone and recounted the experience. "I mean, I know I had it somewhere—it was just in my hand! I forgot to plug it into the charger, so the battery was dead. I couldn't use my mom's phone to find mine. I looked all over for it. I couldn't leave the house without it. My mom was yelling at me to just go, because I was going to be late for school. I was going CRAZY! I was throwing stuff around, searching for it. It took me 20 minutes to find it. My mom and I got into a huge argument about it. I finally found it behind a box of cereal. I'm not sure how it got there. I was so relieved though! I was late for school—AND my mom was really mad at me for a while. But I just had to have it before I left. I mean, I can't go anywhere without it."

Has something similar happened to you? It's not just teens who feel "incomplete" without their cell phones. Most of us adults do, too. What is that weird feeling that we have when we can't find it? Why do we have to have it so badly? In *The Lord of the Rings*, the One Ring cast a powerful spell over all those around it, especially if worn. The hobbit, Bilbo, and his nephew, Frodo, become so obsessed by the One Ring that they couldn't be apart from it for long without becoming increasingly desperate to be reunited with their "Precious." In one scene at the beginning of *The Fellowship of the Ring*, Bilbo misplaces the Ring and starts frantically searching around his house for it. His desperation grows—where could it have gone? Relief washes over his face when he finds it in his jacket pocket.

Jenny, and just about all of us, can relate all too well to Bilbo. We seem to have that same relationship with our cell phones. We are so enmeshed with them that we feel incomplete without them. There's even a term that's been coined for this condition: *nomophobia* (i.e., no mobile phobia).[1] Why do they have such a power over us that we feel compelled to have them, to check them, to post, to comment, and to "like?" Teens and young adults might, at first glance, seem to be more attached to their phones than older adults are, but those phones have hooks in all of us. What is going on here?

In this chapter, we explore the pull of our screens. Understanding the mechanisms behind the pull of our screens will allow us to develop more effective strategies to balance technology in our lives and in the lives of our children.

Our Psychological Needs

Technologies such as texting, social media, email, and gaming seem to have a special power over us that often results in using them reflexively or compulsively. We are not "addicted" to our cell phones in a sense. Rather, our phones become associated with access to other people, news, games, and validation that we desire. After all, an old flip phone that doesn't provide such access is little more than a paperweight nowadays!

Why do technologies, such as texting and social media, have such a powerful grip on us in the first place? One of the main reasons we are all so drawn to the power of these screens is that they provide virtually limitless options with which we can try to meet our psychological needs. After our physiological needs are met (e.g., air, food, water), psychological needs drive our behavior.

According to Drs. Richard M. Ryan and Edward L. Deci's self-determination theory, we all have three psychological needs that underlie intrinsic human motivation:[2]

1. Relatedness: the need to feel socially connected
2. Competence: the need to feel effectiveness and mastery
3. Autonomy: the need to self-regulate one's experiences and actions.

According to their research-supported theory, our psychological health and well-being are dependent upon how well we are meeting these needs. In a sense, relatedness can be considered our most important psychological need because autonomy and competence are generally satisfied within the context of relationships. For instance, if we were stranded on a desert island by ourselves, it would be difficult to experience feelings of autonomy and competence without any social context.

From an evolutionary standpoint, we have psychological needs because they intrinsically motivate our behavior to facilitate survival.[3] Importantly, multiple psychological needs can be met with one activity. For example, if a child is playing *Minecraft* with friends, he or she is likely meeting all of these psychological needs simultaneously to some extent.

Lured Away from Others to Our Screens

At times we can certainly meet our psychological needs through our screens, but this can come at a cost. We evolved to meet these needs in the "real" world, not a digital world. Thus, for secure, healthy attachments to form, in-person contact is essential. We need to look into the eyes of our partners, children, and friends. We need to touch, hug, and embrace. Infants need to look into their caregiver's eyes while feeding in the warmth of cradling arms. Touch is necessary for healthy development and that, of course, is always in person.[4,5] Even if we Facetime or Skype, we don't experience some of the many benefits of in-person connections, such as touch.

Lien, a 26-year-old, adores her six-month-old son, Hyun. Like many young mothers, she uses several social networking apps such as Instagram, Facebook, and Snapchat to share her adoration. She is in almost constant contact with her friends and family through social networking and texting. Quite often she is posting pictures of Hyun and updating her social network with what they are doing. Whether pushing Hyun around the neighborhood in a stroller or nursing him, she is usually on her phone. Even when she reads to him, she has her phone at her side. She takes frequent breaks from reading to him to check it, text, or post.

As our attention, and that of our children, turns from the real world and each other to the digital world, what are the consequences? Many parents, like Lien, are spending more time looking at their screens and less time being attentive to their children.[6] The numerous benefits of our screens can come at a cost when we don't meet our needs in the "ideal" way for which we evolved. Indeed, a number of researchers have found that those individuals who rate their life satisfaction as low (and who are not getting their needs met in the "real" world) are more likely to game or use social media for longer periods of time than those who express higher levels of life satisfaction.[7,8,9] Our position is that *our technologies should be used to enhance and support our in-person social relationships, rather than displace them.*

Why Are We So Captivated by Our Screens?

Trista is a stay-at-home mom with a four-year-old son, Tyson. Tyson has a lot of energy, and his mother has to keep a close eye on him or he's likely to get into some mild mischief. He frequently calls out to her, "Mom, look at me!" or "Look at what I am doing!" in hopes of gaining her attention or approval. Trista is quite active on her phone and is frequently texting her friends and posting to Facebook. She and Tyson often visit the neighborhood park and typically walk there together from their home. Trista usually walks and texts while Tyson rides in front of her on his tricycle. One day, while she is sitting on the bench at the park immersed in her phone, Tyson climbs high atop part of the playscape that is not meant for climbing. After he yells, "Look at me, Momma!" several times, Trista finally looks up from her phone only to see Tyson fall from the playscape into the gravel. She runs to console a sobbing Tyson and feels awful that she wasn't paying closer attention. Fortunately, Tyson only has some scrapes and bruises. Trista knows it could have been much worse.

The preceding scenario is playing out, in various forms, all over the world right now. In addition to parents being preoccupied with their smartphones, kids will spend hours on screens indoors, often at the expense of active free play outdoors with their friends.[10] Teens frequently congregate in groups with one another but are primarily engaged with their phones. If we evolved to meet our psychological and attachment needs with each other, how is it, then, that we keep getting sucked into our screens? *Shouldn't we naturally prefer in-person interactions to the digital?* Why are we struggling with this so much?

The Draw of Supernormal Stimuli

While there are many reasons that we use our screens, the way we evolved also makes us susceptible to the powerful spell they seem to cast upon us. As curious as it may sound, the story of a small fish called a stickleback can help us to understand why our screens can be so alluring that we prefer them over in-person connections.

A male stickleback fish slowly swims around a nest he has built in shallow water in hopes of attracting a female. He is slender, about two inches long, with a red throat. As he circles his nest, another male stickleback swims close by. This triggers a hostile response from the nesting stickleback. He aggressively swims after the intruder and chases him away.

What was the cue that signaled this male stickleback to defend his territory from his challenger? Dutch biologist Dr. Nikolass Tinbergen, a Nobel Prize winner, felt compelled to figure this out. The answer led him to discover what he termed *supernormal stimuli*.[11] Tinbergen noticed how animals, such as the male stickleback, would react to certain stimuli, such as the color red, with instinctive, behavioral responses. In the case of the male stickleback, these fish would strongly defend their territory from other male sticklebacks.

Through his observations and experiments, Tinbergen discovered it was the red throat of the fish that cued these aggressive responses. Then Tinbergen created other stimuli with the color red. For instance, he carved a piece of wood to be roughly the size of a stickleback, painted a vibrant red underside, and placed it in the water near a male stickleback. Sure enough, the stickleback vigorously attacked the piece of wood. Tinbergen observed male sticklebacks in aquariums by a window going into attack mode when a red postal van drove by! Tinbergen was able to provoke the aggressive, territorial responses in male sticklebacks by presenting them with exaggerated versions of the red stimulus, often to shapes that were not even fish-like. Interestingly, Tinbergen was able to get male sticklebacks to respond more strongly *and preferentially* to the exaggerated version of the stimulus than to other male sticklebacks!

As Tinbergen observed other animals, he discovered that many of them would also respond strongly to these exaggerated cues. For instance, mother birds would preferentially sit on larger, more colorful but plaster versions of their eggs than their own eggs. He called these cues "supernormal stimuli" because *they can cause an animal to have a greater response tendency to the exaggerated stimulus than to the natural stimulus to which it evolved to respond.*

Animals, including humans, are hardwired to respond to certain stimuli because they have a survival value in evolutionary terms. Supernormal stimuli, in essence, hijack the natural response tendency and cause animals to respond more strongly, and often preferentially, than to the natural versions of the stimuli.[12] Importantly, in nature, we don't really find supernormal stimuli. As Dr. Dierdre Barrett noted in her book *Supernormal Stimuli: How Primal Urges Overran Their Evolutionary Purpose*, "Animals encounter supernormal stimuli mostly when experimenters build them. We humans can produce our own."[13]

Humans and Supernormal Stimuli

Humans are so much more self-aware than most animals—one would think that we should be able to resist the pull of supernormal stimuli. Unfortunately, we aren't much better than male sticklebacks at resisting them. The almost irresistible pull of supernormal stimuli can lead to a host of negative outcomes.[14] Consider the appeal of junk food. We are naturally drawn to salt, sugar, and fat. In the state of nature, these are in short supply but are important to our survival. Sugar in foods like fruit provides a rich source of calories, nutrients, and energy. However, food manufacturers have learned to capitalize on our natural tendency to be drawn to these foods and provide us with fat, sugar, and caloric nightmares such as Cinnabons, bacon double cheeseburgers, grilled cheese, stuffed crust pizza, and venti frappuccinos. While researchers can't replicate this study in humans for ethical reasons, in one study of rats intense sweetness surpassed cocaine as a preferred reward.[14] A number of researchers have found that supernormal stimuli appear to activate the same reward mechanisms in the brain as addictive drugs.[15,16]

Our attraction to the supernormal stimuli in our foods seems to be responsible, at least in part, for the obesity epidemic that is contributing to countless deaths each year.[17] Consider that the percentage of Americans who are overweight and obese is 68.4%, with an estimated annual health-care cost of $147–$210 billion.[18] Obesity is the second leading cause of preventable deaths in the United States behind smoking. Around 300,000 people in the United States die each year of obesity-related health problems.[19] In comparison, there were about 575,000 American combat deaths in all wars in US history combined, as of 1991 when the Persian Gulf War ended.[20] *Thus, in just about two years, at least as many deaths occur in the United States from obesity as all the military combat deaths in US history combined.* Clearly, the consequences of millions of Americans having an unhealthy diet are very real.

One might think we'd be drawn to raw fruits and vegetables more than junk food. However, the power of supernormal stimuli entices us to select unnatural foods over more natural and healthier options. If fresh fruits and vegetables appealed to us more than junk food, we'd certainly be much better off!

Technology as Supernormal Stimuli

Alexa, a college freshman, is out with her friends at a party on a Saturday night. A live band is playing spot-on covers of some of her favorite songs. Although she is at an exciting party with many of her friends, she always keeps her cell phone in hand. She checks it constantly, and is curious to see what some of her other friends are up to who are not at this party. She disengages from the music and those around her to read and respond to texts and snapchats. She wonders whether her other friends are having more fun than she is having with her current group of friends. She has a fear that she is missing out on a better experience.

So what do technologies such as email, Facebook, texting, gaming, and, yes, even Internet pornography, have to do with supernormal stimuli? Many of the technologies that we are most drawn to can be considered supernormal stimuli.[21,22] That is, they are exaggerated versions of stimuli to which we are evolutionarily predisposed to respond.

Our obsession with texting, for instance, can be explained in part by supernormal stimuli. In evolutionary terms, communicating with others and maintaining strong relationships are critically important for our survival. We are inherently social creatures. Studies consistently show that strong social relationships increase psychological and physical well-being as well as longevity, whereas social isolation and weak social ties have the opposite effect.[23] In terms of self-determination theory, "relatedness" is a powerful psychological need that intrinsically motivates our behavior.[24] A number of researchers have found that social interactions can stimulate the same reward circuits in the brain that are active in drug addiction, particularly in adolescents.[25,26]

But throughout our evolutionary history, we were not texting at all hours to our entire social network, some of whom are across the globe in different time zones, and so on. Thus, at least in part, we might be drawn to both initiate texts and respond to them because they are supernormal stimuli. From this standpoint, texting and social media can be viewed as exaggerated versions of the life-sustaining relationships of our evolutionary past. In essence, these supernormal stimuli serve as powerful lures that hijack our brains and compel us to both respond and reach out to others via texting and social media.

While there are many reasons technology appeals to us, we can see supernormal stimuli in many forms of technology.

Novelty

We are strongly and intrinsically motivated to seek novelty and sensations within our environments. This is because they could provide information critical to our survival.[27,28] For instance, they could signal that a predator, prey, or a mate is nearby. If we did not seek out novelty and take risks, especially during adolescence and young adulthood, our evolution might have floundered. Thus, seeking novelty and sensations is adaptive from an evolutionary viewpoint.[29,30,31] In fact, novelty appears to activate the same reward centers of the brain as other rewards, such as food.[32] Our screens offer endless novelty and sensations in the form of news, social interactions, gossip, games, videos, and so on. We are always just a click, touch, or swipe away from a limitless supply of novelty. Often this novelty beckons us in the form of chimes, buzzes, and push notifications that are irresistible.

Information

Humans, along with many other organisms, are naturally curious because curiosity motivates us to acquire knowledge about our environments.[33] Evolutionarily, we are drawn to seek information because it helps us to make causal connections that enable us to better understand the world in which we live.[34] This, in turn, improves our chances of survival. Researchers have described how humans seem to forage for information in a manner that is similar to the way in which our ancestors foraged for food.[35] Indeed, knowledge is power, and power helps us to survive and thrive. Like novelty, seeking and learning new information activates the reward circuits of the brain.[36,37] It is understandable why we have been compelled to seek information throughout our evolutionary history. For instance, in our hunter-gathering phase of existence, it was important for us to learn which tree was producing ripe fruit, where we could find running water, and who might be a suitable mate.

Interestingly, we often seem to be more drawn to negative news and information. For instance, if we didn't notice which tree bore good fruit, nevertheless we would likely have lived to see another day. However, if we failed to turn our attention to the "news" that there was a pride of lions nearby, we could have swiftly met our end. Thus, people, particularly males, tend to be drawn to negative news over positive news, which is sometimes referred to as a form of "negativity bias."[38] The mud-slinging involved in political campaigning is a prime example of how we are drawn to negative news over positive news. With access to endless streams of intriguing information through the Internet and our smartphones, we are drawn to the supernormal stimuli of the news and knowledge at our fingertips.

Videos and Gaming

Both videos and gaming tap into our natural responsiveness to movement. We experience excitation and physiological arousal from viewing action. We need to pay attention to movement because it can provide important information that could be critical to our survival, such as whether the movement comes from a predator or prey.[39] That's one reason that it is so hard to walk by a TV without stopping for a few moments to watch, regardless of the content. Once again, our technologies provide an endless assortment of movements and actions that are supernormal with respect to what is typically encountered in the natural world.

Pornography

We are naturally drawn to mate and procreate, and thus to be responsive to certain physical characteristics. If we weren't, we wouldn't be here! Internet pornography can override this natural urge and attract our attention to exaggerated versions of the body, sex, sexuality, and novelty.[40] To provide some context, Pornhub, one of the world's most popular pornography sites, reported in 2015 that it receives 2.4 million visitors per hour and that globally, users spent over 4.3 *billion* hours viewing content in that year alone.[41] Put another way, about 500,000 years' worth of human time were spent viewing porn in just one year—on just one pornography site. While there are many reasons that people view pornography on the Internet, it can be argued that its appeal as a supernormal stimulus is one of them.

"Likes"

Why do we like the "likes?" We evolved to care what others think of us. As discussed, strong social connections enhance our survival, so we inherently want others to like us. The likes within social media could be considered as exaggerated versions of our basic psychological need to be liked by others.

Our Psychological Needs

In their recent book, *Self-Determination Theory: Basic Psychological Needs in Motivation, Development, and Wellness*, Ryan and Deci describe how video games, virtual environments, and interactive technologies can be used to meet people's basic psychological needs for relatedness, competence, and autonomy.[42] According to their *need density hypothesis* and consistent with research findings, those individuals who are not adequately meeting their psychological needs in the real world may be especially susceptible to overuse of technology.[43,44] It is usually much easier for people to meet these needs within gaming and virtual environments because such games are often created with a density of features and mechanics to meet those needs immediately and consistently. Although Ryan and Deci don't describe it in this way, one might consider the density and accessibility of need satisfaction access points within gaming and virtual environments as supernormal stimuli. Technology offers exaggerated versions of stimuli to meet our psychological needs. Despite the ability to meet some of our psychological needs within virtual worlds and through interactive technologies, Ryan and Deci caution against its seductive nature, which can cause people to be lured away from authentic living.

Technology has filled our daily lives with supernormal stimuli. In a sense, our devices might be considered "super-supernormal" stimuli; that is, a smartphone provides a single, convenient, ever-present access point to a myriad of supernormal stimuli. It is an aggregator of supernormal stimuli. These supernormal stimuli activate the same reward centers of the brain that are involved in drug addiction.[45] Viewed from this perspective, our smartphones are the digital equivalent of having a fresh, warm Krispy Kreme doughnut always on hand that we can nibble on whenever we desire. Yes, we might resist it sometimes, but eventually we succumb to the cravings and take a digital nibble. Just as taking frequent nibbles of doughnuts throughout the day can begin to have a cumulative negative impact on our health, perhaps out frequent digital nibbles can as well. And then, of course, sometimes we even binge.

Variable Reinforcement Schedules and the "Vegas Effect"

While technology fills our world with supernormal stimuli that are almost impossible to resist, there is another powerful manner in which technology can entice us. Many forms of technology (e.g., Facebook, texting, Twitter, Instagram, email, games such as *Trivia Crack*) can powerfully attract us in the same manner as gambling and even drugs. This is because they often work on what can be considered *variable reinforcement schedules*.[46,47,48]

Dr. Jones is a highly respected archaeologist at a prestigious university. Although his work in the field is often glamorized and exaggerated, few know that the bulk of his work is done sitting at his computer. It takes Dr. Jones a great deal of time to analyze and summarize his findings from the crumpled notebooks he keeps in his satchel during his adventures. He has high hopes that some of his discoveries will be published in the top peer-reviewed journal in his field. Dr. Jones has a little secret, though. He struggles to stay productive at his computer. He receives over one hundred emails a day, from his students, colleagues, museum curators, friends, and family. He compulsively checks his email while he should be working to get his research papers published. He knows this hinders his productivity, but he finds it embarrassingly difficult to stop himself from checking his email long enough to get some solid writing done.

If you ever took an introductory psychology course, chances are you ran across Dr. B. F. Skinner.[49] He was a psychologist and behaviorist who famously looked at how behavioral responses were established and strengthened by different schedules of reinforcement. For instance, a rat in a cage that is taught to press a lever to earn a food pellet might be taught that it gets one food pellet for every three presses of the lever. This would be an example of a *fixed interval* reinforcement schedule.

Although there are a variety of types and subtypes of reinforcement schedules that can affect the likelihood of different behavioral responses, variable reinforcement schedules frequently come into play in our compulsive use of our screens. A *variable ratio* reinforcement schedule occurs when, after a variable number of actions, a certain reward is obtained. The reward will come, but we don't know exactly how many specific actions will be needed to get the reward. Slot machines are a real-world example of a variable ratio reinforcement schedule, which is why this is sometimes referred to as the "Vegas effect."

A variable ratio reinforcement schedule puts us in a state of anticipation because we don't know when we are going to experience a desired reward. When we are in this state of anticipation, a primitive reward system in the middle part of our brains is activated. This includes clusters of neurons called the nucleus accumbens and the ventral tegmental area (VTA), which are deep within the brain. The neurotransmitter dopamine, which is involved in motivation and learning, is released. This dopamine contributes to feelings of eagerness and excitement as we anticipate what might happen next.[50,51] Such feelings motivate us to take action.

One might wonder why variable reinforcement schedules act so powerfully upon our brains in the first place. It seems to come back to learning. In order to survive, it is critical that we learn how our environment works. Our brains need to make causal connections to more successfully navigate within the world. Learning these causal connections allows us to make better predictions within our environment, which, historically, could mean life or death.[52]

The brain's reward system is involved in making predictions about whether certain behaviors will lead to desired rewards.[53] This reward system is highly active when making associations between behaviors and rewards. The difference between predicted and received rewards is known as *reward prediction errors*. Variable reinforcement schedules inherently cause reward prediction errors. The prediction error is caused by the variability.

The reward system in our brains is part of a learning system because it helps us pay attention and make causal connections and associations (e.g., if I do *this*, then *that* will likely happen).[54,55] When relationships are variable, then the reward system in the brain is especially active because of the inherent prediction error. Our predictions cannot be 100% accurate when there is inherent variability. Our reward circuit releases dopamine so that we pay attention and are sufficiently motivated to take actions to obtain the desired reward.[56] Our learning system in the brain wants us to "get" this association because learning can enhance our survival.[57] However, since the relationship is variable or unpredictable, dopamine keeps being released to ensure that we are paying attention in the effort to decipher a potential association. Our brains, in essence, are trying to "crack the code" of variable situations so that we can obtain a desired reward (e.g., news, information, social feedback, or connection).

Imagine that some of our hunter-gatherer ancestors were hunting small game 100,000 years ago in a forested area. If they could discern when certain animals or other foods were most available, they could be more successful in their hunting and foraging endeavors. *What is the pattern of animal movement? Can we predict when they will be most available to hunt? Is there evidence of a predator that I need to be wary of? Does this area of brush have good fruit that we can find and eat?*

The "Vegas Effect" and Our Screens

Again, we fully acknowledge that there are many reasons that we use our devices. But when we examine the way we compulsively check our screens, psychological "hooks" are certain to be involved. This explains why we might ignore friends, or our kids, in our presence in order to check our cell phones, might compulsively check our email instead of working, or may even succumb to the temptation of texting while driving.

Many aspects of our daily technology use (e.g., texting, email, social media use) appear to operate to a large extent on a variable reinforcement schedule.[58] Thus, the primitive reward system in the brain is activated, and we get "hooked" into using our devices. We feel compelled to check our screens as we seek some desired reward, such as information or social connection, and this compulsion is very difficult to resist.[58]

We all know that feeling when our cell phone buzzes in our purse or pocket. As soon as it buzzes, it is very probable that the midbrain reward system is activated, dopamine is released through neural pathway projections into different parts of the brain, and we experience a compelling urge to check our phones. Importantly, it's not that we feel like we won at the Vegas slots every time we view a text. Although there is still some debate in the role of dopamine reward system in the brain, it appears that this system is activated when we are in a state of anticipation.[59] In this sense, it appears to be more involved in "wanting" than "liking."[60] For many of us, it creates the feeling of an itch that needs to be scratched.

The tech industry knows all about the power of variable reinforcement schedules. In fact, tech industry insider and consultant Nir Eyal, author of *Hooked: How to Build Habit-Forming Products*, includes variable rewards as one of the four components of his "Hook Model."[61] While Eyal cautions those in the tech industry against using the Hook Model for unethical purposes, it is clear that variable reward schedules can be found in the many compulsive ways that we use our technologies, such as social media, texting, news and information, and gaming. The variability creates a strong incentive (or hook) that motivates us to engage in specific actions to obtain those rewards.

The Problem of Compulsive Checking

Let's return to Dr. Jones and his struggles with compulsively checking his email. It's certainly having a negative effect on his productivity. On a rational level, he knows this. Despite this "head" knowledge, he still finds himself clicking his mouse to check his email every few minutes. He is not so different from rats that are trained to push a lever to receive a food pellet. When the schedule of reinforcement varies, the rats get hooked into compulsively pressing the lever—just like Dr. Jones is compulsively clicking his mouse to receive his email "food pellet." Recall that both novelty and information activate the same reward circuits as food and other rewards, so we can understand why our esteemed Dr. Jones has such a difficult time resisting his urge to check his email.[62,63]

We compulsively check our texts, email, news updates, social media, and news feeds, and game activity such as *Clash of Clans*. Since we carry our smartphones with us wherever we go, and we almost always have access to cellular service or Wi-Fi, we always have the opportunity to check our devices. Also, others can always ping us, and we receive notifications. Often our experience is that we don't consciously *choose* to check our devices. Rather, it feels more like a compulsion that we *have* to check our devices. As Dr. Adam Alter, professor of marketing and psychology at New York University notes in his book, *Irresistible: The Rise of Addictive Technology and the Business of Keeping Us Hooked*, it is difficult to escape behavioral addictions to our devices because we basically take them with us wherever we go.[64]

A useful way of looking at how we end up compulsively checking our devices comes again from Nir Eyal in *Hooked: How to Build Habit-Forming Products*. Eyal describes how investors often want to know if new products or services that they might fund are "vitamins" or "painkillers." *Vitamins*, in this context, satisfy users' emotional needs, while *painkillers* relieve some pain point. Technologies such as social media often start out as "vitamins" that are perceived to enhance our lives in some way. However, we often become hooked into them as painkillers so that we feel bad if we don't check or respond. In this sense, resisting the urge to check our devices is more "painful" than simply checking. Like many addictive drugs, it could be the case that we compulsively use technologies such as social media not to feel good, but to stop from feeling bad when we don't check them.

Brittany is an 18-year-old high school senior. She often keeps her smartphone in hand and, while driving, she keeps it on her lap. While on the way to school one day, it buzzes as she is pulling into the school parking lot. She looks down at it for just an instant, which happens to be when the car in front of her abruptly stops. She ends up rear-ending one of her classmates. Fortunately, no one is hurt, but both cars are damaged.

There is a compulsion to be in the loop and in the know. Many teens and young adults suffer from a "fear of missing out" (FoMO) that arises due to concerns that they are missing out on rewarding experiences that their friends and acquaintances might be having.[65] Curiously, this fear leads to the frequent checking of social media posts. Teens in particular might experience some social consequences for not being responsive to texts and social media posts. In our digital world, prompt responses are expected. These fears, coupled with the pull of supernormal stimuli and variable reinforcement schedules, keep us all checking, and checking, and checking.

Classical Conditioning

It can be argued that another powerful "hook" of technology that makes it so irresistible comes in the form of *classical conditioning*. Dr. Ivan Pavlov (1849–1936) was a Russian physiologist who first described and investigated this form of behavioral conditioning, which is a type of learning.[66] In a series of landmark studies, Pavlov was able to behaviorally condition dogs such that, by repeatedly pairing the tone of a metronome (conditioned stimulus) with food (unconditioned stimulus), he was able to get dogs to salivate in anticipation of food (unconditioned response) with merely the sound of the metronome (conditioned response). So, for the dogs that were classically conditioned in his experiments, he could then just ring the metronome and the dogs would salivate in anticipation of food. Studies have found that the midbrain dopaminergic reward system is activated in classical conditioning paradigms.[67,68,69]

Classical conditioning isn't just for the dogs. These mechanisms can powerfully affect humans as well.[70] In addition to innumerable studies involving classical conditioning and humans, we have our own direct experiences with the phenomenon. Perhaps the scent of a particular cologne instantly conjures positive feelings about your dad based on childhood experiences. Maybe hearing Nirvana's *Smells Like Teen Spirit* on the radio evokes images from hanging out with your friends in the college dorms because that same song was repeatedly played by a buddy (or everyone!) on your quad. The iconic golden arches of a McDonald's sign might elicit visions of a cheeseburger and your own salivation response. For a heroin addict, the sight of a hypodermic needle may elicit overpowering cravings.[71,72]

From an advertising and marketing standpoint, branding involves classical conditioning principles such that the goal is to have consumers associate positive thoughts and feelings with a brand or image.[73] For example, if we see enough ads featuring young, beautiful people drinking Coke and having fun, then if the advertising works on us the familiar image of the Coca-Cola white across a red background will evoke positive feelings. The hope for the advertisers, of course, is that these positive feelings will motivate us to purchase Coke over similar products.

When it comes to technologies, particularly our smartphones, we might be responding quite a bit like Pavlov's dogs. Our phones provide access to powerful rewards in forms such as connection, novelty, and information. Thus, the chimes of our phone (e.g., text notification) may activate the reward system in the brain through classical conditioning mechanisms. Through what is considered "second-order conditioning," just seeing our cell phones might activate a conditioned response and result in us feeling compelled to check our phones—or at least to consider doing so. Classical conditioning principles might be used to explain why the mere presence of a cell phone can diminish both the quality of social interactions as well as our cognitive performance.[74,75]

We have all developed powerful associations from our long-term use of our cell phones. Access to our friends, newsfeeds, videos, and games are all just a touch away. As such, the behavioral cues in the form of various chimes and buzzes that are associated with our phone uses (e.g., texting, social media posts and alerts, tweets) are likely to trigger emotional, cognitive, and physiological responses that are beyond our conscious control. Like Pavlov's dogs, we can't help ourselves from having such responses. Instead of salivating, our behavioral response is to check our devices.

It's important to restate that supernormal stimuli, variable reinforcement schedules, and classical conditioning all appear to activate the same reward centers in the brain as addictive drugs. In this sense, our daily technology use seems to be compelled, at least in part, by three different mechanisms that are synergistically activating the same reward circuits in the brain. For example, the buzz of our smartphones (classical conditioning) alerts us to supernormal stimuli (e.g., connection, news, novelty), but the access to the supernormal stimuli is variable (i.e., the "Vegas effect") because we don't know exactly what we will get. Thus, it is possible that the combination of variable reward schedules, classical conditioning, and supernormal stimuli create a veritable "triple-whammy" of irresistible motivation to check our devices—or at least to react to them.

Death by a Thousand Walnuts

Regarding how technology is affecting our brains, *what* we consume might not be the most problematic aspect; it may be *how much* (or how often) we consume it. Let's go back to the public health model for a moment and consider fats. Although vilified at times, fats are an essential part of our diet. There are some fats that are considered "good" fats, such as unsaturated and omega-3 fats, and that are a necessary part of a healthy diet (e.g., nuts, avocados, extra virgin olive oil). Then there are other fats, such as "trans" fats or partially hydrogenated oils that are, arguably, never healthy to consume (e.g., cookies, French fries). In this manner, it might be said that a doughnut is never a healthy food.

We have all heard of the expression, "death by a thousand cuts" and we referred to this in Chapter 1 in reference to our use of technology. Is our frequent use of technology throughout the day like death by a thousand cuts? Perhaps this is not the best analogy because even one cut is bad. They are to be avoided altogether. In contrast, technology is often beneficial. But our frequent use of it amounts to a death by a thousand walnuts.

How is this so? Going back to fats, eating foods such as walnuts can be a great way to reap the benefits of these nutritious fats. However, eating a thousand walnuts would amount to about 26,000 calories and 3,000 grams of fat. This, indeed, could lead to our death by a thousand walnuts.

Internet pornography, cyberbullying, sexual predators, distracted driving, and graphic violence are all legitimate concerns of screen use. They might rightly be considered the "junk food" of our tech use. These forms of tech use and others can all cause harm to users, and kids are likely to be particularly vulnerable. However, we believe that the more pervasive and insidious harm of technology comes with the frequency and amount of our use.

Let's say every text, email check, and social media post is like eating one walnut. By the end of the day, one has consumed hundreds of digital "walnuts." Too many walnuts on a daily basis could result in digestion problems and weight gain. Similarly, the frequent use of technology throughout the day might be having a cumulative negative effect on our attention, well-being, and relationships.[76] Indeed, there seems to be a "dose effect" of technology such that the negative effects come into play with greater usage.[77,78,79] Researchers Drs. Andrew Przybylski and Netta Weinstein found evidence supportive of the "Goldilocks hypothesis" with regard to teens' use of technology.[80] In their research, they found that frequent use of technology was associated with negative effects on well-being, whereas moderate technology use was not found to be harmful and might even have benefits. The old saying rings true *there can be too much of a good thing.*

"Average" Does Not Mean "Healthy"

As with the average food consumption of Americans, it might be said that the average or typical way in which we use our screens is not healthy. Using data from the US Department of Agriculture, the Pew Research Center found that the average number of calories consumed by Americans went up 23% between 1970 (2,025 calories/day) and 2010 (2,481 calories/day). Not surprisingly, researchers have found that the rise in caloric intake has contributed to the rise in obesity rates.[81] Thus, when it comes to our diet, one can say that the average calorie intake of Americans is not healthy, and we pay a price for that.

As our kids use their screens to play games, check social media, and stream content, we might also assume that their use isn't unhealthy because their screen use is typical of most kids. However, given the amount of time we and our children spend on our sceens and the frequency with which we check them, we must be careful not to conflate "average" or "typical" with "healthy." While we and our children may indeed benefit from moderate screen use, it can be argued that the typical amount and frequency with which we use them is beyond moderate.

The Takeaway?

We feel the pull of our screens, often hundreds of times per day. We are so conditioned to its call that even when someone else's phone rings or buzzes, we reflexively reach for our own devices. Most of us experience "phantom" buzzes or rings in which we think our phone vibrated or chimed only to realize that it didn't—*or did it?* While extreme dangers of screen use such as sexual predators do exist, just about all of the most severe dangers of screen use are nested within our daily use. The more that we are hooked into our screens, the more likely that we, and our children, become exposed to more extreme dangers.

It might just be our day-to-day usage that is causing the greatest problems, at least on a societal level. We often seem to get sucked into our screens at the expense of our in-person relationships, physical activity, sleep, and sustained attention. While there are many reasons we are drawn to our screens, including positive uses, we all experience the feeling of being compelled to check our screens. The ways in which our screens tap into primitive reward systems in our brains in the forms of supernormal stimuli and variable reinforcement schedules seem to be two of the main reasons that we get so "hooked" into our screens. Classical conditioning principles seem to be at work as well, with the sounds and sights of our devices evoking unconscious reactions. We evolved to live in a world very different from this digital world. Old parts of our brain are often being hijacked by our devices.[82]

Many who work in the tech industry know how to exploit these old parts of our brains to great profit. They want our eyes on screens because that's how they make money. While that might not be inherently bad, the cumulative effect of many companies all competing for our attention through our screens might come at a cost. There are good reasons to believe that companies will continue to do so and will become even more effective at it. As renowned Silicon Valley investor Paul Graham observed, "The world is more addictive than it was 40 years ago. And unless the forms of technological progress that produced these things are subject to different laws than technological progress in general, the world will get more addictive in the next 40 years than it did in the last 40."[83]

We are affected by how we spend our time. Our experiences, in part, shape who we are. Nowadays, we are all consuming *a lot* of digital walnuts. While some of our screen use clearly has benefits, our eyes, and the eyes of our children, are often more on our screens and less on each other. Time on our screens can displace other need-satisfying activities, especially in-person time with each other.

There are clearly both benefits and consequences to our screen use. In Chapter 5, we explore the effects of our screen use on us and our kids. Knowledge is power, and arming ourselves with knowledge about the effects of technology can help us to get the most out of our screens. But we must always keep in mind that we evolved to get our needs met with each other in person. So we believe that our screen use, no matter how beneficial, will become harmful if its use undermines and displaces our in-person relationships excessively.

5

The Effects of Technology on Children and Families

In 1973 Woody Allen released the movie *Sleeper*, in which his character, Miles Monroe, thaws from a cryogenic hibernation 200 years in the future. The scientists who observe him are surprised at his breakfast request:

> DR. MELIK: He requested something called wheat germ, organic honey and tiger's milk.
> DR. AGON: [laughs] Oh, yes. Those were the charmed substances that some years ago were felt to contain life-preserving properties.
> DR. MELIK: You mean there was no deep fat? No steak or cream pies? Or hot fudge?
> DR. AGON: Those were thought to be unhealthy, precisely the opposite of what we now know to be true.
> DR. MELIK: Incredible.[1]

And in our present, nonfiction world, what is the current wisdom from nutrition science? Eggs are bad for you. Or eggs are good for you. Wait, what does the latest research say? We feel frustrated when scientific research about nutrition provides strong recommendations (i.e., *lower your consumption of dietary cholesterol*) and later read about contradictory findings (i.e., *it's fine to eat eggs and dairy because they won't significantly affect your blood cholesterol*). But perhaps we shouldn't be surprised when we see conflicting reports, given the methodological weaknesses of the studies and the tendency for scholars, journalists, and policymakers to overstate the findings. For those of us who want to eat healthy meals, we depend on good science to inform our choices, yet we're hard pressed to find reliable guidance in this area. For example, author Nina Teicholz wrote in the *New York Times* that even the most basic dietary recommendations lack sufficient scientific support, noting that "[i]t's possible that a mostly meatless diet could be healthy for all Americans—but then again, it might not be. We simply do not know."[2] So, should we eat eggs? Or hot fudge? Drink wine?

The consumption of digital media has something in common with the consumption of eggs: research findings are preliminary, inconclusive, mixed, and often overstated. Keep in mind that we've been studying people eating eggs a lot longer than we've been studying people using smartphones and consuming social media. So all research on the effects of new digital technologies is, well, *new*.

In this chapter we summarize some of the research about the effects of technology on our relationships, mood, productivity, and other important areas for children and families. This is not meant to be an exhaustive review, but we want to highlight some important areas of concern. Technology is such a sprawling landscape that attempting to summarize how our screens affect us is like trying to summarize how life affects us. Our experiences in the digital world, just like the real world, can range from good to ill. Sometimes the effects are for good *and* ill simultaneously.

In reviewing this research, we'll underscore the fact that while the research is still young and technology changes rapidly, there are some solid reasons why our kids should not be given unbridled access to screens. That being said, based on the research and what we've discussed in previous chapters, we also want to offer some guidance as well as food for thought. Ultimately, we must become very mindful of how our screens are affecting us and our families. Before we dive into the research, we first want to tell the story of a product that many parents bought because they believed it would make their kids smarter.

Lessons from Baby Einstein

Juanita is a mother of two children, aged one and four. She also runs a small business and volunteers at her community library. She enjoys reading to her children and playing with them outside, but also needs some adult quiet time so that she can accomplish tasks for her business. From time to time, she will sit her kids in front of the television and play an educational video so that she can have some quiet time to work. She feels a little bit guilty about this but tries to make these screen-time moments rare.

Remember *Baby Einstein*? In the late 1990s a series of videos for babies were produced and sold to parents as educational materials. The products were wildly successful and the Baby Einstein Company was bought by the Walt Disney Company for $25 million in cash in 2001, and became a popular franchise that also included toys and other products.[3] As researchers began to study the effects of viewing Baby Einstein videos, some intriguing (and conflicting) results emerged. Allegations that the products didn't have a positive effect on cognitive development ultimately led to Disney's decision to offer refunds to parents. What are the effects of "screen time," whether it's exposure to videos, tablets, or other digital devices, on the minds of infants and toddlers?

Based on a review of research on the effects of technology on developing minds, the American Academy of Pediatricians (AAP) has made recommendations regarding screen time and young children. In their 2016 updated recommendations, AAP advises, "For children younger than 18 months, discourage use of screen media other than video-chatting" and "[f]or parents of children 18 to 24 months of age who want to introduce digital media, advise that they choose high-quality programming/apps and use them together with children, because this is how toddlers learn best. Letting children use media by themselves should be avoided."[4]

Given such a clear and strong recommendation from a prestigious medical organization, why would so many families sit their kids in front of Baby Einstein videos? After all, the AAP recommended no screen time before age two during the height of Baby Einstein's popularity. It's possible that many parents are not aware of media guidelines for infants and toddlers, given the fact that commercially available products are marketed more heavily than are physicians' recommendations.[5] Perhaps some parents are willing to try something that may help give their kids a cognitive edge in a competitive world. Did the research support the idea that these videos made a positive difference?

One study suggested that those children who watched the videos showed no improvements in language development over kids who didn't watch the videos.[6] Another study found that children who watched videos knew fewer words than those who did not watch,[7] but an independent analysis of those data did not reach the same conclusions.[8] Looking at the body of research on television/video viewing by children under the age of two, we can conclude that there do not appear to be any clearly documented benefits, nor do there appear to be any clearly documented cognitive/language declines. Parents may ask then, what's to be gained by showing baby-oriented media to children under two, and at what cost?

A recent review of the developmental research on television viewing found that infants learn very little from television and "there is evidence that the constant presence of background television frequently gets young children's attention and distracts them during play, reduces their focused attention, and diminishes parent-child interaction."[9] We know that during the first year of life, learning occurs best when infants interact with adults and other children, and that time in front of a screen is time that's not spent engaged with a human.

What happens when parents and children watch educational videos together? Not surprisingly, the quality of parent-child interactions decreases when the television is on, and when parents watch educational videos with infants that are designed to enhance learning, engagement suffers.[10] Consistent with the "dose effect" of other technologies, while there may be some benefit in small doses, lots of time in front of the television appears to do more harm than good.

Considerations Regarding the Effects of Technology

Earlier we provided a case example of Juanita, whose children are one and four years old. As a busy parent, she may not have time to sift through the AAP recommendations and research articles on screen time and young children. If she did set aside time to review the research, she would likely find some conflicting results. Juanita may also have her own concerns about time in front of the television as time that could be better spent in active play, exercise, or social interaction. As she searches for answers, she may also look within to ask herself why she feels uncomfortable or guilty about showing videos to her kids so that she can have some work time. She may also consider the amount of screen time in her decision-making. There's a big difference between five hours of screen time per week for young children and five hours per day. Ultimately, parents who are trying to make decisions about children's use of technology must engage in some cost-benefit analysis by asking not only what is gained by screen time, but also what is lost.

There may very well be gains. For example, the use of a smartphone app that helps a child learn the alphabet may produce some positive, measurable learning outcomes. Importantly, the fact that children learn from the app does not necessarily mean that this kind of learning is *superior* to learning from a parent or other adult. The app certainly can't capitalize on an emotional bond during the learning process, or connect the letter "O" to the oatmeal that the child had for breakfast that morning. Kids learn in lots of different ways, and it may be helpful for them to learn from both humans and apps. But overreliance on a device to teach, babysit, or entertain will likely limit opportunities for family members to interact, socialize, play, and connect, which are all important components of healthy development.[11] As we discussed in Chapter 3, there are opportunity costs associated with spending time in front of screens. With a finite amount of time in every day, screen time subtracts from opportunities to participate in other important activities.[12,13]

We all long for clear answers and guidance in raising our children, especially with regard to technology. But the reality is that technology, like life, is complicated. Researchers find it virtually impossible to explore all of the many nuances of the effects of technology as it continues to evolve. This makes summarizing the research into rock-solid recommendations a challenge. To better illustrate these challenges, let's more closely examine the effects of video-game violence on children, as that is often near the top of parental concerns about technology.

The Effects of Video-Game Violence on Kids and Teens

Li Zhou is a 14-year-old Asian-American boy who generally does well in school. Like most boys his age, he enjoys playing video games. He has been playing them in various forms since he was about four years old. His parents managed and monitored what he played and for how long throughout his childhood. They used ratings from the Entertainment Software Rating Board (www.esrb.org) to guide their decisions on what games they allowed him to play. They tried to limit his game playing to about one hour per day with some extra time allowed on weekends, holidays, and special occasions. As Li grew older, they allowed him more freedom on his game play. They reasoned that he had many friends, wasn't a discipline problem, maintained high marks in school on his own, and had a number of other hobbies, including tennis and piano. Also, since becoming a teenager, they knew they needed to give him more autonomy than he had as a child.

Li recently started playing a game in the Call of Duty *series,* Infinite Warfare. *This is a first-person shooter, and Li enjoys playing on a team online with several of his friends. It is rated "M" for "Mature" (ages 17+) by the ESRB. Li's parents have watched him play and are concerned that the gratuitous violence could have a negative impact on him. Might he become more violent and aggressive? They have talked to Li about it, and he dismissed their concerns. "Mom, Dad—it's just a video game! I'm not going to turn into some psycho-killer because of this! I'm just having fun with my friends! Besides, my friends and I have all outgrown* Mario *games. This is what they all play now." Although Li's parents understand his point of view, they don't entirely agree with it. They wonder whether such a violent game could be having a negative effect on him and other players, especially since Li is playing it around two hours per day and more on the weekends.*

Since their entry into popular culture in the late 1970s, the violence in video games has alarmed parents, politicians, and child development experts. For example, giving his personal opinion on the subject in 1982, former US Surgeon General Dr. C. Everett Koop stated that there is ". . . nothing constructive in the games . . . . Everything is eliminate, kill, destroy."[14] Acclaimed Stanford psychologist Dr. Philip Zimbardo echoed these feelings in 1983 when he stated, "Eat him, burn him, zap him is the message rather than bargaining and cooperation. Most games feed into the masculine fantasies of control, power, and destruction."[15]

Starting in the 1980s and using a body of research supporting a causal relationship between viewing television violence and increased aggression, researchers also pursued and found this link with video game violence.[16] Numerous studies continue to support a connection between playing violent video games and negative outcomes such as increased aggressive behavior, feelings of hostility, and decreased prosocial behavior.[17,18]

However, the body of research linking violent video-game play to such negative outcomes is not without its critics. Indeed, in an open letter to the American Psychological Association (APA) in 2013, 228 academics and scholars wrote to express their concerns that the APA's Task Force on Violent Media came to strong, overgeneralized conclusions about the negative effects of media violence that were based on weak or insufficient data and publication biases.[19] A closer examination of the research literature on the effects of video-game and media violence shows why there is room for debate and ongoing research on this issue. A number of researchers have *not* found a relationship between playing violent video games and negative outcomes, such as increased aggression and hostility, desensitization to violence, or decreased empathy.[20,21,22] In a study published in *Journal of Pediatrics* in 2009, psychologist and Stetson University professor Dr. Christopher Ferguson, who is co-author of *Moral Combat: Why the War on Violent Video Games Is Wrong*, and sociologist and Texas A&M International University professor Dr. John Kilburn analyzed the research literature on the relationship between media violence and negative outcomes, such as increased aggression, and identified a systematic publication bias favoring studies that showed such a relationship. When they statistically controlled for this publication bias, the relationship between media violence and negative outcomes, such as increased aggression, virtually disappeared. In a 2015 meta-analysis of the effects of video game violence, Ferguson concluded that ". . . video games, whether violent or nonviolent, have minimal deleterious influence on children's well-being."[23]

Even the large body of research associating the negative effects of television viewing on kids and teens is not without noteworthy limitations and critics. For example, University of Nebraska at Omaha criminology professor Dr. Joseph Schwartz and Florida State University criminology professor Dr. Kevin Beaver conducted a comprehensive re-examination of the literature claiming a causal relationship between television viewing and various forms of criminal behavior, including violent behavior.[24] They concluded that genetic influences, which were not adequately controlled for in other studies, appeared to be causally related to these negative outcomes and not the television viewing per se.

Still, this is not to say that video games (or other media forms, such as TV) have no effect on kids and teens. To put it simply, video games create experiences, and our experiences affect us. With this concept, it is also clear that experiences have a greater influence the more one engages in them. We all know this intuitively and from our own lives. The more we practice at something, the better at it we become. Practicing guitar or chess or learning a foreign language for one hour per week will only allow us to progress so far, whereas 10–20 hours per week of dedicated or deliberate practice will more quickly develop expertise. Consistent with this idea, a number of researchers point to a "dose effect" of gaming such that any positive and/or negative effects are more likely to appear the more frequently children play these games.[25,26,27]

While there is still some debate about the extent to which video-game violence results in negative effects such as increased aggression in players, it appears likely that whatever contribution they have to the overall level of societal violence is small.[28] It has been well documented that levels of violence have fallen precipitously over the past 30 years in the United States, including levels of adolescent and young adult violence.[29,30] In his comprehensive and compelling book, *The Better Angels of Our Nature: Why Violence Has Declined*, Harvard psychologist Dr. Steven Pinker statistically supports the position that we are, despite what the media might have us believe, living in the most peaceful time in human history.[31]

This drop in societal violence has occurred despite a proliferation of increasingly sophisticated violent video games, a fact noted by the academics and scholars in their open letter critical of the APA's stance on media violence.[32] There is no question that video-game violence continues to be quite popular. For instance, since the middle of the first decade of the 2000s, the M-rated first-person shooter, *Call of Duty*, and its sequels have sold almost 250 million copies globally as of

June 2017.[33] Although it's difficult to get precise figures on how many kids under the age of 17 play such games, one study found that most boys and many girls do.[34] While the factors that influence aggression are many, one would think that, if these violent games profoundly elicited the aggressive behavior that many fear, then we would see a tremendous spike in societal violence levels. We just aren't seeing that.

It is most certainly not the case that moderate exposure to the typical violence levels found in many video games turns kind, compassionate, responsible kids into psychopaths or highly aggressive bullies. But could playing *certain* violent video games in *sufficient* quantities influence *some* kids to be more hostile and aggressive and less empathetic to *some* extent? Undoubtedly the answer to that question is "yes." Even so, the variables that contribute to the development of violent behavior are many and complicated. As such, a number of researchers have noted that a nuanced approach is needed to more accurately describe the effects of video-game and media violence on children and teens.[35,36,37,38]

So, what are we to do as parents? Should we restrict our kids from playing violent video games altogether because they could become more aggressive and less empathetic? Should we limit their exposure to television violence as well? As in all of life, definitive answers and certainties are hard to come by in the social sciences. If we are wondering about the effects of these games, we might ask questions such as the following:

- How old is the child? How developmentally mature is he or she? Does he or she have a history of mental health issues? Does the child have a history of aggression and hostility?
- Which video game is it? What is it rated? What types of violence does it depict? Is it realistic? Can the child play the role of the "bad guy?"
- What medium (or platform) is the game being played on (e.g., smartphone, tablet, console, virtual reality headset)?
- How long is the child playing the game per day, over what period of time?

- Are family members, peers, and community accepting of violent behaviors and attitudes?

At this point, you might be wondering if we are going to offer any guidance regarding video games! We offer a more extensive list of recommendations in Appendix 2, but here is a short list of recommendations:

- Check the ESRB ratings and select games that are appropriate for your child's age/developmental level. While playing typical violent video games in moderate amounts is unlikely to be extremely harmful, there is a potential for negative effects. Thus, we believe it is better to err on the safe side.
- Steer your child toward less violent games, particularly if the violence depicted is realistic or allows him or her to play the role of the "bad guy." There are literally thousands of fun, engaging, low- or nonviolent gaming options available for kids these days.
- Given the issue of the "dose" and "displacement" effects, limit your child's gaming time to perhaps an hour per day during the week and two hours per day on the weekends.
- If you notice increases in your child's anger, hostility, or aggressive behavior when playing certain games, it may be time to step in and redirect him or her to other options. When such problems arise, your child is likely at the Yellow Light Level of our Tech Happy Life model. We discuss how to address such challenges in the following chapters.

Relationships

Peter comes home from school with a level of excitement that can hardly be contained. He runs to his father and begins to talk about the mummy project his class is starting this week. As he begins to describe how, with the help of his teacher, he and his peers will make and bury a mummy, Peter's father absentmindedly nods his head as he texts a colleague while Peter is talking. There's no eye contact, nor any real connection, and Peter realizes that his father isn't really listening.

Healthy relationships are central to our overall well-being and happiness, so a closer look at how technology may enhance or disrupt our relationships deserves our attention.[39] Our earliest attachments to parents and caregivers form through face-to-face interactions, yet the introduction of tablets and smartphones has the potential to take our eyes away from the faces of others. An emerging body of research shows that infants who have poor eye contact during the first year of life may be at greater risk for psychological difficulties later in life.[40] Although it's unclear how much parenting and heredity factor into this risk, one can turn to other research findings to draw connections.

Interestingly, researchers have shown that cutting back on screen time for even short periods of time can improve some skills associated with better relationships. In one study, preteens spent five days at a summer camp without screens and were then compared to peers with screens on the ability to recognize nonverbal emotional cues in others. Those who were without screens for five days (with greater opportunity for social interaction) showed greater improvement in recognizing the emotional cues than their peers who had access to screens.[41]

Developing and maintaining healthy relationships also require our focused attention. To truly connect with family members, we need to attend to and acknowledge the nuances within our social interactions. By giving and receiving undivided attention, we communicate to our loved ones that they're important and that they matter. Active listening, eye contact, and reciprocal communication help us develop empathy, build our social relationships, and ultimately promote our well-being.

We all want to feel important and that we have worth. Others' focused attention on us, particularly with unconditional positive regard, allows us to experience, on a fundamental level, the feeling that we matter in the eyes of others. When we turn away from others in real life and focus our eyes on screens, we may send the message that whatever is on our screen is more important than the person who is physically with us.

We are social creatures and thrive when we are in good relationships with one another, and relatedness to others is essential for our overall well-being.[42] Given the importance of our connections to each other, understanding the impact of technology on our relationships is critical.

The Internet, smartphones, social media, and e-mail offer us ways to connect with one another, and advocates of communicating through digital media suggest that technology has the potential to bring us closer together. Consider the following:

- The child in Texas who can have a live video conversation with her grandparents in California
- The Italian foreign exchange student who can email pictures of himself in New York to his parents in Florence
- The capacity for multiple teens to converse online after school about homework, relationships, and pop culture.

Even so, what happens when brains that evolved to communicate face to face begin to communicate more through texts, tweets, and Facebook posts? What's the impact on interactions within the home when we're, as Dr. Sherry Turkle describes, "alone together," looking at our separate screens, communicating with those who are not physically present? Take a moment to think about your own family and take this short questionnaire:

1. The quality of my relationships with the people in my home is negatively impacted by screen time. (Circle one: Yes / No / Sometimes)
2. Smartphone, video games, or computer time interferes with family time. (Circle one: Yes / No / Sometimes)

3. Technology has made it harder to leave work at work. (Circle one: Yes / No / Sometimes)

If you circled "Yes" or "Sometimes" for any of these statements, consider how you would like your family time spent, what high-quality family interactions would look like, and how technology may affect you and those you love.

Recall that in our Tech Healthy Life model, healthy relationships and technology can coexist, so long as we maintain some boundaries and prioritize our relationships over our devices. As parents, we have the responsibility of modeling this for our children by giving them adequate attention and eye contact, showing them how to engage face to face, and separating our family time from our screen time. Demonstrating these behaviors, in which we show kids how to live a balanced life that includes tech-free play, eye contact, interpersonal communication, and authentic engagement, falls squarely in the foundation of our Tech Happy Life model: relationship building. We must invest in our relationships with our kids in order to build and maintain their capacity to relate to others. This is central to their (and our) well-being. Through our relationship with our kids, we are able to most effectively use our Green Light, or level one, preventive strategies. Here we are preventing excessive use of technology that has the potential to interfere with our relationships and well-being.

Liz is a 13-year old girl who enjoys using social media and taking photographs. She aspires to be a visual artist and posts images of her drawings and photos on Instagram, as well as pictures of herself and her friends on Facebook. The positive feedback she receives from others makes her feel good, and she has quickly learned to dismiss or block unsavory comments and hurtful responses. Social media facilitates connections to others, and even led to a scholarship in a summer art program in her city. More recently, she has become interested in politics and has used social media to stay informed about current events and to dialogue with others about issues that are important to her, such as funding for the arts, women's rights, and poverty.

Much of the literature on screen time concerns include difficulties in relationships. In fact, a great deal of research on the topic of *problematic internet use* (PIU) has linked excessive time spent online (i.e., a dose effect) with a variety of relationship problems.[43] There seems to be a chicken-and-egg question surrounding relationships and PIU, as some point to poor relationships as a precursor to PIU, whereas other studies cite PIU as a cause of poor relationships. Some scholars refer to PIU as an addiction to the Internet or an impulse control disorder. Obviously not everyone who uses the Internet has significantly challenging relationship issues, but it comes as no surprise that those who spend too much time in front of screens may have interpersonal difficulties. These concerns may be related to preoccupations, mood disorders, social skill deficits, or irritability.

We're still learning how family life, parent-child interactions, and happiness are affected by increased use of smartphones, video games, and the Internet. However, a large body of research in the areas of developmental psychology, child development, and family systems tells us that healthy, well-adjusted individuals feel connected to those around them.[44] When we fail to form and maintain our most intimate and loving relationships, we fail to take care of our most basic needs. When technology disrupts these relationships, families have to find ways to reconnect to each other, even if it means disconnecting from devices.

Mood

How are you feeling? It's a question family members ask each other, though perhaps not often enough. When we're at our best, we listen carefully to the responses of the ones we love. If we're taking good care of ourselves, we also look within and ask, *How am I feeling?*

These are important questions to ask in the context of technology and screen time as well. For example:

- To the kid who has spent three hours playing video games: *How are you feeling?*
- To ourselves, after scrolling through social media posts for an hour: *How did that make me feel?*
- To a romantic partner who has been working on the computer all day: *How are you? What does it feel like to be in front of a screen for so much time?*

We recognize that digital media are not inherently bad, and that the quality and quantity of the media are important factors to consider. Even so, "problematic media" (e.g., video-game violence, online gambling, and pornography) in large doses are associated with negative outcomes.[45] Regarding social media, in one study involving 180 college students, the more time students spent on Facebook, the more likely they were to experience mild depressive symptoms.[46] The researchers concluded that these negative feelings were primarily caused by unfavorable social comparisons. Other researchers have found that negative feelings brought on by Facebook use might be caused by the perception that the time spent was not meaningful.[47] FoMO, or the fear of missing out, is associated with low levels of life satisfaction and unmet psychological needs.[48]

Given that our screen use can have negative effects on our well-being, it's important to be mindful of how it is affecting us. Taking time to look at the well-being of our family members can help the process of screening for potential problems. So, suppose you have set some limits on the quality and quantity of screen time in your home and want to know whether your kids are at risk for problems at current consumption levels. A rough screener might include questions like the following:

- Do kids complain of boredom when they don't have access to screens?

- Does screen time produce lethargy or irritation?
- Are family members irritable around the use of the Internet?
- Are screens the go-to place when family members feel sad or lonely?
- Does having to turn off or put away screens cause irritability, emotional outbursts, or conflicts?
- Has screen time significantly replaced meaningful family connections and other activities?

Our Family Assessment of Screen Time (FAST) tool, which can be found in Appendix 1, can also help with this process. The focus here is on self-assessment, as well as understanding the effects of technology on our family members. Technology affects us in different ways, and while quality and quantity are important factors, individual differences also play a role. Sometimes by looking at our patterns of behaviors and associated moods we can gain insight into what's working in our lives and what isn't. This kind of information may be right in front of our noses, but without some focused attention and self-awareness, we may not see it. Younger children will need guidance from adults to better understand how technology affects them.

Consideration of technology's effects on mood should also take into account that which is displaced by screens. Our mood is dependent on a variety of factors, including sleep, exercise, and social interaction. We know that play is essential for healthy child development, yet many kids have limited opportunities to play freely at school.[49] Every hour that children spend in front of screens takes away an hour of play, social engagement, and language development.[50] When these important developmental needs aren't met, our children are at greater risk for cognitive, social, and emotional challenges. As addiction specialist and the author of Glow Kids, Dr. Nicholas Kardaras, observed, "Not getting the right kind of human contact and nurturing support at key developmental periods in childhood can lead to profound emotional and psychological problems."[51]

Productivity

Try to imagine growing your own food, making your own clothes, and building your own home. Technological innovations have made modern life much more convenient in many ways that free up time for other pursuits. Writing this book without the benefit of a computer and Internet access would certainly have taken a lot longer. Given the ease and rapidity with which we can now communicate, share resources, and create, we might think of technology as a great gift in terms of our productivity.[52] There's certainly some truth to this perception, but there's another side to the coin.

The effects of new technologies, including the ways in which screen time may affect the brain, are still emerging, though some research suggests that we should proceed with caution, particularly with young children. For example, some animal studies have demonstrated that overstimulating the brain as it is developing may have a detrimental impact on cognitive (thinking) skills, including memory.[53] Though technology may be designed to improve productivity, we should think twice about eroding the cognitive potential of young children and how that may impact future productivity.

Emerging research suggests a relationship between screen time and attention-deficit hyperactivity disorder (ADHD). While it is certainly true that technologies such as smartphones and video games are not at the root cause of ADHD, researchers have found that more hours spent in front of screens is associated with greater attention problems.[54] Interestingly, the researchers believe that the potential for eroding attention does not necessarily come from the screens, but perhaps from the high-paced, choppy nature of modern entertainment, including video games that require the user to make many rapid decisions.[55] In another study of over 3,000 children in Singapore carried out over three years, Iowa State University researcher Dr. Douglas Gentile and colleagues found evidence of a bidirectional, causal relationship between video-game playing and ADHD.[56] Thus, video-game playing predicted subsequent increases in attention problems, even when prior attention problems were statistically controlled. Given the importance of sustained attention for learning and work, these findings are concerning.

Though today's young adults were not exposed to iPads and smartphones as toddlers, they too struggle with the distractions of digital technologies. Consider this 19-year-old psychology major's experience:

> When my friends and I get together to study, we can't go more than five minutes without checking our phones. I'm really bad, but one of my friends is even worse. Last time we got together I had to take her phone away from her so that she could focus on her studies. It's ridiculous!

In our daily lives, technology has become omnipresent with the advent of smartphones and smartwatches. We carry devices everywhere we go and may even feel naked without them. Moreover, they push notifications to us that take us out of the here and now. Consider the parent who is reading a book to his child and is interrupted with texts and Twitter notifications. Even the mere presence of a smartphone can interfere with cognitive capacity, draining our brains of our finite ability to process information, which may interfere with learning, problem-solving, and creativity.[57] Ironically, devices that are promoted for increased productivity may actually interfere with their stated goal.

We may think of ourselves as good multitaskers, capable of cooking dinner, sending emails, giving our kids attention, and checking the weather app. In reality, we're generally poor multitaskers. Alarmingly, high levels of multitasking are associated with greater levels of depression and social anxiety.[58]

Rather than true multitasking (e.g., a teen texting *while simultaneously* writing an essay about William Shakespeare), we instead rapidly toggle back and forth between tasks (i.e., task-switch).[59] Transitioning from one task to another results in what researchers have termed "attention residue."[60] That is, as we transition between tasks, some of our attention is left with the prior task.

In general, we cannot abruptly transition our attention from one activity to the next without a loss in productivity or effectiveness. The frequent interruptions that come from living in this hyper-connected world can cause "attentional blinks" that disrupt our cognitive control and weaken our accuracy, response speed, and performance across basically any task requiring sustained attention.[61,62] Turns out, we're much more productive when we focus on one task at a time. This is a challenge for those who work on a computer that not only has word processing and other productivity applications, but also Facebook, texting, and other distractions. Despite solid research evidence to the contrary, the typical teen and young adult believes that he or she can effectively juggle six to seven media forms at once.[63] In a partial backlash to "multitasking," the importance of "monotasking" or "unitasking" is now being trumpeted by some.[64]

A Deficit in Awareness?

There is another concerning problem about the way in which we use our devices that makes it difficult to address some of the negative effects of our screen use. We're often unaware (or in denial) of how our screen use is affecting us (and possibly others). For example, in one study comparing estimated smartphone use to actual smartphone use, young adults checked their smartphones twice as often as they thought they did.[65] In a different study conducted by University of Texas School of Business professor Dr. Adrian Ward and colleagues documenting the "brain drain" caused by the mere presence of smart phones, the vast majority of study participants surveyed indicated that they did not think that the presence of the phone affected their task performance.[66] Teens believe they can effectively juggle multiple screens at once without affecting their performance. In one study, young adults who tended to multitask the most performed worse on laboratory tests of multitasking than those who multitasked less frequently in their daily lives.[67] This finding prompted the researchers to conclude that "participants' perceptions of their multi-tasking ability were poorly grounded in reality."[68] A sobering insight from these and similar studies is that we are unlikely to be motivated to address a problem that we don't recognize is even there.

The Takeaway?

In this chapter we have tried to describe the way technology intersects with important areas of our lives. The potential for technology to impact our functioning, both positively and negatively, is significant. Although the research on the effects of technology is, in many ways, still in its infancy, there are some general findings that we take from the review of the current research literature:

- The negative effects of screens tend to come from overuse (i.e., a dose effect), while moderate, developmentally appropriate use can often be beneficial. While there is still room for debate about whether wine or eggs are healthy for us, too much of them surely is not! This seems to be the case with our screen use as well—extreme levels of tech use is not good for us.
- There appears to be a bidirectional influence such that, at least in many cases, those individuals who tend to overuse technology have some preexisting condition (e.g., depression). The overuse, in turn, can exacerbate the preexisting condition (e.g., greater levels of depression from overuse of social media).
- We tend to be unaware of how multitasking and technology can negatively affect us (e.g., decreased productivity from multitasking). We often underestimate our screen use.
- Those who overuse technology seem to have lower levels of life satisfaction and this, in turn, seems to stem from not

adequately meeting their psychological needs for relatedness, autonomy, and competence in the "real" world.

- The effects of technology are very nuanced, with many variables influencing how and to what extent users are affected (e.g., age of child, personality differences, nature of content, platform, frequency of use).

As parents, these challenges provide us with an opportunity to self-examine, reflect, and then put into action plans that address our basic needs of having fulfilling relationships, maintaining healthy moods, and being productive contributors. In her review of the scientific research on the developmental benefits of touch, journalist and author Lydia Denworth noted, "In a society that so often substitutes virtual communication for personal contact, the findings on affective touch remind us to relish every embrace and hold hugs even a few seconds longer. Those moments may be the bedrock of our richest relationships."[69]

There are valid reasons to "embrace" digital technologies to enhance our relationships, mood, and productivity. However, these same innovations may also interfere with meeting our needs and goals in these areas. The bottom line is that when our screen use causes us to stray too far away from living and interacting in the way that is consistent with our evolutionary heritage, there will be consequences—the most serious of which may be a reduction in our authentic intimacy with others.

The technologies are not going away. Our mindful use of them is critical. By raising awareness of how technology can affect relationships, mood, and productivity, family members may be better able to gain the benefits and avoid the pitfalls.

In the next chapters, we'll apply our Tech Happy Life model to help families strike a better balance. Our model starts with the foundation of the relationship. Not only are relationships the foundation of our model, they can be undermined if we don't find this balance.

6

Foundations of the Relationship

It is another typical day at the Miller residence. Meghan has been critical of her 10-year-old son, Jackson, all morning. He was slow to get ready for school, left his pajamas on the floor, barely caught the bus, left his cereal bowl on the kitchen table, and left his partially completed homework in his room. When he gets home from school, she tells Jackson about all of the things he did wrong that morning. He tells her that he will go into his room to finish his homework. He trudges to his room and shuts the door. An hour later, Meghan explodes when she finds Jackson has been playing Geometry Dash *on the iPad instead of doing his homework like he promised. He continues playing on his iPad and says, "I've never beaten this level before! I'll get to my homework in just a minute!" "You never get off of that darn iPad!" his mother says sharply through clenched teeth. An argument over his reluctance to stop playing games on the iPad escalates. Meghan literally yanks the iPad away from Jackson's clutched hands. Jackson is in tears because he had almost completed a very difficult level of the game. The long, emotional struggle leaves them both tired and resentful.*

Does this situation sound familiar? As parents, we all encounter similar challenges with our kids at times. Arguments over screens have taken a toll on families. We are proverbially, and sometimes literally, in a tug of war with our kids over screens. What's the best way to navigate through these challenges? In the preceding example, how can Meghan get her son off the iPad more effectively?

Where Do We Start?

Perhaps asking how Meghan can get her son off the iPad is the wrong question. Although we want to provide help for parents like Meghan in these difficult situations, we would prefer to reduce the frequency of such conflicts in the first place. In this chapter, we'll formally discuss the foundation for our Tech Happy Life model—the relationship. The public health model begins with preventive efforts. However, for preventive efforts to be successful, a strong, healthy parent-child relationship must be established. Everything starts here.

Our Influence Through the Relationship

We are inherently social creatures who evolved to be in relationships with one another. Thus, the need for close relationships is hard-wired. We are quite literally dependent upon one another for survival. If we think of our best times in life, those were most likely with other people—family, friends, and loved ones. Because neurochemicals associated with warmth and attachment are activated in the context of social relationships, it *feels* good to be connected with one another.[1,2] Indeed, relationships are so central to our well-being that scientists have found that social rejection activates some of the same areas of the brain that are involved in the experience of physical pain.[3] We suffer when we struggle in our relationships.

As parents, we want our kids to grow up to be happy and healthy with a balanced use of technology that influences them in beneficial ways. This helps increase the odds that their opportunity to live happy, content lives is not undermined but enhanced through their technology use. This is the key: *Our influence as parents is strongly dependent upon the quality of the relationship that we have with our children.* A large body of research supports the idea that the stronger the relationship we have with our kids, the more likely it is that we can have a positive impact on their well-being.[4,5] In a sense, the relationship is a conduit through which we influence our children.

Importantly, research supports the idea that parents influence their children's health beliefs and behaviors throughout childhood, and this influence persists into young adulthood.[6] It is true that as kids become teens they will naturally want to distance themselves from their parents as peers become the focus of their social world. This is expected because teens have psychological needs for both autonomy and competence that become especially important to satisfy during their teen and young adult years. This is why they often distance themselves from us as they transition from childhood to adolescence. That's how we might become "uncool" virtually overnight! Still, what remaining influence we can have on our teens is still highly dependent on the quality of the relationship that we have with them.

We meet our psychological need for relatedness through our connections with one another.[7] While some people exercise power over others through fear, intimidation, and other coercive means, in the long run, we more effectively influence others through close, warm, positive relationships.[8] Through healthy and secure connection with our kids, we allow space for them to grow and develop so they can meet their psychological needs for autonomy and competence. So it is critical that we build and maintain our relationships with our kids in order to have a positive influence on them. This parent-child bond starts in infancy and is often referred to as *attachment*.

Attachment theory stands out as one of the most important developments in twentieth-century psychology and has had a profound impact on parenting, education, and our understanding of mental wellness. The basic premise of attachment theory is that the early bonds that infants and young children develop with primary caregivers are integral to our development and health throughout the life span.[9] Ideally, babies develop a "secure attachment" to one or more caregivers when basic physical and emotional needs are met. For example, an infant bonds with a mother who provides emotional warmth (cuddles), food (breast milk/formula), and responsiveness (diaper changes, soothing in response to crying). This kind of parenting communicates to the child that the world is a safe place and that there's someone who can reliably provide love and care. Those who have this secure attachment go on to feel comfortable exploring and engaging with the larger world, knowing that they can return to the caregiver as a safe base.[10] As children grow older, their behaviors and social circles become more complex, but this attachment remains the foundation on which different styles of parenting are built.

Preventing Screen Problems Through the Relationship

Parenting can be challenging, even under the best circumstances. The pervasiveness of our screens is affecting all of us, creating unique challenges for families, and it is the source of much ongoing tension and conflict. There are no simple solutions. However, preventing these problems in the first place is a much more effective strategy than focusing on solutions to problems that emerge.

Our parenting styles, as well as our beliefs about how we should relate to our children, will likely drive our behavioral decisions when it comes to technology use. Some of the most influential work in the area of parenting styles, produced by the psychologist Dr. Diana Baumrind, helps make sense of how we relate to our children around themes of control and warmth.[11] Imagine that a parent's level of control with children can be measured from low to high (where low control means that the parent is permissive and high control indicates much more setting of limits). You might ask yourself at this point, *where would I fall on a continuum from permissive to controlling as a parent?* Keep in mind that though there may be parents that exhibit high levels of permissiveness or control, most fall somewhere along the continuum.

Now, imagine that a parent's level of warmth could also be measured from low to high (where low warmth means that the parent is neglectful or indifferent and high warmth suggests a great deal of

TABLE 6.1 Parenting Styles

Authoritarian	Authoritative
(low warmth, high control)	(high warmth, high control)
Permissive Neglectful	**Permissive Indulgent**
(low warmth, low control)	(high warmth, low control)

nurturing engagement). Now, apply this to your own parenting by asking yourself, *where would I fall on a warmth continuum?* Again, most parents fall not at the extreme ends, but somewhere in between.

As you think about this framework (Table 6.1) for understanding parenting styles, keep in mind that our styles vary across situations. We may exhibit less warmth when we are cranky or ill, or we may be more permissive around holidays and special occasions. However, by thinking about our typical ways of interacting with our children in the context of control and warmth, we can place ourselves in one of four common parenting styles: authoritarian, authoritative, permissive neglectful, and permissive indulgent.

Last year, Micha's screen time was fairly limited. Occasionally he played games on his parents' phones, but did not have his own device. However, his grandparents gave him a laptop for his birthday and since then he has been spending a lot of time in his room watching videos online and playing games. His parents feel like it's too much screen time for a 10-year-old, though they aren't really sure how much time he is actually spending on the computer. They're also concerned that the screen time is beginning to replace other activities, such as reading, playing outside, and engaging with family members. They don't feel like this has become a significant problem, but worry that this may be the beginning of a "new normal" that makes them feel uneasy.

How would you advise Micha's parents? Remember, it's not just about screen time. It's about the relationship, too. When screen time has taken up too much time from other important domains of childhood (e.g., outdoor play, family time, educational activities), parents may have to withdraw some of the electronics to make room for developmentally appropriate and healthy activities. Simply shutting off the gaming system will likely produce conflict. Applying parental control mindfully in the context of the warm and loving relationship will more likely yield the desired results with minimal disruption. In the case of Micha's family, they may decide that he may continue to use his laptop, but with some clear time limits and only in the living room (supervised).

Using an authoritative parenting framework, consider how Micha's family might address the screen-time concern. In the following we show how each of the four parenting types might shape the way Micha's parents respond to the growing concern that he spends too much time on the computer.

- *Authoritarian*: Micha's parents express a desire to nip this screen-time problem in the bud. They take away the laptop to set a firm limit. They decide he can no longer play video games. His anger and hurt feelings are brushed aside. They sign him up for soccer whether he likes it or not because they've decided it's good for him. The approach here is to put your foot down and don't budge, because if you give kids an inch, they'll take a mile.
- *Permissive neglectful*: Micha's parents don't pay much attention to his needs or the appropriateness of screen time for a boy his age. Consequently, he is permitted to do as he pleases. They provide little guidance or oversight regarding time spent on the computer or the nature of the content he consumes. They do not display awareness or concern regarding how technology may be affecting his well-being or shaping his development.
- *Permissive indulgent*: Micha's parents want to keep him happy and show a great deal of warmth, but in doing so may satisfy his immediate desires without much regard for his long-term

needs. When he wants computer time, they let him have it. When he asks for a new gaming system and/or video games, they get him those promptly. They don't attend to the appropriateness of the games for his age or developmental level.

- *Authoritative*: Micha's parents understand that he will benefit from consistent, reasonable limits and boundaries, and they are careful to set those limits in a warm and supportive manner. They help him understand that screen time may be fun and beneficial, but that it must also be balanced with other wants and needs.

Be Flexible Within a General Approach

These four styles should be thought of as very general approaches that parents may use when raising children, and we acknowledge that the simplified organization of types doesn't accurately match the realities of day-to-day parenting. In our experience, there's often a gap between our parenting ideals and how we act across situations that vary due to unique circumstances, stress, and other factors that are beyond our control. Even so, being able to recognize different parenting strategies and to set goals for ourselves gives us the capacity to envision the way we want to parent, and that's a step in the right direction.

As psychologists, we read and evaluate the parenting research to determine what seems to produce the best outcomes. In the case of Baumrind's work mentioned earlier, the data point toward high warmth and high control (authoritative) as a recommended style because young children need both love and boundaries.[12,13,14] Authoritative parents communicate and reason with their children to guide their behavior. They create the type of environment that, in terms of self-determination theory, enables children to meet their needs for relatedness, autonomy, and competence. The authoritative style fits well with our Tech Happy Life model since the foundation of a strong relationship is considered.

As Children Grow and Develop, Parenting Must Adapt

From our perspective, children become more adaptive teens and young adults when the parental control gradually decreases over time as children gain greater skills and responsibilities. This enables them to meet their psychological needs for autonomy and competence. Consistent with self-determination theory, parenting practices that support greater autonomy are associated with more positive outcomes.[15] When teens push back against excessive parental control, the parent-child relationship can suffer. This can undermine the need for relatedness, and can lead to resentment toward parents, contributing to insecure attachment.[16] We should then ask ourselves, "What's more important? Maintaining control, or maintaining the relationship?" Keep in mind that growth and development may be inconsistent, sometimes looking like one step forward and two steps back. Just as children's physical development is uneven, so is their cognitive, emotional, and social development. Conflict over boundaries is where warmth and control intersect. When a parent tries to set limits and the child balks, parental warmth reminds the child that he is still loved, even when the parent needs to say "no."

The combination of control and warmth may also be easily seen in a three-step approach to setting limits that's appropriate with younger children. Suppose a child wants to play a video game that isn't developmentally appropriate (e.g., a violent, first-person shooter game for a six-year-old). The parent using the *authoritarian* strategy might simply say "no" (high control, low warmth). But the parent using the *authoritative* strategy may use the three-step approach known as the ACT model (acknowledge, communicate, target):[17]

1. Acknowledge: "Sweetie, I know you really want to play *Call of Duty* . . . " (acknowledging the child's desire).
2. Communicate: "But that game is meant for people 17 and older" (setting the limit).

3. Target alternatives: "You can play *Mario Cart* or *Cut the Rope* instead" (providing an alternative).

This three-step approach requires us to be a bit more thoughtful about limit setting, and it has some clear advantages over simply saying "no." By acknowledging children's desires at step one, we're communicating to them that they are important and worthy of consideration. We're acknowledging that they have desires and are helping them develop effective ways of coping with disappointment by providing other opportunities to meet their needs (as the Rolling Stones sing, "you can't always get what you want"). At step two, we're setting an appropriate boundary with some rationale (you're too young), and at step three we're helping by directing the child to an alternative way of getting the need (or want) met. For younger children, offering two alternatives may be helpful.

For older kids, we want to strike a balance between respecting their developing independence and warmly setting age-appropriate limits. One of the best examples of this approach that we've seen is Dr. Ross Greene's *Collaborative and Proactive Solutions (CPS)*.[18] The model, which was formerly known as *Collaborative Problem Solving*, has been successfully applied in both home and school settings. It provides adults with a refreshing alternative to punitive methods that have been tried (with very limited success) to address behavioral concerns. Within Dr. Greene's CPS approach, it is acknowledged that children already have positive goals. For instance, they want to be liked by others, do well in school, stay out of trouble, and ultimately be successful in life. We haven't met a child or adolescent yet who, when being completely honest, says she doesn't care if she fails out of school and lives with her parents far into her adult years. Greene's CPS approach fits squarely with Ryan and Deci's self-determination theory, which describes how humans are intrinsically motivated to meet their psychological needs for competence, autonomy, and relatedness.[19]

Rather than emphasizing punishment, CPS is based on the idea that "kids do well if they can" instead of "kids do well if they want to." This means that many of the struggles of kids and teens are viewed through the lens of a skills deficit rather than the result of apathy or delinquent intentions. Parents then are encouraged to partner with their children to, in essence, help them achieve *their own goals for themselves*. Parents and kids are on the same team, trying to collaboratively find solutions to shared problems.

The Takeaway?

Although many factors contribute to the well-being of our kids, our relationship with them is one of the most crucial. It begins with building and maintaining nurturing, secure attachments. Then, as our kids get older, we should attempt to use an authoritative parenting style that is characterized by both warmth and limit setting. It is within such a relationship that our kids can best meet their needs for relatedness, autonomy, and competence. So, developmentally, we should endeavor to be sensitive to these needs so that we control and manage less as our kids get older. We have to keep in mind that they want to be successful in life, and it is our job as parents to provide an environment that is both safe and allows room for them to grow. This can be a tough balancing act, particularly as they enter adolescence.

The proliferation of technologies in our hyper-connected world represents a new and rapidly evolving challenge for parents. Yet, we must view this challenge as still within the framework of effective parenting practices, which are in turn dependent upon a strong, healthy parent-child relationship. This is one of the keys to our influence as parents. In our next chapter, we cover some strategies that can help build and strengthen this relationship.

7

Building the Relationship

Meghan and Jackson make chocolate chip cookies from scratch together. They have a good time and enjoy sampling their freshly baked cookies with cold milk. Afterward, Meghan reminds Jackson to put away the toys in his room. Although he frequently argues with his mother or passively avoids such responsibilities, he agrees to go put his toys away without a fuss. While in his room, Jackson is briefly tempted to play on the iPad, but he knows his mother will be upset. So, he puts his toys away with the satisfaction that his mother will be pleased. Meghan notices that Jackson has put away his toys and remarks, "Jackson, thanks for much for putting your toys away like I asked. I really enjoyed making those cookies with you, too!"

Any parent will note how quickly time seems to pass. Infants become toddlers in the virtual blink of the eye. Before we know it, they are becoming teens and talk turns to college and career options. The days are long, but the years are short.

How do we want to spend this time? It's a limited resource that seems to ebb away all too quickly. When want our children to grow to be healthy, happy, and successful adults. As difficult as it may be to do, we have to accept that we cannot totally control our children's future. Somewhat ironically, in order for them to achieve these goals, we have to step back somewhat as they develop. We must allow them the space to meet their needs for autonomy and competence. Ultimately, they need to be able to take responsibility and credit for their own well-being and achievements.

That being said, how we parent our children *does* matter. We make a difference in their lives from infancy and beyond. Children generally respond best to an authoritative parenting style in which we strike the balance between warmth and setting limits. As our children develop, we provide space and opportunities for them to meet their increasing needs for autonomy and competence. Establishing and maintaining a healthy relationship with our kids is one of the best predictors of their life satisfaction.[1] Moreover, our relationship with them is the channel through which we can best influence them.[2,3] So, it benefits both children *and parents* to invest in building a strong, positive relationship.

In the following sections, we will cover two powerful ways in which we can strengthen our relationships with our kids: spending quality time with them and using the "magic ratio."

Spending Quality Time with Our Kids

Spending quality time with our kids doesn't guarantee that they will listen to us or follow our directions. It's not a panacea. We could do everything "right" as parents and our kids still might struggle because kids, like the rest of us, have free will and will flex their need for autonomy. Other factors, such as genetics, peer groups, the school environment, teachers, community, and chance events, also affect their behaviors. But investing in our relationships with our kids improves the odds that they will respond favorably to us.

A skeptic might consider this a form of manipulation. We don't see it that way. This is a case of win-win. It is our responsibility as parents to guide our children in positive ways. A strong relationship that is characterized by warmth, caring, and quality time together helps us to achieve that goal. In addition, family members are likely to be happier when the family system is harmonious.

Just to be clear, we are *not* advocating that parents step back and just have an "anything goes" attitude. Kids need parental limits and guidance. Discipline definitely has its place. However, it is important to remember that discipline is about teaching, not punishing. The root word of "discipline," after all, is "disciple." Telling our kids what they should be doing and promising rewards, or threatening them with punishments if they don't, isn't necessarily instructive. Those are forms of external control. Ultimately, we want our kids to be able to self-regulate (i.e., controlling emotions and behaviors to meet situational demands), which falls within the construct of autonomy. So, it's critical that they learn how to develop this skill.

If our relationship with our kids consists primarily of commands and criticisms, it isn't much of a relationship. For instance, a sampling of Meghan's verbal interactions with Jackson might include the following:

- *Clean your room.*
- *Do your homework.*
- *Put your shoes away.*
- *How many times do I have to tell you to TURN OFF the iPad?!*
- *Quit horsing around and get to bed!*
- *Take out the trash.*
- *Eat your vegetables.*
- *What grade did you get on that math quiz?*
- *You are making a mess at the dinner table.*
- *You weren't playing your position in the soccer game.*

Meghan isn't a "bad" mother for such statements. In fact, all of us make similar statements to our own kids. They need direction and guidance, but we want to interact with our kids in other ways that build the relationship. It's critical that we do activities *with* them instead of just *to* or *for* them.

We want to be able to teach and guide our kids as best we can without being overly controlling or coercive. You might recall the old proverb, "Give a man a fish, you feed him for a day. Teach a man to fish, you feed him for a lifetime." Controlling our children's actions is effectively giving them a fish. We need to teach our children to fish.

Activities That Build the Relationship

To be a positive influence as parents, we need to figure out how to be involved in our kids' lives in ways that build the relationship. When our kids are meeting their needs in the real world and within healthy family relationships, it can reduce the chances that they will be seduced into meeting their needs with their screens.[4] A great place to start is to find some activities that you can enjoy doing together. Some examples include:

- Cooking
- Arts and crafts projects
- Building models or Lego sets
- Making jewelry
- Playing catch
- Hiking or biking
- Going out to eat
- Going to the park
- Flying a kite
- Collecting insects
- Playing tag, board games, card games
- Reading with them or to them
- Teaching them a sport or training them in one.

It's great to tell our kids how much we love and care about them, but doing activities with our kids sends the clear message, "I love you. I care about you. I want to spend time with you." On the flip side, what messages are we are sending our kids when our eyes are on our screens more than on them? You might be old enough to recall the life lesson in the iconic Harry Chapin song, *Cat's in the Cradle*—if we don't invest time and attention in our relationships with our kids now, we will likely not have much of a relationship with them at all later.

Using the "Magic Ratio"

In addition to spending quality time with our kids to build the relationship, there is another general strategy that is backed by scientific research. Drs. John and Julie Gottman of the Gottman Institute have studied romantic relationships for decades. One of their discoveries is "the magic ratio."[5] They have found that a ratio of five positive interactions for every one negative interaction is predictive of relationship success and satisfaction within romantic relationships. This ratio is found in other contexts as well, including leadership relationships in work environments.[6] Consistent with this body of research, in a meta-analysis (i.e., a study of studies) on the effectiveness of parent training programs, researchers found that one of the best predictors of positive outcomes was increasing the frequency of positive parent-child interactions.[7]

Just as plants require sunlight, water, and fertile soil to grow, our relationships with our children blossom when showered with positive interactions. This doesn't mean that we send a non-stop stream of disingenuous praise toward them. Praise must be genuine and specific. Moreover, praising effort over abilities tends to foster what Stanford University's Dr. Carol Dweck calls a "growth mindset";[8] that is, kids who believe that they can improve through effort are more likely to take on challenges and persist when faced with setbacks.

Juan, age seven, loves playing games on his parents' tablet. His parents, Maria and Emilio, have to set limits on his screen time, and often it's a struggle. Weekends can be particularly tough. As they try to catch up on household chores, they find it tempting to allow Juan to play for two to three hours at a time. However, they're trying to get his eyes off the screen and on some of the many toys and games that they have around the house. They pulled out a marble run set out of their game closet to see if he would enjoy it.

With this toy, kids can build various structures and see how well the marbles roll through the multicolored wheels, chutes, and ramps. The last time Juan tried playing the marble run, he became frustrated and gave up quickly. But that was almost a year ago. With a little help from his parents, Juan begins to build structures. Sometimes the structures fall or his marbles get stuck. Both Maria and Emilio sprinkle encouragement while he plays. "Juan, you are really focused on that! You are working so hard!" When he finally completes a large structure that works, Juan beams with pride. Emilio exclaims, "Nice job, Juan, you really stuck with it! I love what you built!"

Importantly, these positive interactions need not be verbal. Some examples of these positive interactions include:

- Hugs
- Pats
- Warm smiles
- "Thanks for putting your shoes away."
- "I like how you got right on your homework when we got home!"
- "Nice hustle on the soccer field today—you really gave it your all!"
- "I really enjoyed going with you on the hike!"

Regarding the use of positive interactions, a particularly useful strategy is to use praise to address recurrent areas of concern. For instance, if your child often does not put his shoes away after kicking them off at home, praising him *when he does put them away* is likely to increase this desired behavior. Similarly, whatever your screen-time struggles are with your kids (e.g., turning off the screen when his game time is up), noticing and praising them for when he does this quickly (e.g., "Joey, I appreciate how you turned off the game right away when your time was up—that's awesome!") is an effective, positive strategy for improving desired behaviors and decreasing challenging behaviors. Sometimes this strategy is referred to as "catching our kids when they are being good."

To summarize, we want to influence our children in positive ways. The relationship is the conduit through which we influence our kids. The quality of our relationship increases our effectiveness as parents, so it's critical that we spend quality time with our kids to build and strengthen this relationship. Also, we want to use the "magic ratio" with our kids so that we have around five positive interactions for every negative interaction. Targeting our positive interactions to "catch" our kids when they are engaging in desirable behaviors during challenging situations can be especially helpful. Taken together, our positive interactions with our kids provide the nourishment that helps our relationships thrive.

Why It's Important to Foster Internal Motivation

According to *self-determination theory*, it is generally beneficial to foster internal motivation rather than using external motivators (e.g., earning rewards, losing privileges, avoiding punishments) to promote well-being and success.[9] As noted previously, Dr. Richard Ryan, a psychologist and professor at the Institute for Positive Psychology and Education at the Australian Catholic University, and Dr. Edward Deci, a psychologist and professor in the Department of Clinical and Social Sciences in Psychology at the University of Rochester, co-developed self-determination theory to explain human behavior and motivation. Consistent with their self-determination theory, creating an environment that supports an individual's experience of autonomy, competence, and relatedness fosters greater motivation, creativity, and persistence, and enhances performance.[10]

Optimally, we need to parent in a way that helps kids meet their psychological needs for autonomy, competence, and relatedness. Doing so, in turn, helps them to be more internally motivated to meet their own needs so that they can be successful and happy in life.[11] Certainly, there is a time and place for everything. *All of us* manage, command, control, coax, and coerce our kids. It is very tempting to simply tell our kids what they need to do. Parents know what's best, right? However, there are a number of reasons to be careful when trying to manage our kids' behavior, especially if we come to rely on coercive measures. Ironically, trying to control our kids can often backfire.

Reasons for this include the following:

- People, particularly kids and teens, do not like to be controlled. Trying to manage our kids' behavior undermines their fundamental psychological needs for autonomy and competence. In essence, we are restricting their freedom and sending the message, "I don't think you can manage your life effectively, so I'll do it for you." When others try to limit our freedom and control us, we have a strong inclination to resist external control and reinstate our autonomy and power. As parents, we notice this in our kids all the time. They often resist what we are trying to get them to do—even when we are "right."

   For example, we might try to get our kids to dress in warmer clothes when we know it is going to be cold out. Curiously, sometimes they can be highly resistant for the simple reason that we are telling them what they *should* wear. Kids, especially teens, are infamous for "cutting off their nose to spite their face." In line with this reasoning, researchers found that parents' technology-focused parenting practices have greater influence on younger kids than on teens.[12] Moreover, the researchers noted that controlling efforts by parents can be viewed as intrusive by adolescents and may be outright rejected, even if the parents' rules and restrictions could be helpful if followed. There's even a term for this human tendency to resist control: *psychological reactance.*[13] When a person perceives that his or her behavioral freedom is being limited, he or she will be motivated to act in ways to re-establish his or her autonomy. This inclination is very much in line with the need for autonomy that is central to self-determination theory.

- If we rely on controlling strategies as parents to get our kids to "behave," what happens when we are not able to exert these controls? Often kids will go a little bananas (or a lot!) when they finally have a taste of freedom from these parental controls. You might have seen some of these teens go completely overboard when they began college because they didn't know how to use their new freedom responsibly. Perhaps you were even one of these college kids!

- In order for our children to grow to meet their needs for autonomy and competence, they need to learn how to use freedom in a responsible way. If we use too many controlling measures as parents, we deny our children the opportunity to learn to develop their own competence because we are making too many decisions for them. Competence and self-regulation are skills that children develop over time with the right amount of support and guidance from their parents. Thus, it's critical that parents provide opportunities for their children to practice using freedom responsibly, develop self-competence, and learn to regulate their own behavior.

Just so there is no confusion on this issue, we are not saying that we as parents shouldn't use any controlling measures. When kids are younger, we have to set more limits and boundaries. Still, these should come from a secure base of warmth and caring that characterize the relationship. As our kids get older, we gently back off some of our control and allow them opportunities to meet their intrinsic needs for competence and autonomy. This, in turn, enables them to gain greater independence from us as parents as they transition to becoming responsible adults.

Being a Role Model as a Parent

Building a strong, positive relationship with our kids forms the foundation that allows us to most effectively use the preventive,

Green Light approaches that will be discussed in Chapter 8. These relationships, in turn, help our kids live a balanced life in a technological world. Another benefit of building this positive relationship with our kids is that we can then serve as more powerful role models. A wealth of research indicates that we are more likely to influence others as role models when we are held in high esteem by the other person.[14]

A critical point that all parents need to remember is this: *If too much of our attention is on our own screens instead of our kids, we undermine our efforts to build the type of relationship necessary to influence our kids in a positive manner.* "Be the change you want to see in the world" are words of wisdom often attributed to Mahatma Gandhi. When it comes to parenting, a slight twist that can work well as a mantra is, "Be the change you want to see in your kids." Perhaps nowhere is this more important today than in how we use technology. Our children's technology use presents one of our greatest challenges. However, modeling balanced screen time as parents, which includes espousing these family rules and values and following them ourselves, is an effective way to reduce our own kids' screen time.[15,16]

Be the Change

Mr. and Mrs. Park are concerned with their 10-year-old son Marlon's eating habits. At his annual physical, Marlon's physician suggested that Marlon needed to lose about 20 pounds. Marlon is self-conscious about his weight and has experienced some teasing at school. He prefers processed food and rarely eats fruits or vegetables. He seldom exercises and typically chooses to stay indoors playing video games rather than playing outdoors with the neighborhood kids. Mr. and Mrs. Park also struggle with maintaining a healthy weight. Though they aspire to eat better, they often dine out or buy fast food. Like Marlon, they rarely exercise. They work long hours and are often at their respective computers. Evenings and weekends are usually spent working, watching Netflix, or going to the movies.

First, let's refrain from judging the Park family. We all have the same struggles, to some extent. Recall our discussions of supernormal stimuli. We are hard-wired to be attracted to unhealthy foods. Moreover, the advertising industry works relentlessly to entice us with their products. But imagine that Mr. and Mrs. Park are trying to tell Marlon to eat carrot sticks and then to go play outside with the neighborhood kids; yet, they are sitting at their computers eating potato chips. This just won't fly. We can't ask our kids to start eating healthy foods if we are not. Likewise, we can't tell our kids that they need to rein in their use of technology if we haven't reined in our own. *We cannot realistically expect from our kids what we do not demonstrate ourselves.*

There may be many times in the Park family that find the parents on their computers or devices instead of spending quality time with Marlon. As adults, if confronted by our children for our own screen time, we might be tempted to argue, "Wait a second! I'm working on my computer! I'm not playing *Clash of Clans* or on Facebook!" From our kids' perspective, the experience of not getting desired or needed attention just because our screen use is work-related still stings. They receive the message, "What mom or dad is doing on the computer (or cell phone, tablet) is more important than me." Ouch! Likewise, this is one of the main reasons we get so irritated with our kids and friends when they won't get off *their* screens. They are choosing whatever is on their screens over us.

The Gift of Our Undivided Attention

We all long to be viewed as important and worthy in the eyes of others. We dearly want others to approve of us and to like us. Think of all the lengths that we go to in order to get positive attention from others: selfies, expensive handbags, designer clothes, "likes" within social media, school popularity, luxury cars, plastic surgery, Botox injections, grueling workouts for the "perfect" body, and so on. Our quest for attention from one another is profound. Thus, our undivided attention on others is so powerful because it sends the message, "*You* are important. I care about you."

Our undivided attention to others is a form of caring and validation. You can think of your own experiences with your favorite mentors, coaches, clergy, and teachers over the years. Chances are, when you were interacting with them, they gave you undivided attention. This let you know that, at those times, you were the only person that mattered in the whole world. Here's the greatest part: *We all have that power*. We can give others the invaluable gift of our undivided attention. It is especially important that we give this gift to our kids.

When it comes to having our kids make more responsible and considerate choices regarding their screen time, we first must demonstrate that ourselves. We need to honor our time that is spent in person with others by setting boundaries around our screen usage. We want to convey the message to our kids, partners, and friends that *they are more important than whatever is on our screens.*

Are We Giving Our Kids the "Right" Amount of Attention?

We are not the best judges of how our screen time affects other family members. They are. If our screen usage bothers other family members, it's a problem. *It only takes one person who experiences it as a problem for it to be a problem.* In order to find out how much our own screen time is affecting other family members, we might ask questions like the following:

- Does my screen time bother you?
- On a scale of 1 to 10, with 1 being "not at all" and 10 being "an extreme amount," how much does my screen time bother you?
- Do you think I have a problem with my screen usage?
- When does my screen usage bother you? When do you feel like it is too much?

The Family Assessment of Screen Time (FAST) scale we developed, in Appendix 1, is designed to help family members understand one another's perspectives regarding screen use. Importantly, the mere asking of such questions is role modeling what we want to see in our kids. We want them to value us, their siblings, and their friends more than their screens. We understand that they are often connecting with their friends *through* their screens. There is truth to that. However, it is also true that we evolved to be in face-to-face relationships. In order to develop the strong, deep, need-satisfying relationships that are necessary for our happiness, we need to set limits on our screens and carve out uninterrupted time for our in-person relationships.

Demont, age 11, and his brother Rashan, age 9, went with their parents to a popular restaurant on a Saturday night. The boys were both passionate gamers and liked to play their favorite game, Clash Royale, on their respective iPads whenever possible. Demont and Rashan begged their parents to let them bring their iPads so they could play their game while on the drive and at the restaurant. Although their parents sometimes allowed this, they began to worry that the boys hardly looked up from their screens when the family went out to eat. They decided it was best that they use these outings as a time for the whole family to connect. Knowing that they had to set a good example, the parents were careful to keep their cell phones off and out of sight throughout dinner.

Although we understand that Demont and Rashan, like many kids, wanted to play their game, we can see that it's a slippery slope. The encroachment of technology into our in-person relationships won't stop unless we draw some boundaries. Our kids are watching whether and how we set these boundaries. It doesn't mean they will necessarily like it when we do! In fact, oftentimes we will get pushback. However, it is our responsibility as parents to set these boundaries and to lead by example.

It's Okay to Make Mistakes

Sophia, age 16, was excited to come home from school to tell her mom, Ann, about an "A" she had just received on her English test, for which she'd worked hard to prepare. When Sophia walked in the door, she found her mother with her laptop on, looking at Facebook. Her mother didn't get up from her computer to greet her or ask her about her day. Sophia wondered why her mother didn't ask her about her test. "She knew that I had studied hard and that it was a big deal!" Sophia thought to herself. When she told her mother about her test grade, her mother didn't look up from her computer or fully acknowledge what Sophia had said. Frustrated, Sophia exclaimed, "Mom! Can you please get off Facebook and listen to me!" At that moment, Ann realized what she had done. She got off her computer and apologized profusely to Sophia.

The allure of the screen is strong and persistent. We're far from perfect. We don't always keep our own lives in balance in this hyper-connected world. Like Ann, sometimes we are paying more attention to our screens than to our kids. However, it's critical that we don't beat up on ourselves, or judge ourselves as "bad" parents, when we make mistakes. Being kind to ourselves despite mistakes enables us to re-cover from them more quickly.[17,18]

Imagine that we were trying to run a marathon and someone phys-ically beat us up. Well, it would be quite challenging to continue the race! Similarly, beating up on ourselves for our mistakes as parents makes it more likely that we will make such mistakes in the future. If our goal is to reduce the likelihood of such mistakes, self-compassion is essential. It's okay to judge an action as a "mistake," but we don't want to judge ourselves as bad, incompetent, or a loser for making such a mistake. Judge the behavior, not the self.

Going back to the importance of role-modeling, we want to model for our kids how to handle making mistakes. After all, when our kids make mistakes, we don't want them to react by saying things like, "I'm such an idiot!" whether this is aloud or in their heads. Instead, we want to model self-compassion, accepting responsibility, asking for forgiveness, and addressing the problem in the future.

For instance, Ann might say something to Sophia like the following: "I'm so sorry that I didn't stop what I was doing right away when you came home. That was my mistake, and I'm really sorry. I just got sucked into that darn Facebook again. I'm going to set a timer for myself to get off early so that I can be sure to greet you when you get home. Can you please forgive me? Now, I want to hear all about your 'A' on that English test!"

By admitting her mistake, asking forgiveness, and taking steps to correct it in the future, Ann has modeled what she'd like to see in Sophia. She is sending the message to Sophia that she values the relationship over her screen and is taking steps to ensure that the priority is maintained. In essence, she has turned a "fail" into a "win." Also, note that Ann is not promising to never use Facebook again. Rather, she is trying to put a boundary on its use so it doesn't interfere with her relationship with Sophia.

Importantly, it's basically impossible for Sophia to be defensive about what Ann is saying since Ann is correcting her own behavior. Kids and teens can get very defensive when we are trying to correct their out-of-balance screen time. But, when we are correcting our *own* behavior, we get a free pass. We are leveraging the power of our relationship and modeling the change that we want to see in our kids.

The Takeaway?

As parents, we must invest in our relationship with our kids if we are to help them have a healthy, balanced relationship with technology. We need to prioritize our kids over our screens. Directing our undivided attention on them sends the message that we care deeply about them. Through a relationship characterized by both warmth and limit-setting (i.e., authoritative parenting), we create an environment that enables our children to most effectively meet their psychological needs for relatedness, autonomy, and competence. In the following chapters, we'll show how an authoritative parenting approach can be applied to prevent screen-time challenges (Green Light), address emerging concerns (Yellow Light), and intervene for serious problems (Red Light).

8

The Green Light Level

Prevention

The allure of the screens is both powerful and ever-present. Given the strong pull that our screens exert on us, we need to focus much of our efforts on preventive strategies. It's much easier to instill healthy tech habits to begin with than it is to break unhealthy habits. We invest in the relationship to build a strong foundation so that we can more effectively implement Green Light, or preventive, approaches. Within our Tech Happy Life model, the Green Light Level indicates that there are not any chronic or major problems occurring with technology use. The parenting work within the Green Light Level is meant to keep it that way.

We find it richly rewarding to be engaged in activities with other people in the real world; yet, the constant pull of our screens often results in us turning our attention to devices instead of maintaining engagement in the real world and with each other. While our screens offer many options to (try to) meet our human needs for relatedness, competence, and autonomy, we evolved to meet these needs through in-person connections. Consequently, we need to make efforts to ensure that we take time to fully engage in real-world relationships and experiences. We still want to reap the benefits that screens offer without paying too high a price. If we can learn to keep our screen use in check, we can open doors to more deeply rooted happiness *and* enjoy the many positives of our screens.

The focus of this chapter is on efforts that you can use to prevent family technology use from getting out of control. This may be particularly relevant to young families with small children who are not yet heavy users of technology. Preventive efforts become much more challenging with teens and tend to be less effective.[1,2] However, we also believe that these approaches are suitable for all families because they are essentially healthy habits that can be acquired at any time.

Earlier we introduced the concept of parenting styles and endorsed the authoritative style (high on warmth and control) as the optimal approach. In the next few chapters we'll illustrate how authoritative parenting can be used to employ Green, Yellow, and Red Light strategies for technology management. Let's begin with Max.

Max is six years old. For several years his parents have tried to strike a healthy balance of technology in his life. Aware that technology could offer Max a wide range of benefits, they carefully selected age-appropriate opportunities for him to become familiar with electronic devices, particularly when there appeared to be educational elements to the screen time. On the other hand, they were concerned about minimizing some of the potential drawbacks of technology. By being proactive, they managed to mitigate or eliminate some of the harms by establishing their own family rules and guidelines around screen time. Limits were made explicit and boundaries were held. For example, no screens were allowed at mealtimes. His parents also used ratings and reviews from the Entertainment Software Rating Board (esrb.org) and the app store to ensure that games and apps were developmentally appropriate. They limited his recreational screen time to one hour during the week and two hours on weekends. Because Max's parents were thoughtful and prevention oriented, conflicts around screen time occurred less frequently than in many other families. By employing an authoritative parenting style, Max's parents display warmth toward Max and simultaneously hold their ground on reasonable limits. Max experiences their love and warmth and feels safe and secure, knowing that his parents have reasons for their rules (even if he doesn't always agree with those rules). Most important, Max's parents have conscientiously built a strong, positive relationship with him that serves as a foundation on which day-to-day parenting can securely rest.

The fact that Max's parents have been thoughtful and proactive does not preclude challenges around screen time. What's noteworthy about Max's family is that the mindful approach to parenting and technology make the challenges easier to overcome. Small difficulties around screen time remain small, thanks to the positive relationship and authoritative parenting style. In other families, particularly those with an authoritarian style (high control, low warmth), minor disagreements often escalate to the level of blowouts and meltdowns. Here's a typical conversation between Max and his mother about screen time to illustrate the authoritative style:

Max gets out some construction paper, folds the sheets, and staples the edge to make a small book.

MOTHER: Hey there Max, looks like you're working hard at something.
MAX: I'm making a book of colors, of what the colors are like.
MOTHER: Tell me more about your book.
MAX: You know, red is like fire and makes you feel hot.
MOTHER: So your book is all about colors and what they're like.
MAX: Yes, but I need to get on the computer to search for what the colors are like.
MOTHER: You want to use the computer for this, but we're not getting back on the computer today. You can think about how colors make you think and feel and make your book about colors.
MAX: I can do that. Blue makes me think of water.

We'll revisit Max later to see how parenting style and strategies may be applied as he gets older and technology plays a more prominent role in his life. Here we focus on Green Light strategies, starting with involvement in healthy activities.

Getting Kids Plugged in to Life

Let's start with a strategy that can be used within the Green Light Level that involves getting our children plugged in to other activities in life. The accessibility and variety offered by our screens make it too easy for our kids to default to turning their attention toward them. Unfortunately for parents, it is often too easy for us to *allow* our kids to default to their screens. Sometimes we really benefit from the "electronic babysitter." That's certainly fine from time to time. However, we have to remind ourselves that for our kids to get their needs met and experience deep-rooted happiness, they must be engaged in real-world activities. Their engagement in real-world activities will reduce the pull of the screens and will decrease the likelihood of problems that can arise from excessive screen use. When our kids are getting their psychological needs met in the real world, they are less likely to overuse technology in an attempt to get these needs met online.[3,4,5] Consider Lucas:

Lucas is an 11-year-old who loves video games but also happens to be an avid reader of fantasy books, such as the Harry Potter *and* Percy Jackson *series. He and his parents had heard of "Camp Half-Blood," a Percy Jackson themed summer camp for kids located at a nearby state park. The camp was filled with outdoor games, contests, and adventures inspired by the books. Not only was Lucas happy to leave his books and video games behind to go to the day camp, he made a number of new friends. One of these new friends introduced him to* Magic the Gathering, *a tradable card game. Lucas has found a new obsession and now collects cards, plays the game with a new group of friends, and attends local tournaments. While he does play an iPad version of the game as well, he has a passion for the physical version. He and his friends have endless discussions about cards and strategies. Lucas has even taught the game to his younger brother, Ian (age 9). His parents are supportive of his card game because it has led to many in-person interactions and friendships.*

Lucas's parents did not want to be in the position of battling him over screen time during the summer. They realized that this was a losing proposition. Even if they could manage to limit his screen time, they knew it would be an ongoing struggle. Also, they didn't know what other activities would engage him at home.

If you have younger kids at home, you might hear variations of "I'm bored" when they are not on the screen. At this point, we might be tempted to launch into a "back in *my* day" lecture. Rather than fight that battle, here is where an ounce of prevention comes into play. *It's essential to get your children involved in need-satisfying activities that don't involve screens.*

We are not advocating that you fill their every waking hour with activities. There can be problems with over-scheduling a child, for certain. There is much value in free time and free play. Still, if we leave it all up to our kids, there are legitimate reasons that they will be pulled into their screens. So as a preventive strategy, we suggest one of the first steps is getting our kids engaged in other need-satisfying activities. This naturally limits their screen time without having to fight it directly.

Here are a few ideas for getting your kids unplugged from the screens and more plugged in to life:

- Team or individual sports
- Martial arts
- Learning a musical instrument
- Art
- Cooking
- Math pentathlon

- Chess clubs
- Robotics
- Boy/Girl Scouts
- Volunteer/Community service
- Choir
- Gardening
- Going to the neighborhood park
- Card games such as Magic the Gathering
- Fantasy role-playing games such as Dungeons & Dragons.

Of course, it's great to do some of these activities with our children, but it is also important for kids to develop their own interests and skills apart from us to fulfill their needs for autonomy and competence. We recommend that kids be involved in at least one extracurricular activity. It is not an option for kids to *not* be involved in an activity. However, they do have the freedom to choose which activity (or activities) they want. Also, kids need not be required to commit to an activity for multiple years in a row. It's important that they try different sports and activities as they learn what they like the most. This could even be that they just like variety. There's nothing wrong with that. However, once they are signed up, they generally should be obliged to stick with that activity until that season/cycle is complete.

When we require our kids to be involved in activities, we can trust that they will find some that meet their psychological needs. Importantly, this process will naturally place some boundaries and limits around screen time. Thus, we won't have to fight their screen use constantly because the activity naturally displaces it.

Over time, when kids have experienced the positive benefits that such activities offer, they will likely be motivated to continue them on their own. Such activities satisfy our psychological needs at such a fundamental level that there will be a natural inclination to return to them. However, kids must experience these activities in order to know that they are need-satisfying. It's up to us to provide opportunities and a little encouragement for them to have such experiences. Of course, we should also be role modeling involvement in hobbies, sports, and activities ourselves! If we develop our own need-satisfying lives out of view of the screen, our kids are more likely to as well.[6] An authoritative parenting approach enables us to more effectively use Green Light strategies to prevent problems with technology from emerging. However, we fully acknowledge that this is a vast, complicated, and controversial topic. Moreover, it is a moving target, as technologies evolve rapidly while our kids are simultaneously changing developmentally. To complicate matters further, if you are a parent of multiple children, you probably have found that what works great for one child doesn't always work so well for another. So we can say that we don't have all of the answers. And we realize that parents have different values, beliefs, and expectations.

However, as we have mentioned, all caregivers share the common goal of having our kids grow up to be happy, productive members of society. We just don't always agree on the best way to go about achieving those ends. Even using an authoritative parenting approach doesn't provide all the specific answers. Rather, the authoritative parenting style provides a framework. We all have to figure out what works best for our respective families and acknowledge the challenges posed by this formidable, moving target. That being said, we are going to share some ideas that we believe are worth considering as you try to parent around the issue of technology.

Lessons from Odysseus

In Homer's *Odyssey*, Odysseus and his crew needed to sail their ship past the Sirens, magical beings whose entrancing song was known to lure sailors to dash their ships upon the rocks. Odysseus wanted to hear the song of the Sirens, but knew that he would wreck his ship and drown if he did. So he had his men tie him to the mast and to tighten his restraints should he beg to be released. He also had his men put beeswax in their ears so that they would not be enticed by the Sirens' call. Odysseus was thus able to listen to their song without endangering the ship or their odyssey.

Odysseus didn't choose to listen to the call of the Sirens without first taking preventive measures because he knew he wouldn't be able to avoid the temptation of their song. We need to think and act like Odysseus to save ourselves from ourselves. We should not pick the losing battle of trying to fight the temptation of technology. As mentioned previously, *we cannot win a war against the primitive parts of our brains.* The variable reinforcement schedule and the supernormal stimuli that are embedded within our technologies make them especially enticing. We are also classically conditioned to react to our technologies. The Sirens' call is virtually impossible to resist, so we need to think smarter. Using Odysseus's approach as one of our Green Light strategies will help prevent these technologies from becoming habits in the first place.

To this end, we have developed some preventive recommendations. We developed these based on our understanding of how screen use can become a habit. Habits can turn into addictions, so *preventing the formation of unhealthy habits also prevents the formation of addictions.* The line between "a bad habit" and "an addiction" is indeed blurry. We aren't going to try to split hairs over these terms. But in both cases, prevention is the key.

One might rightly point out that Odysseus devised and implemented his own approach to dealing with the Sirens. Eventually, we do want our kids to self-regulate. Importantly, they will be able to self-regulate as they learn to meet their needs for competence and autonomy. We can't always force the Odysseus approach on our kids and then expect them to learn to do this for themselves. However, we believe that it's best for parents to implement some of the strategies we suggest when kids are younger. As our kids get older, we will need to gradually back off. We can't teach self-regulation if we regulate everything *for* our kids. We can't control them into self-competence and autonomy.

It's important to remember that preventing the formation of habitual screen use also maintains the primacy of our relationships. Our influence with our kids depends upon us having a strong connection with them. If too much face-to-face interaction time is displaced by screen time, then we don't create that strong bond that allows us to have the positive influence that we are seeking. The preventive recommendations that follow are inspired by the powerful example of Odysseus.

Preventive Recommendations

Sylvia is in the fourth grade at a public elementary school. Some of her classmates are getting smartphones already, and she really would like to get one as well. She begs her parents, Joyce and Callie, to get one for her main Christmas present. Joyce and Callie are empathetic with Sylvia. They acknowledge her desire to get a smartphone and hear the reasons why she thinks she should have one. However, they gently but firmly tell her that she will need to wait a while longer. They both expressed concerns that she is too young to effectively manage the responsibilities and challenges that come with smartphones. Sylvia tearfully expresses her frustration to her parents. She storms to her room and slams the door. Joyce and Callie give her space to calm down, and check in with her after some time passes. Although Sylvia is still upset with her parents and disagrees with their decision, she still loves them both and can't stay upset at them for long.

In the previous section, we discussed the importance of using the Odysseus approach to prevent technology from causing problems in the first place. In the preceding scenario, Joyce and Callie used this approach with their daughter, Sylvia. They realized that, although Sylvia would love to have a smartphone, it was likely going to create too many problems for their comfort level. While it might be tough for them to stand their ground with Sylvia, they used an authoritative parenting approach to set limits with warmth in order to prevent greater potential problems from arising in the future.

There is a body of research indicating that parents' beliefs, behaviors, attitudes, and family rules around screen time significantly affect their children's level of screen use.[7,8] In the following subsection, we list some of the main preventive approaches within the Green Light Level. We think Odysseus would approve. In Appendix 2, we have a more comprehensive list. You might also have suggestions of your own that have worked for your family, so please submit suggestions you have to www.techhappylife.com/tech_tips/. We will revise and update our list of recommendations periodically.

Since we are to be role models for our children, please note that most of these recommendations apply to our kids *and to us*. These preventive strategies are about saving us from ourselves and our kids from themselves.

General Recommendations

- *Wait until technologies are developmentally appropriate before giving your child or teen access to them.* Just because your child wants a certain technology doesn't mean he or she is ready for the responsibility and challenge that it represents. So, whether it is a smartphone, gaming system, or social media access, avoid letting your child become an "early adopter" of these technologies.

- *Turn off as many chimes, buzzes, and push notifications as possible.* It is neurologically impossible to avoid turning our attention to these. If you need to have some on, just use the bare minimum. Even consider turning off social media and text notifications. We want to check these *when we want to*, rather than *when they are telling us* to check them. Though the absence of notifications may pose an inconvenience, in general, the pros outweigh the cons. One can always enable notifications in situations in which it is extremely important to receive them right away. Be sure to teach your children this strategy as it is critically important (e.g., when installing a new game to the phone, don't allow the game to send alerts or push notifications).

- *Only have one screen on at a time.* Thus, when you or your kids are watching a movie, they shouldn't also be playing a video game. A single screen is already stimulating enough without having to look back and forth between multiple screens.
- *When not actively in use or needed, put away devices.* All too often we keep our devices with us or within line of sight or hearing range. This makes them a source of almost constant distraction. While at home, we want to get in the habit of having uninterrupted connecting time. Unless we are expecting an urgent message, we can usually get by with only checking our devices about every 30 minutes or so.
- *Make a habit of unitasking (or monotasking).* Try to focus attention on one activity at a time. Set boundaries around screen use so that you are honoring the person (or task) in front of you with the gift of your undivided attention. Thus, when walking or waiting in line, don't have your smartphone out. When watching your child at an event (e.g., soccer game, graduation), keep your smartphone put away and silenced (unless taking a quick photo or video). Use the opportunity to engage with the people around you—to meet new people or build friendships. Remember, it's OK to be bored! Use that time to introspect or daydream. Through setting such boundaries around your screen use, you are trying to instill these same values in your children.

Home Recommendations

- *Keep screens, such as TVs, computers, and gaming consoles, out of bedrooms altogether.* That way, you can keep an eye on what your kids are doing on the computer *and* when they are doing it. If your house has a study area, then we recommend that the computer be kept there.

- *Children and teens should be allowed to have their portable devices in their bedrooms only up to a certain time of night.* While it is virtually impossible to prevent kids/teens from having their screens in the bedrooms altogether, there is too much temptation for them to access their devices past bedtime if left in their rooms. Ideally, devices should be out of the room and off (or at a charging station) about an hour before bedtime. If you do decide to allow your teen to use a laptop in his or her bedroom, have him or her unplug it and leave it outside of the room at bedtime.
- *Dinner and mealtimes are sacred spaces.* Thus, no cell phones should be present during mealtimes at all. They should be silenced and put out of sight. Meals are a communal time that can be used for conversations and bonding with the people present. Even when a person is eating by him- or herself, discourage screen use.
- *No devices are allowed in certain rooms in the house.* For instance, you might have a reading or sitting room in the house in which screens are not allowed. Also, we recommend that devices not be allowed in bathrooms. There are many reasons for this, some of which have to do with hygiene. Yes, it's difficult to restrict teens from doing this. However, we want to help them develop the habit when they are young.

Recommendations for Travel

- *Cell phones should not be used by the driver at all.* Even Bluetooth phone calls increase the chances of accidents.[9] Cell phones should be put away, perhaps in the glove compartment, center console, or trunk, to avoid the temptation. Alternatively, there are apps that disable calling or texting while the car is being driven that could be installed.
- *Children shouldn't be allowed screen time, as a standard, while in the car.* Travel times are great for conversations or enjoying

music together. We might make exceptions for long trips, but that still shouldn't mean unfettered screen access. Alternatively, as Depeche Mode sang, it's good to "enjoy the silence." There is value in quiet and even boredom. Providing "down time" for minds to wander can result in greater creativity.[10] See how one parent used Green Light prevention for travel in the vignette below.

- *No cell phones or devices at restaurants.* We want to create a shared experience with meals, including when we go out to eat. Again, mealtimes are sacred times. Kids need to learn to manage their attention and behavior without a screen to occupy their minds. Smartphones should be put away, as their mere presence is distracting.

Alice was looking forward to a Thanksgiving road trip with her children to visit family for the holiday, but was concerned about the amount of screen time her kids would have on the long drive to her brother's house. She felt that some screen time would help make the trip more comfortable for everyone, but she didn't want her kids to emerge from the minivan like zombies following excessive viewing. To prevent too much screen time, and to minimize battles over limit setting, Alice let the kids know that they would get one hour of screen time after the family had traveled for an hour. After that hour of screen time, then no more screen time for the remainder of the ride. This was the typical arrangement with the kids on long car trips. The kids brought some books and toys along for the ride, knowing that their screen time was limited. They also made some music playlists and downloaded some audiobooks for the ride for the whole family to enjoy. As a result, everyone's needs were met and there was no parent-child conflict over screens.

A United Front Instead of a House Divided

When it comes to successful parenting, if you have a partner, communicating about and agreeing on limits may help establish parental authority around screen usage. The importance of forming a united front with your partner doesn't just apply to parenting about screen time. Rather, it is critical in a more general sense for effective parenting. This is why we view forming a united front as a preventive strategy within the Green Light Level. Consider the struggles that Bob and Claire are having with technology in their home.

Bob and Claire were at odds over screen time in their house for their two boys, Evan (age 12) and Griffin (age 8). Bob grew up playing video games and still plays them frequently on the family's Xbox One, as well as on his smartphone and tablet. He tends to set few limits regarding their screen time when he is with the boys. Claire, on the other hand, believes their boys have too much screen time as it is, and tries to limit gaming to one hour per day. She also doesn't allow the boys any screen time in the car. She is frustrated when she leaves Bob in charge of the kids and, upon returning home after running errands, finds that the boys have been playing games for four or five hours at a time. In addition, Bob and Claire get into frequent arguments because Bob always lets the boys play games on their devices when he is driving them.

When our kids are getting conflicting rules, standards, and messages from parents, they experience a great deal of confusion. Moreover, inconsistency with regard to parents' rules about screens can result in a lot of conflict between partners and between partners and kids. For instance, when Claire drives the boys and doesn't allow Evan and Griffin to be on their screens, they frequently beg her to allow them game time. "Dad lets us!" is their frequent refrain. Claire's efforts to set limits are being undermined by her husband. Perhaps Bob believes that his efforts to allow the boys to have fun on their games are being undermined by Claire.

Importantly, the pendulum can swing too far in either direction. Claire isn't always "correct" about the way that she sets limits about screen time. She might restrict their screen time in ways that are arbitrary or unnecessary. For example, she might not budge on allowing more screen time than one hour per day even on special occasions such as sleepovers or holidays. In such a case, Bob could make a strong case for greater flexibility on Claire's part.

Parenting, like life, can be messy. There are few black or white answers to be found. This is especially true of rules around screen time. Forming a united front allows parents to reduce the many problems that would naturally arise from a house divided. Consistency is one of the keys to successful parenting. So parents need to discuss their concerns, perspectives, and hopes "offline" to try to get on the same page.

With Great Power Comes Great Responsibility

We are borrowing this quote from the 2002 *Spider-Man* movie, in which Uncle Ben tells Peter Parker (aka Spider-Man), "With great power comes great responsibility." When we consider the power in our smartphones and other devices, we need to heed the advice of Uncle Ben. We should not just hand these powerful devices over to our kids without first having some discussions with them about what responsible use of these devices looks like *and doesn't look like.*

Since one of our goals is to help our children meet their needs for autonomy and competence, we recommend having ongoing discussions with our kids about responsible use of their various technologies. This doesn't mean that kids get to dictate the terms of use to us. But it is important to hear what their perspectives are. They need to learn to reflect on the pros and cons of their tech use. They need to consider how their tech use affects themselves and others. Importantly, this isn't just one conversation. It will need to be an ongoing discussion about screen time—theirs and our own.

The Issue of Setting Time Limits

We have already noted that there are innumerable studies linking many of the negative health and psychological outcomes associated with technologies such as viewing television, playing video games, and using social media to excess. This is in line with our position that no matter how need-satisfying technology can be, it can displace ways of more effectively meeting our needs in the real world. These negative outcomes might be caused by limited or frequently interrupted face-to-face interactions, and decreased physical activity, sleep, and time spent outdoors.

The importance of limiting screen time applies to everyone, not just the kids. So we are in favor of setting time limits within an authoritative style framework. This is much easier to do with infants, toddlers, and younger kids. As kids get older, especially when they get a smartphone, this becomes increasingly challenging to manage. Teens will exert their needs for autonomy and competence, which can make enforcing screen time limits very difficult or even counterproductive.

Ideally, in line with the American Academy of Pediatrics recommendations, we believe it is best for kids under the age of two to have basically no or very limited screen time. We know this is a formidable challenge in this digital age. Parents of infants and young kids sometimes require a "sanity break," as caring for infants and toddlers, as we all know, can be extremely taxing even under the best of circumstances. In particular, single parents who cannot "tag out" with a partner might be especially susceptible to being maxed out with stress. In these circumstances, if the alternative is aversive interactions with a young child, it is probably best to allow the child some screen time. Just be sure to have a few apps and/or videos that have slow pacing and developmentally appropriate material. Try to keep such screen time as infrequent as possible. It's too easy to become overly reliant on the electronic babysitter. If we notice that we are too frequently providing screen time for our infants or toddlers, this could be used as a cue to attempt to problem-solve.

Forensic cyberpsychologist Dr. Mary Aiken makes an important point in her illuminating and thought-provoking book, *The Cyber Effect*, regarding when to first introduce kids to screens.[11] She flips the question around to ask when parents should be introducing their children to *their own* screen use. Although many parents might keep their babies and toddlers from gaining access to screens, they often don't limit their own screen time enough while with them. So, they might binge watch a TV series while nursing, text while strolling their baby, or use social media while spoon-feeding their infant. Consistent with both our evolutionary needs and attachment theory, it's important for parents to limit their own screen time when they are with their babies and toddlers.

In line with AAP, we recommend no more than one hour per day of recreational screen time during the week and closer to two hours on weekends for children ages two to five years old, with more time for older children as appropriate. But we view this as a general guideline to aim for, rather than a rigid policy. Rather than using apps and other devices to impose a strict electronic cutoff, we believe it is better to have ongoing discussions regarding family values, expectations, and time limits with our kids within an authoritative parenting style. Parents also should consider the unique developmental characteristics of their children and their needs for sleep, in-person connection, and physical activity. The time limits are established and agreed upon ahead of time.

Let's return to Max at age eight and see how Max's dad sets time limits. Max's dad uses an authoritative approach within our Green Light Level.

MAX: It's 4 o'clock. Can I have my afternoon game time now?
DAD: Sure thing, bud. You did a great job of waiting to ask until 4. You just need to put your toys in the living room away.
MAX: Aw, ok! (Max puts his toys away). Now can I play?
DAD: Yes, you get one hour. I'll start a timer.

MAX: Wait! Don't start the timer! I haven't started the game yet!

DAD: OK. Tell me when you are ready to start.

MAX: OK! You can start the timer!

DAD: I'll let you know when you have 5 minutes left, OK? (Starts a timer for 55 minutes. Timer goes off.) OK, Max. The timer went off. Time to start wrapping up. (Dad sets timer for 5 more minutes).

MAX: Okay, but I have 5 more minutes! I'm about to fight the boss.

DAD: Okay. Just wrap it up right after. (Timer goes off). Okay, Max, it's time to stop.

MAX: Wait! I've almost beat him!

DAD: OK. Just finish this battle. But you have to stop whether you win or lose.

MAX: Ah! I lost! Can I try to beat him just one more time?

DAD: Oh, man! I'm sorry you lost that battle. That's frustrating. I know you really would like to fight him again, but your time is up. You can have another crack at him tomorrow. Let's go to the pool.

MAX: Aw, please, please!

DAD: I'm really sorry, but your time is up. Let's go to the pool. Let's bring those super soaker water guns. I challenge you! I'm the boss—let's see if you can defeat me! I double dog dare you!

MAX: (Max turns off the tablet). You wanna piece of me?! You are going down!

DAD: Bring it! Hey, and thanks for turning the game off. We can't forget the super soakers!

You can see that Max's dad used a number of strategies to help prevent problems:

- He used an authoritative approach characterized by both warmth and limit-setting.

- They had already established some family rules, expectations, and limits around screen time.
- In line with the "magic ratio," he complimented Max specifically about abiding by the family rule regarding when his afternoon game time can start.
- He used a timer and gave a 5-minute warning to Max.
- He allowed some flexibility by allowing Max to finish the boss battle.
- He empathized with Max regarding loss to the boss.
- He held firm on not allowing Max to battle the boss in the game again, despite Max's pleas.
- He offered a transition to a mutually enjoyed activity (in line with the foundation strategy of building the relationship through quality time).
- He engaged in playful banter with Max.
- He acknowledged and thanked Max for turning off the tablet.

We realize that setting limits with kids on games doesn't always go this smoothly. However, Max's dad didn't just get lucky in this scenario. He laid the groundwork over a long period of time, and he used many positive strategies throughout the interaction. This increases the odds of successfully navigating these challenging situations.

The Issue of Contracts

There are many professionals and parental advisors who recommend creating some form of contract with kids before giving them access to new technologies. For instance, before kids are given a smartphone, they must agree to a kind of "terms of use" contract. Within this contract, there can be a list of "dos and don'ts" as well as consequences for misuse. We cannot definitively say whether parents should create such contracts with their kids. To our knowledge, there are no empirical studies on the effectiveness of such tech use contracts. They could work great for some families but not for others. We believe, however, that it is a good idea to at least go over some ground rules, expectations, and consequences prior to giving kids access to new technologies.

The downside of such contracts is that they can get rather lengthy and cumbersome. Think of your own experiences with such contracts. Did you ever have one as a kid or teen? Did your parents make you sign one when you got your first bike, phone line, or your driver's license? There are many developmental privileges that kids have traditionally received that didn't require a contract. How would you have reacted to a four-page contract upon getting your own phone line when you were a teen? Think of how you react now to terms of use contracts. Have you ever fully read one for Apple's iTunes or Google's Gmail before agreeing? Neither have we.

If you do decide to create a contract with your kids regarding certain technologies (e.g., social media, smartphone, video game system), we recommend that you keep it concise. Try to cover main themes such as when and where they can use their screens, how to limit overall use, and what are the consequences of misuse. Also, it's important that the contract be created with some input from your child/teen. After all, we are trying to teach them to become more responsible. If the contract is created entirely with a "top-down" approach, our kids/teens don't have the opportunity to problem-solve. They are more likely to abide by a contract when they have skin in the game. Although we're not giving our kids the final say, we at least need to hear them out and offer compromises when possible. On this point, in the timely documentary, *Screenagers: Growing Up in the Digital Age,* physician and documentary filmmaker Dr. Delaney Ruston and her husband tried to implement a contract regarding smartphone use with their tween daughter.[12] This contract was not successful until they renegotiated the terms with their daughter's input.

It might be useful to tell kids that the smartphone is being "lent" to them, rather than that they own it completely. After all, kids seldom pay for their devices outright, and even fewer pay for monthly cellular charges. However, to help them learn to be more responsible, it's a good idea to have them pay for at least some of the fees, especially for the entertainment features.

The Issue of Parental Controls

Most computers, devices, and gaming consoles have ways of using parental controls to restrict access to certain content, such as pornography. Also, one can install various types of Internet security programs onto personal computers that have parental control features. Finally, there are a number of apps that parents can install that allow them to manage their kids' screen use (e.g., what apps they can use and when, the ability to block them from apps for periods of time). While it is beyond the scope of our book to review these, we can recommend Common Sense Media for a review of options.[13]

In general, we recommend using parental controls, especially for younger kids. It is extremely easy for kids to access woefully inappropriate material without some kind of parental controls in place. The average age at which kids first view Internet pornography is 11 years old.[14] Often, this is inadvertent. Things that are seen by our kids' young, inquisitive eyes cannot be unseen. Also, we don't want their sensitive, developing brains to become habituated to the extreme content that they could access. While, of course, there are ethical (and commonsense!) reasons that experimental design studies cannot be conducted on the effects of viewing pornography on young kids over time, a number of correlational studies suggest that pornography can shape kids' views of boys and girls, men and women, and sex in unhealthy ways, as well as increase risky sexual behaviors.[15]

Regarding the apps that can be used to manage our kids' time on their smartphones, tablets, and other screens, many of these vary in quality and effectiveness. This is such a rapidly changing landscape that peer-reviewed research on the effectiveness of such apps has not been established to our knowledge. Ideally, parents don't have to use such apps because other preventive strategies, discussions, limit-setting, role-modeling, and problem-solving are effective enough. For younger children, though, such apps might be used within the Green Light Level. Teens, who are much more sensitive about controlling efforts from their parents, are not likely to respond well to parents' use of such apps. Plus, teens might find ways around them (e.g., use their friend's phone to access certain apps). So, perhaps these screen-control apps are not used with teens unless problems emerge (Yellow Light Level). Even then, we believe that these apps should be used when the pros seem to outweigh the cons, and then only sparingly. Teens should be involved in discussions about the use of these apps. Ultimately, they need to meet their needs for autonomy, which includes self-regulation, as well as competence. We interfere with the development of these needs if we are too controlling, even if we do so through the use of apps.

Consider that the Internet is like some vast, sprawling world with both wonders and terrors to behold. It is both a mirror and a lens; it both reflects and magnifies what is best and worst in all of us. We wouldn't just plop our kids down in the middle of an unfamiliar city and let them explore on their own to their heart's content, right? Sure, most people are good, but there are some shady characters out in the world.

Still, as kids get older, we want them to learn to self-regulate and meet their needs for competence and autonomy. It is also essential for them to build and maintain healthy relationships with others without us looking over their shoulders. Therefore, it's critical that we relinquish some control as our kids become teens. In this dance of parenting, we take the lead when our kids are younger, but then they slowly take the lead as they get older. As our kids make responsible choices and show that they can be trusted, we gradually continue to back off. Importantly, this should be discussed with both our kids and our partner in an ongoing way. These conversations are woven into our relationship with them, which is why it is so important to invest in that relationship.

The Issue of Monitoring

We should first distinguish *monitoring* from *surveillance*. For the most part, we want to be involved in our kids' and teens' lives so that we generally know who their friends are, what leisure activities they are involved in, what video games they are playing, and so on. In this sense of monitoring, we believe that parents should strive to be involved in their kids' lives. We want to develop the type of relationship with our kids that encourages them to be willing to self-disclose information to us. This in turn enables us to help them work through their challenges, so our monitoring is within the context of a healthy relationship.

Although the issue is not black and white, we think of electronic surveillance as a controlling approach that is more in line with an authoritarian parenting style. Electronic surveillance might include things like checking your teen's phone with or without his permission, reading his texts, viewing all of his social media posts, and reading his email. This type of over-involved and over-controlling parenting is sometimes considered "helicopter" parenting. Researchers have found that helicopter parenting is associated with lower levels of need- and life-satisfaction in young adults.[16] So there are good reasons to be wary of taking a surveillance approach with kids and teens.

That being said, kids need to know that parents reserve the right to view anything on their phones, email, or social media accounts at any time. Our recommendation, though, is that parents don't exercise this right without "probable cause." *Electronic surveillance of kids, while sometimes warranted, should be justified.* Thus, within our Tech Happy Life model, we don't believe in clandestinely viewing our kids' electronic interactions. Nor do we believe that we should demand access to their phones, social media, or email accounts and scour through their interactions as an approach within our Green Light Level. At the Yellow or Red Light Levels, when our kids have broken our trust and engaged in online behaviors that have caused serious harm, or have the potential to, then some level of surveillance might be warranted.

We are not advocating that we be uninvolved in our kids' screen use, even with teens. We do need to be aware of what apps, games, and social media platforms they are using and, to some extent, with whom they connect online. We need to have ongoing discussions with them regarding our family rules, values, and expectations. If they have broken our trust or have shown they cannot handle the responsibilities of screen use in a healthy manner, we may need to restrict their use and/or use some surveillance for a while. However, we need to provide opportunities for them to earn this trust back and, when they do, then we need to loosen the reins on our restrictions.

We realize this is a controversial and touchy subject. It can be very upsetting and embarrassing for kids to have their parents observe every conversation they are having. Imagine that your parents had eavesdropped on all of your interactions with your friends when you were growing up. If you are like us, you would have been absolutely mortified if your parents had heard many of your jokes, conversations, stories, musings, gossip, and revelations.

Remember that our leverage of influence as parents is through the relationship. Relationships, at least in part, are built upon trust. If we are constantly managing our kids within their digital worlds, we are sending them the message, "I don't trust you to make good choices." Kids and teens are likely to push back and become angry about perceived breaches of privacy. Think of how many of us have been upset by the collection and monitoring of our data by the National Security Agency (NSA). As discussed, we all have a fundamental psychological need for autonomy. Electronic surveillance can cause us to feel that our liberty to think and speak freely is being restricted.[17]

Many of us hold our freedoms dearly and are quite upset when we believe our privacy has been breached. Kids and teens can react that way as well to parental surveillance. If this surveillance causes severe tension and conflict, the relationship can be damaged. A damaged relationship, in turn, can undermine our influence as parents. So, we must tread carefully with regard to electronic surveillance of our kids.

In support of this position, in a longitudinal study of parental efforts to monitor middle-school students, research found that parents' monitoring efforts, regardless of whether they were solicitations or controlling, did not predict children's delinquency over time.[18] However, youths' willingness to disclose information to their parents was predictive of delinquency (i.e., kids who were willing to self-disclose to parents were less likely to engage in delinquent behaviors over time). This suggests that it is critical to have a strong relationship with our kids such that they are more willing to talk with us and share information. Complimenting these findings, other researchers have found both parent-child cohesion and parental involvement to be associated with lower rates of teens' online risky behavior (e.g., gambling, violent and sexual content).[19,20]

Another important issue to consider regarding monitoring or surveillance is whether we can do it effectively at all. Teens can be quite tech savvy these days. This can be particularly true when it comes to ways to hide screen use, such as texting and social media activity, from parents. When sufficiently motivated, many teens can probably find ways around most blocking and surveillance. Just Google that and see how many results you get! When it comes to hiding their screen activities, motivated teens will likely be a step or two ahead of us. Regardless, if our relationship with our kids has devolved into some elaborate cat-and-mouse game of electronic surveillance, *we've already lost*. This is not the type of relationship that we want with our kids.

This might be an odd way to think about this, but when we think of managing or restricting our kids and teens from screen use, what is the goal? Usually, the answer is something like "to protect them." From what, though? Harm is the general answer. We want to protect our kids so that they don't suffer some form of harm.

Now, the ironic part of this is that our attempts to restrict, block, and control our kids can also result in harm. This comes in forms such as anger from our kids toward us, heated arguments, and decreased positive interactions. Thus, as parents, we need to weigh the harm that our kids might experience from their (inappropriate or excessive) screen use versus the suffering caused by the fallout from us attempting to restrict or oversee their screen use.

An Antidote to Our Digital Distractions?

We want to introduce one overarching "meta" preventive strategy that can be quite powerful when it comes to resisting the pull of our screens. In a sense, our screens take us elsewhere. Whether it is in a game, newsfeed, social media, or texting, our minds are no longer where our physical bodies are. We are in cyberspace and "absent present." Although it is a virtual space, it can have as profound an effect on our thoughts and feelings as any physical space. For a number of reasons, including those "hooks," we continue to be enticed to be anywhere but where we are.

From one perspective, an antidote to the pull of our screens is *mindfulness*. You might have come across this term, as it has entered our popular culture in the past decade. While there are a number of variations on the definition of mindfulness, renowned author, scholar, teacher, and pioneer in the field Dr. Jon Kabat-Zinn defines mindfulness as "the awareness that emerges through paying attention, on purpose, in the present moment, and nonjudgmentally to the unfolding of experience moment by moment."[21] Although it is often associated with eastern religions, such as Buddhism, mindfulness is present in nearly every major spiritual tradition. However, one need not be of any particular religious faith to benefit from mindfulness.

Mindfulness is not about emptying our minds. It is about focusing our attention. It can be on our breath, sensations in our bodies, or just aspects of the world around us. Our screens give us unlimited access to endless novel stimuli that are enticing. Mindfulness is about training ourselves to maintain focused, conscious awareness on one thing that we choose.

Why is mindfulness important? As discussed previously, our focused attention is at the heart of everything we do. The quality of our productivity and relationships is dependent upon our focused attention. For the many reasons described previously, we keep being enticed into believing that we need things that we don't already have. We think that "more" or "new" is somehow better than what we have. We have difficulty being satisfied with what we have, yet consuming more doesn't make us any happier.

Mindfulness is about learning to "stop and smell the roses." Those roses are right in front of us if we can slow down long enough to appreciate them. Those roses may literally be roses, but they are also the smiles of our kids, laughter, a sunset, a hot cup of coffee on a cold morning, conversation over dinner with friends, the embrace of our partner, or the warmth of the sunlight on our faces. Those are the "roses" in which true happiness is found. Yet, if we don't slow down and pay attention to those, we miss the very sources of deep happiness and contentment that are all around us. Practicing mindfulness enables us to attend to what matters most in life. At the same time, mindfulness can liberate us from ruminating on negative thoughts that frequently contribute to our emotional suffering (e.g., regrets about the past, self-criticism, worries about the future).[22,23]

We can only be in charge of our own state of consciousness and our own behavior. If you are interested in the many benefits of mindfulness, we recommend that you start with yourself. Any effort to change, improve, and grow requires our focused attention. Mindfulness allows us to practice this skill of attention that is fundamental to our growth, productivity, relationships, and well-being.

In recent years, there has been a flood of research supporting the many benefits of mindfulness practice.[24] Some of these benefits include the following:

- Reduced stress
- Reduced rumination (i.e., spinning negative thoughts)
- Less emotional reactivity
- Increased focus

- Improved working memory
- Increased relationship satisfaction
- Improved cognitive flexibility.

Sounds pretty good, right? Perhaps the best part of mindfulness is that it is free. In can be practiced anywhere at any time because the present moment is always with us. Spiritual teacher Ram Dass captured this sentiment nicely in his book entitled *Be Here Now.* Some good introductory books on mindfulness include Kabat-Zinn's *Mindfulness for Beginners: Reclaiming the Present Moment and Your Life* and Thich Nhat Hanh's *The Miracle of Mindfulness: An Introduction to the Practice of Meditation.* Importantly, mindfulness is now being used successfully with kids and teens as well as formally taught to and practiced with students in schools.[25,26] There is also a growing body of research on "mindful parenting" that indicates that mindful parenting contributes to a number of positive health outcomes in children, including a strong parent-child relationship.[27,28] Moreover, several researchers and scholars have advocated for the use of mindfulness practices to manage behavioral addictions, as well as to resist the pull of technology and use it in a more balanced way.[29,30]

Getting Our Needs Met Through MET (Mindful Engagement with Technology)

Mindfulness has the potential to be a powerful tool in dealing with digital distractions. In a way, it is more than a strategy. It is an approach to living life and has the potential to be transformative. From a neuroscience perspective, mindfulness practices activate many of the areas of the brain, such as in the prefrontal cortex, that are involved in higher-order thinking. The areas of the brain strengthened through mindfulness practices are associated with the regulation of attention, awareness, and emotion.[31] In contrast, the primary reward circuits of the brain involve the midbrain, a more primitive area. So, in a manner of speaking, mindfulness practices enable us to use our conscious awareness and higher order thinking skills to adjust our responses to our situations, environment, and internal states.

There is a quote that, although probably wrongly attributed to Albert Einstein, is some variant of the following: "A problem cannot be solved by the same kind of thinking that created it." Regardless of who actually said or wrote this, it contains deep wisdom. With regard to our technology use, we cannot adequately address the problem of our screen use by staying at the reflexive level of habitually checking our screens. Given the tremendous pull of technology, we have to be more conscious (i.e., mindful) of its enticing tug on us, as well as its effects, in order to take steps to reduce them. Through the application of mindfulness practices, we are more aware of our own screen use and, with this increased awareness, can choose to attend to our children over our screens. This sends them the powerful message that they are more important than our screens.

Dr. David Greenfield, a psychologist, professor, author, and founder of the Center for Internet and Technology Addiction, discusses the importance of "conscious computing" given the manner in which technology can hook us.[32] We will present our version of that idea with a slight twist. Since we have explained the many benefits of mindfulness as well as the importance of meeting our physiological and psychological needs, we want to promote a "meta" strategy of MET, or Mindful Engagement with Technology. For our happiness and well-being, we must learn to engage mindfully with technology. We want to be intentional and strategic with our use of technology, rather than using it mindlessly and habitually. We can get our needs met through MET. We want our children to learn MET as well, but we start with ourselves. Through using MET ourselves, we have the potential to more effectively model the healthy use of technology that we want to see in our children.

A Caution About Cognitive Biases and Blind Spots

No matter how objective and mindful we try to be, we all have cognitive biases and blind spots that prevent us from seeing ourselves and the world as they really are. Many of these biases seem to be a form of unconscious attempt to enhance our sense of self.[33] At some level, we all want to feel good about ourselves and would like to think that we are above average. In fact, there is even a specific cognitive bias known as *illusory superiority* that has been captured in studies. In short, in comparison to others, most people tend to rate themselves as being above average in positive attributes and below average in negative attributes. However, statistically, *most* people can't be above average.

When it comes to the effects of technology, it might be easy for us either to deny or to be unaware of how it can have a negative impact on us. This might be from some self-enhancing cognitive bias, or perhaps they are just blind spots. For instance, as discussed in a prior chapter, in University of Texas at Austin marketing professor Dr. Adrian Ward and colleagues' study of how the presence of smartphones caused "brain drain" (i.e., decreases in cognitive performance), most study participants rated that they believed that their performance was totally unaffected by their presence.[34] In a separate study of teens' views of sexting, teens expressed a belief that others were more harmed by sexting than themselves.[35] In pilot tests of our scale, we have found that kids tend to view others as having greater struggles with technology than themselves.

So, how can we use MET if we don't even know how we are being affected by technology? That's a challenge! This is when at least a general knowledge of the research comes into play and why we have grounded most of our recommendations in the research. We have to accept that we, just like others, can be negatively affected by our screens at times. For example, if we know that the research indicates the texting while driving increases our chances of an accident, then we should use MET to prevent us from doing that (e.g., put the smart-phone in the glove compartment).

The Takeaway?

The idea behind the Green Light Level of our model is preventing problems from arising in the first place. In particular, we need to set boundaries around screen use so that our kids don't learn to habit-ually use technology. It is this habitual use of technology that can undermine their relationships, productivity, and happiness, and can open the door to a host of other problems (e.g., cyberbullying, sexting).

As we see time and again, it is much more effective to spend our efforts on preventing problems than on addressing them once they do occur. Within an authoritative parenting style, we engage in these preventive efforts. We always pay special attention to our children's psychological needs for relatedness, autonomy, and competence, knowing that we will need to make adjustments as they grow and develop. Mindful parenting, which includes Mindful Engagement with Technology (MET), can help us more skillfully and wisely choose how to use our technologies, set limits with our kids, and re-spond to their wants and needs. However, even with such preventive approaches in place, it's possible for problems to arise. What do we do when these problems start to emerge? We need to find effective ways to address them, which is the topic of our next chapter, the Yellow Light Level.

9

The Yellow Light Level

Addressing Emerging Concerns

The old story of the boiling frog serves as an apt metaphor for technology in family life. It goes something like this: if you drop a frog in a pot of boiling water, it will jump out to escape the scalding water. However, if you put a frog in a pot of lukewarm water and gradually heat it, the frog will not notice the subtle change in temperature over time and will die (note that we don't encourage readers to try either of these). Though any herpetologist would be quick to point out that this is false, it's illustrative of how the effects of technology can subtly creep up on us. We're not suggesting fatal consequences from the increased presence of technology in our lives. But the metaphor resonates for many parents who ask themselves, *how did we get to this point?*

Lauren is trying to spend more time outdoors with her three sons, ages 5, 9, and 12. On a recent Sunday afternoon she decided to take the boys to the park and play, even though she was feeling like she needed to catch up on her work emails. After spending some time shooting hoops at the park, she took a break to read her email and lost track of time. When she looked up, she saw that all three boys had retrieved devices from the car and were playing video games. Lauren gently encouraged the boys to turn off the games and play, but her suggestion was ignored. This wasn't what Lauren had in mind when she planned the outing, and she struggled to make sense of how they had gotten to this point of spending what felt like too much time in front of screens. How did this happen?

Like the frog in the pot of cool water that was gradually warming, Lauren didn't notice the incremental increase in technology and apparent dependency in her family until it reached a point that alarmed her. In retrospect, some of the early signs were obvious. For example:

- Kids are asking for more screen time than they had previously.
- Family members experience frustration when others are attending to screens more than they are to each other.
- Screen time interferes with attainment of other goals.
- Checking devices has become a habit.

Recall that in our Tech Happy Life model, level one (Green Light) focuses on prevention activities for families, aimed at avoiding some of the problems associated with technology use. Just as health prevention activities like hand washing may prevent some but not all illnesses, so do our strategies within the Green Light Level prevent some but not all screen-time problems. Most families will, at some point, experience tension or conflict around the intersection of technology and family life. As these initial, relatively minor concerns begin to emerge, they are signs that we are at the Yellow Light Level of our Tech Happy Life model. Strategies are applied to address issues before they become serious problems. Like a traffic signal's yellow light, level two conveys a sense of caution.

Here are some signs that Yellow Light concerns are emerging:

- Screen time begins to eclipse other activities (e.g., time outside, in-person time with friends, physical activity).
- Kids experience frustration when screen time is denied.
- Children complain that they are bored if they don't have screen time.
- Grades are declining with increased screen time.
- Kids or teens are losing sleep because of screen time.

- Screen time is displacing in-person peer interactions or, when kids are together, they are primarily on their screens.
- Battles over screen time are affecting the parent-child relationship.

For some families, Yellow Light problems emerge when kids' usage of parent-approved technologies begins to spill over into usage that has not been approved. This may show up as playing video games that are rated M (for mature, or age 17 and older), social media access that puts them in contact with content that is not age appropriate, or simply a gradual erosion of time limits. In such cases, parents may feel a need to pull back on access, to have some conversations with kids about healthy media use, to re-establish limits, and perhaps to set new boundaries.

Even parents who have worked hard to prevent screen-time challenges by using preventive strategies within the Green Light Level are likely to encounter some difficulties at the Yellow Light Level. Screens are pervasive and often are accessible to children who are otherwise given limited access. For example, kids who spend very little time in front of screens at home may be granted access when visiting the homes of relatives or neighbors. Many schools provide tablets and computers to young children, and screens are increasingly available in restaurants, retail outlets, medical waiting rooms, and community centers. Anecdotally, many parents report to us that once kids start spending more time in front of screens, pulling back to previously lower frequency is hard to accomplish.

In this chapter we focus on how parents can use authoritative parenting strategies within a Yellow Light Level of concern to manage these emerging problems, which sometimes calls for curtailing screen time in a way that both addresses the concern and maintains a high-quality parent-child relationship. Though giving in to a child's desire to spend more time in front of screens may initially appear to be easier than fighting a battle over an iPad, the short-time avoidance of conflict may only exacerbate the long-term problem.

This is why the permissive parenting style yields instant gratification for the child but poorer skill development for future success, whereas the warm parenting style with clear rules and expectations (authoritative) will likely be most helpful in achieving your goals. That being said, we cannot be too rigid as parents. We must consider that kids don't all develop in exactly the same time frame, that technological advances create new challenges, and that there are many situational variables that can come into play (e.g., special occasions and situations, and visits to friends' homes that have different rules and limits).

The Yellow Light Level

As we have discussed, our Tech Happy Life model has three color-coded levels: Green (level one) is for preventing problems; Yellow (level two) is for addressing emerging concerns; and Red (level three) is for intervening when things get really difficult. Our focus in this chapter is on the Yellow Light strategies that families can employ when they start feeling like the negative aspects of technology use may start overtaking the positive side.

We describe some of these strategies in the context of positive parenting, collaborative and proactive solutions, and parenting style or strategy. Ultimately, we all have to decide which approaches best fit our unique circumstances. There's no one-size-fits-all strategy that will work for everyone, and none of these is a cure-all. Rather, these strategies demonstrate *how* we can be effective parents who set limits around technology while maintaining and strengthening our relationships with our kids. The *what* (as in, *what* to do) will come from each of us as we think about our unique family values and needs. In this sense, the specifics of the *what* are nested within the overarching *how*. The *how* is to use an authoritative parenting approach with a developmental consideration of the child's needs for relatedness, competence, and autonomy.

If you find yourself in a pot of boiling water that was initially cool but gradually is warming, it will be helpful to take the temperature now and then assess your situation. Similarly, you may find yourself with kids who are starting to engage with screens more and more at the expense of quality time with you and others. How can you begin to address this concern? Some of the recommendations that follow are extensions of strategies that are primarily used within our Green Light Level. However, because problems are emerging, you must now set stricter limits, and you must enforce them.

In essence, the crux of the challenge of parenting often comes down to this: At what point do we as parents intervene and use more controlling measures because it is for our kids' "own good?" Put that way, we can see that the answer is often not very clear. Usually it comes down to some version of "when the benefits of intervening are greater than the benefits of not intervening." Still, the answers are not always apparent, but this is the question that we must ask ourselves when we are at the Yellow Light Level.

Once we have decided that we need to intervene, we must start using more controlling measures within our authoritative parenting framework. The "control" dial is turned up because it is necessary to do so. When setting rules and limits, parents should be explicit about rules in order to avoid misunderstanding, and should be consistent in maintaining the limits. Here are suggestions:

1. *Establish some tech-free areas and times.* For example, you might strictly enforce a screen-time curfew. Also, you might not allow video games after school during weekdays. In doing so, you're setting some clear boundaries that will enable family members to connect (to each other, not to the Internet). It's important to acknowledge here that parents should follow these rules, too. It may be helpful to explain this rule to your kids. We're reminded of a billboard seen in Canada that read, "If you're texting, who's driving?"[1] Explain to your kids that

just like someone can't drive a car without giving it their full attention, one can't engage fully in a relationship while looking at a screen. Naturally, we need to model this behavior for our kids by focusing our attention on them without devices, too. Seeing something modeled is a much more effective learning tool than being told to do something.

2. *Establish the understanding that recreational screen time is a privilege to be earned, not a right.* Families can develop a shared understanding that work must be completed before playing on devices, and that there are time limits around screen time that need to be maintained. Parents should always consider the developmental needs of children when making determinations about how much screen time is appropriate (generally less time for younger kids).

3. *Separate work devices from leisure devices.* When we use one computer for work and leisure, we tend to drift between work and recreational use. This often results in poorly completed work that takes much more time than was necessary to complete it well. The temptation to go off task to highly rewarding video games and social media posts is simply too strong to resist in a consistent way. For example, when a group of college students was asked whether they turn off their phones while studying, they acknowledged that they probably should power down the phones, but instead kept them on while trying to focus on academic tasks. At home, parents can support their kids by setting up a work computer that provides limited functions (e.g., word processing for writing) and lacks some of the more distracting apps and features, or use a public library computer for school work and a home computer for entertainment. Many schools are now loaning tablets or laptops to all students during the school year. In these cases, parents should work with their kids to ensure that no gaming, social media, or other recreational apps are installed on the school's device. This may help kids work while they work and play while they play.

4. *Collaboratively develop, communicate, and uphold limits.* As we described earlier in our mention of Dr. Ross Greene's work, adolescents often don't respond well to top-down limitations.[2,3] After all, the adolescent brain has the capacity to question rules and authority, and frequently chooses to exercise these newly developed abilities. In doing so, teens are seeking to meet their needs for autonomy and competence. The idea behind this more collaborative approach is to get ahead of the ball and talk about the concern before an unsolved problem gets heated. Certainly, when we're upset about a given situation, it's hard for us to think rationally about it. Moreover, this collaborative approach can help develop the skills that meet kids' needs for autonomy and competence. Consider the following conversation between a parent and a 13-year-old:

FATHER: Miguel, you've been playing video games for three hours now. Time to turn it off and start your homework.

MIGUEL: Hang on Dad, I've just gotten to a new level and I can't stop right now. I need just a few more minutes.

FATHER: No, you've been on too long already. Your homework is more important than video games. I'm shutting this down. (Turns off computer).

MIGUEL: (temper flaring) No! You've ruined it! You don't understand how important this is!

FATHER: You're grounded for a week!

Miguel, engrossed in a game that, though not important to his father, has a lot of meaning to him, doesn't yet have all of the internal resources he needs to engage in a collaborative discussion about balancing leisure and academic work. Considering Miguel's attention and emotional investment in the game, compounded by his anger at being disrupted, one would not expect a good outcome here. However, once Miguel's struggles with gaming have emerged, he is at the

Yellow Light Level. Now, his father knows that he needs to take action to keep this problem from recurring or escalating.

At this point, Miguel's father might sit down with him and collaboratively develop a better plan to address the ongoing screen problems. The current approach is clearly not working out well! When they work on this plan, it should be *when the problem is not occurring*. The midst of a power struggle is not a good time for problem-solving and plan generation. When they come up with a plan for success, it may include one or more of the following collaboratively derived options:

- Video games are played after homework is completed.
- Video games may be played during designated time periods.
- A warning alarm goes off 15 minutes prior to his time being up. This can give Miguel the time he needs to wrap up levels.

Prevention isn't always effective, so we rely on more controlling approaches when problems have emerged, and we are at the Yellow Light Level. Even if Miguel's father had started preventing screen-time problems as soon as Miguel was born, there may be external influences from peers, school, and other sources that result in too much time in front of screens. If Miguel's father believes that this is the case, he will need to find a way to work with Miguel, in the context of a warm relationship, to set and hold some new limits. This may be challenging, as kids are often unreceptive to the imposition of greater restrictions after they've experienced increased access. While the initial rollback of screen time my be difficult, the newly established limits, if consistently enforced, will become the new normal.

Collaboration and Consequences

When problems emerge, it is important to come up with more restrictive rules and limits. Still, it's important that we maintain warmth and strong boundaries, as described earlier. As parents, we must remember that being collaborative requires us to listen to our kids, compromise, and encourage. Simply dictating a list of rules falls short of the criteria for collaboration. Consistent with self-determination theory, collaboration is a better way to meet our kids' needs for autonomy and competence. Eventually we want our kids to competently and independently make healthy decisions. Guess what? They do, too! Now, they aren't always very effective at doing so, but they need opportunities to practice. If we are too controlling and dictatorial, we don't provide them the growth opportunities to meet their intrinsic psychological needs.

When parents try setting limits around technology use, they often struggle with the application of consequences. Many feel that misbehaviors, such as sneaking in more screen time after a limit has been set, must be met with punishment. Unfortunately, the consequences we dole out are often ineffective. Suppose Miguel's father had set the limit of no more than two hours of screen time per day, but later discovered that Miguel got on the computer after his parents went to bed and spent an additional four hours gaming. What would be an appropriate consequence? We want to avoid punishment that is arbitrary, excessive, and unrelated to the problem behavior, so grounding Miguel for an entire month would be inappropriate. We also want to consider the developmental needs of the child and tailor the consequence so that it accounts for age and maturity.

Natural consequences occur without parental intervention. For example, Miguel may be exhausted the next day and perform poorly on a test or in a soccer game after a night of gaming on the computer. *Logical consequences* come from parents and are linked to the problem behavior (e.g., "because you had six hours of screen time yesterday and the limit is two hours per day, you won't have screen time for the next two days").

When we find ourselves delivering the same consequences over and over again, we know that they are ineffective and that we need to try something else. That may be a good opportunity to try something more collaborative. We're often surprised and delighted when we ask kids what they think may work and they provide their own solutions.

A child's plan for success is one in which he or she can take ownership, which leads to greater feelings of autonomy and competency.

Ernie's parents gave him permission to play a new video game that had been recommended by a friend. As Ernie became increasingly engaged with the game over several weeks, his parents became concerned about the violence to which he was being exposed. When they told Ernie that he couldn't play the game anymore, he became quite upset and begged them to change their minds. As parents with an authoritative parenting style, Mark and Daniel empathized with Ernie, listened to his concerns, and maintained their boundary around age-appropriate video games. Though Ernie misinterpreted his fathers' refusal to concede as a lack of understanding, Mark and Daniel held their ground and provided other options, including access to games that lacked the graphic violence.

Debbie and her kids live in a large, urban center high-rise apartment without easy access to outdoor play spaces. When she needs to occupy her children so that she can get some work done, she sometimes gives them some screen time so that they will be occupied and entertained while she accomplishes her goals. Lately she has noticed that unanticipated problems have emerged, such as tantrums from the three-year-old when technological challenges with the iPad generate frustration, or when the seven-year-old appears to be increasingly dependent on devices for contentment. To address this problem, Debbie incrementally decreased the frequency of screen time access and replaced it with age-appropriate games and activities (coloring, Legos, etc.) that did not require much parental supervision.

In the following example, parent and child find a way to collaboratively address and resolve a screen-time problem. Note that the mother uses a variety of parenting skills to connect with her daughter.

Bernadette, age nine, is allowed 30 minutes of screen time every day after school, but often is in conflict with her mother about turning her device off when the 30 minutes are up. This scenario is particularly vexing for her mother, Louise, when they are transitioning from screen time to the commuter train for Bernadette's piano lesson in the city. Each Wednesday, Louise asks Bernadette to get off the computer so that they can drive to the train station, but Bernadette invariable argues with her, stating that she's in the middle of an important chat with a friend. These interactions are stressful for Louise, as she worries about missing the train and the piano lesson. Though she feels that Bernadette benefits from screen time, she does not like the way this has become a source of tension between them. At her book club, many of her friends reported similar problems when they ask their children to transition from screen time to other activities.

Unsure as to how she should handle this situation, Louise decided that she would start by talking with Bernadette about the problem when they were not in conflict with each other, knowing that talking during a calm moment would likely be more productive. One Saturday morning they decided to bake a cake for Bernadette's grandmother, and Louise opened the conversation while they were making the frosting.

LOUISE: I know it must be hard for you to have your screen time interrupted when it's time to go to your piano lesson. Can you tell me about that?

BERNADETTE: Yeah, it's like you're not aware that what I'm doing is really important and you just rush me to end it right away.

LOUISE: I understand it's important to you. I also want you to understand that catching the train on time is important to me.

BERNADETTE: I get that. It's just that your demand to turn off the computer just comes out of the blue without any warning, and I need some time to wrap things up.

LOUISE: That makes sense, and I know that it's not helpful for us to be in conflict over that. Do you have any ideas of how we can fix this?

BERNADETTE: Maybe give me a five-minute warning before we have to go?

LOUISE: That could work, but I think you may need more than five minutes to transition. What if you had your 30 minutes of screen time after the piano lesson? That way you could end it without feeling so rushed.

BERNADETTE: I'm willing to give that a try.

LOUISE: Great!

When ongoing screen problems have emerged, we know that we are at the Yellow Light Level and we need to take some action to improve the situation. The strategies described in this chapter within an authoritative parenting framework are general guidelines that can be adapted to meet the unique needs of our families, taking into consideration family values, developmental levels of children, and other factors that are specific to individual situations. We acknowledge that any given strategy may be useful to one family and useless to another, so consider what is realistic when selecting an approach. We also understand that sometimes being collaborative is easier said than done, particularly when there's a lot of resistance to parent involvement. It's our job as parents to keep trying, to be warm, and to uphold a firm boundary against which children with developing autonomy can safely push, knowing that they will still be loved at the end of the day. Importantly, even when our kids don't accept our efforts to collaboratively problem-solve, the gesture still counts. It still conveys a positive message that connects with them on some level, even if they don't always acknowledge or seem to appreciate it.

You also may find that some of the strategies across the levels overlap or perhaps seem redundant. Some strategies are indeed more particular to our different levels within the Tech Happy Life model than others. However, the Green, Yellow, and Red Light Levels of our model have more to do with the manner and degree to which we are intervening within our authoritative parenting framework based upon the severity of the problem. When we are at the Green Light Level, problems have not emerged and our parenting strategies have to do with prevention. At the Yellow Light Level, problems have emerged that necessitate greater levels of control within the authoritative parenting framework. Finally, at the Red Light Level, the severity of problems requires us to intervene more forcefully.

Keep in mind that preventive strategies discussed within our Green Light Level are not abandoned when Yellow and Red Light Level problems emerge. In fact, it's critical that these preventive strategies are maintained. Just as health prevention and promotion efforts (e.g., eating healthy foods) are not discontinued when someone becomes ill, our efforts to maintain a balanced use of technology and to build healthy relationships must persist when problems emerge. However, we do adjust our levels of parental control based upon developmental factors. While we maintain an authoritative parenting style throughout our Tech Happy Life model, we need to more strictly enforce the rules, limits, and consequences as problem behaviors have emerged at the Yellow Light Level.

In the previous chapter we introduced Max at age six to illustrate how his mother used her relationship and some prevention to deny a request for screen time and to redirect him. We return to Max, who is now older, to show how we use parenting strategies within an authoritative parenting framework when some problems have surfaced.

By age 11, Max has gained greater access to technology and, by virtue of his increased maturity, requires less supervision. His parents are becoming concerned that Max is spending too much time in front of screens now, noting that outside play and face-to-face social interactions are being eclipsed by video games and texting. They recognize a need to decrease the amount of screen time, but anticipate difficulties doing so now that technology has become such an integral part of their lives. Utilizing their authoritative parenting style and practices, they explain to Max that though they have been relatively lax recently in enforcing screen time limits, it's now time to make sure that technology doesn't interfere with other important parts of their lives. They sit down with Max and collaboratively make a list of some reasonable rollbacks on screen time and agree as a family to stick to the new plan. Though Max does not like it, he appreciates the warm and respectful approach that his parents have taken in addressing this concern.

MOTHER: Max, we've given you a lot of freedom with the computer and have not set a lot of limits with you.

MAX: That's true.

MOTHER: And you've been great about not abusing the privilege. You've played age-appropriate games and have followed our rules about online safety. My concern now is that you're spending too much time in front of screens.

MAX: I don't think it's too much.

MOTHER: I understand that, and I think it's normal for parents and kids to have different ideas about how much is too much. But it's my job to take care of you, just like I need to make sure you wear sunscreen and eat carrots.

MAX: I don't like cooked carrots.

MOTHER: Right, so I give you raw carrots with hummus.

MAX: So do you want me to play video games with hummus?

MOTHER: I want you to spend less time in front of screens and more time playing outside. We'll need to agree on the amount of screen time you can have and stick to a schedule.

MAX: Like two hours a day?

MOTHER: I think right now, for your age, one hour per day on school days makes sense. And two hours a day on the weekends.

MAX: You always say that you have a reason for your rules. What's this one?

MOTHER: My reason is that there are only 24 hours in a day. For each hour that you're in front of a screen, that's an hour that you're not getting needs met in other ways. A little less screen time means a little more time for cooking, climbing trees, and going fishing with me.

MAX: Can we go fishing?

MOTHER: Sure, let's plan a trip.

Is Max's mother going to totally remedy this Yellow Light challenge with one conversation? We seriously doubt it. We expect that they will have a number of conversations around this issue, and that Max will test limits at times. How will his mother respond? Let's take a look at how this might play out.

In the following exchange, Max has deliberately exceeded the time limit that his mother set. He has been showing more struggles with screen time and repeatedly tests limits. His mother has talked to him several times about this, but that hasn't resulted in changes to his behavior. She let him know that, moving forward, she would start imposing some consequences if he disobeys the rules about screen time.

MOTHER: Max, I told you that you had 5 more minutes of screen time left, but that was 30 minutes ago. What's going on?

MAX: But the app wasn't working and then I was in the middle of a level. I can't just stop in the middle of a level!

MOTHER: I know that the game is important to you. Tell me more about it so that I can understand.

MAX: It's just that I love it so much and it's so hard to stop.

MOTHER: Right, I know you want to keep playing because you love it. Even so, we have to stick to the time limits.

MAX: But one hour a day isn't enough time!

MOTHER: You feel like you need more time. I think for your age you have enough screen time, and that you'll have more when you get older.

MAX: But I need it now!

MOTHER: One of your jobs as an 11-year-old is to learn how to stop sometimes. My job is to help you with that so that you'll continue to grow happy and healthy.

MAX: I'll be happy if you give me more time with my games.

MOTHER: Like I said, you'll get more time when you're older. For now, it's important that you stick to the time limit. Since you have broken our rule, you know what the consequence will be. You will lose 10 minutes of your 60 minutes of game time for tomorrow.

MAX: (Getting tearful). Mom! That's not fair!

MOTHER: I know you are very upset right now and that you think that our rules are not fair. But for now, you need to stop playing. If you continue, you will lose another 10 minutes of game time tomorrow.

MAX: (Turns off the game). OK!

MOTHER: It's time to prepare dinner. I sure could use some help. How about you crack the eggs for me?

MAX: I don't feel like it.

MOTHER: Well, if you change your mind, I sure would love the help. Remember you have some library books checked out. Maybe you could read some of those for a bit.

MAX: Maybe. (Walks off to his room).

The scenario between Max and his mother was tense. He broke a rule, and he received a logical consequence (loss of some game time tomorrow). She used the logical consequence because her other efforts to problem-solve and more gently set limits were not working. Consistent with an authoritative parenting style, his mother remained calm and empathetic throughout the exchange. She gently but firmly applied the consequence. She decided that it was only necessary to have him lose 10 minutes of game time, because she believed that is all that will be needed to change his behavior. She made attempts to switch him to some other need-satisfying activities after their exchange, but perhaps Max needs to cool off a bit first. She has invested a lot of time and effort into building a strong relationship with Max, so she feels confident that he will cool off fairly quickly and reconnect with her.

The Takeaway?

Even the best efforts to prevent screen-time challenges can't prevent all problems from emerging, so parents will likely need to address some difficulties at the Yellow Light Level. By using authoritative parenting strategies and leveraging good parent-child relationships, parents can address emerging screen-time issues effectively. Rolling back access, collaboratively developing solutions, maintaining boundaries, and using logical consequences are among the most effective ways for parents to deal with escalating screen-time challenges.

In the next chapter, we consider how families may address the most challenging screen-time problems. Though less frequent than the more typical screen-time challenges at the Yellow Light Level, the behaviors at the Red Light Level of our model can create a great deal of stress and unhappiness for families. At this level, screen time has become habitual (or addictive) and has eroded relationships, sleep, and in some cases, basic self-care. Also, kids and teens at this level might be engaging in risky online behaviors, such as exchanging nude pictures or texting and driving, that could result in severe harm or legal consequences. Sometimes situations may require more serious intervention and, when this becomes necessary, we are at the Red Light Level.

10

The Red Light Level

When Strong Intervention Is Necessary

The young man is clearly distressed, and watching him scream and moan generates considerable unease. In the YouTube video, which has racked up millions of views, the young man in his early twenties confronts a father who has adopted a "tough love" approach to excessive time spent on video games.[1] Perhaps the video is a fake, intended to look authentic, but the pain, whether real or contrived, is palpable. The father, after creating a pile of his son's video games in the yard, threatens to destroy the games with a riding lawn mower.

> FATHER: I'm going to mow them over so that maybe you'll get out of your room for a little while and maybe get a job.
> SON: Gaming is going to be my job! I'm good at it!
> FATHER: You got student loans, you got car payments, you got insurance.
> SON: I'm really [expletive] good at it!
> FATHER: Yeah well you've gotta make money while you do it.
> SON: This cost me like hundreds of dollars. It's an expensive hobby.
> FATHER: I don't care. You have to get a job.
> SON: What does this achieve? What is this going to do, mowing my games over?
> FATHER: Maybe you'll quit playing for a while and get a job and pay some of your bills.

SON: I'm never going to quit playing![Father mows over games]
SON: (Screams and howls, rage and despair)

Dealing with Serious Problems

In this chapter, we focus on the most challenging and problematic concerns with screen time (the Red Light Level). The Green Light Level in our Tech Happy Life model encourages prevention; the Yellow Light Level aims to address problems when early warning signs emerge; and the Red Light Level is when parents must strongly intervene to correct addictive or maladaptive use of technology and/or address significant concerns. Serious problems require creative, time-intensive solutions delivered mindfully. Problems at the Red Light Level were not prevented with Green Light efforts nor solved using more controlling and limit-setting approaches within the Yellow Light Level. So, now we must resort to more extreme measures in dealing with them. Please note that, depending on how extreme the problems are, when we are at the Red Light level, sometimes help from a mental health professional is required.

When Is It a Serious Problem?

Take any introductory psychology course and you're likely to encounter a unit on abnormal psychology. When describing abnormal or deviant behavior, psychologists are careful to point out that just because something is unusual or strange does not necessarily mean that it falls under the category of *psychological disorder*. What's the difference between an avid interest in a subject and an obsession? What's the difference between an eccentric person and someone who has a diagnosable mental disorder? The behaviors of various entertainers are outlandish, but also functional. In many cases, the determining criterion is whether the individual has impairments in his or her social, occupational, or educational functioning. In other words, does the behavior interfere with his or her relationships, work, education, or self-care?[2] Also, a serious problem might be said to occur when screen use breaks the law or could result in severe harm to self or others (e.g., exchanging or posting nude photos of underage people, using screens to facilitate the sale of drugs, texting while driving).

We also acknowledge that a serious problem for one parent may not be so serious for another, as we have different levels of tolerance, varying expectations, and our own ways of coping with frustration. One person's Yellow Light concern may be another's Red Light problem. Rather than setting rigid boundaries across the levels of our model, we advocate for some flexibility and fluidity.

Can a Person Really Have an Internet Addiction?

The *Diagnostic and Statistical Manual of Mental Disorders* (5th ed., *DSM-5*) is often referred to as the "Bible" of psychiatric diagnoses. Published by the American Psychiatric Association (APA), the *DSM-5* is used by professionals to determine whether an individual has a disorder. While screen-time problems are not included in the catalog of mental illnesses, the current edition lists *Internet Gaming Disorder* as "a condition warranting more clinical research and experience before it might be considered for inclusion in the main book as a formal disorder."[3] Citing research that has largely come from Asia, the APA's fact sheet on Internet Gaming Disorder suggests that the neural pathways of compulsive gamers are similar to those of individuals who are addicted to substances. A number of studies support the idea that the neural pathways and reward circuits involved in behavioral addictions are the same as those involved in drug addictions. Though it's certainly possible that future editions of the *DSM* may formally recognize Internet Gaming Disorder and/ or other screen-time problems as diagnosable mental illnesses, no such diagnosis currently exists. Creating a formal diagnosis would have a wide range of implications, including health insurance reimbursement for treatment.

Dr. Ronald Pies, Professor of Psychiatry at SUNY Upstate Medical Center, has argued that there is currently not enough research to support the idea of Internet addiction (IA) as a unique disorder. Even so, he acknowledges that some people have serious screen-time problems that need treatment.[4] Others have argued strongly that behavioral addictions such as IA should be included in the *DSM* as disorders based on what scientists know about the neuroscience of addiction, and that the APA has inappropriately and arbitrarily excluded them from the *DSM-5*.[5] There's little doubt that the "addictive" use of screens is associated with serious psychological difficulties, but researchers are not clear about the cause and the effect. In other words, do people with mental health disorders become heavy users of social media and video games, or does excessive screen time cause mental illness?

One large-scale study of over 20,000 individuals ages 16 and older found that addictive technology use (video games and/or social media) was associated with attention-deficit hyperactivity disorder (ADHD), obsessive-compulsive disorder (OCD), anxiety, and depression.[6] To say that screen time and mental illness are positively correlated means just that—that higher levels of screen time are associated with higher levels of mental illness; however, this does not mean that one causes another. One of the conclusions drawn by the authors of the study is that adolescents with ADHD, OCD, depression, or anxiety may be at risk for developing screen addiction and therefore could be identified for prevention efforts.

Based on the available research findings, it appears that heavy screen use and mental health issues both influence each other through the "dose effect" that we discussed in Chapter 5. As individuals use their screens more heavily, mental health problems such as depression worsen because the person is not getting his or her basic physiological (e.g., sleep, physical activity) and psychological needs (e.g., autonomy, competence, relatedness) met. Also, heavy screen users are likely to see their performance in areas such as school and work drop. This, in turn, can lead to negative outcomes that can feed back into depression, social withdrawal, and increased screen use. Thus, a person can become caught in a vicious cycle as he grows increasingly dependent upon screen use to avoid experiencing recurrent negative thoughts and feelings. With regard to ADHD, some research is supportive of a bidirectional influence of video games such that kids who have attention and impulsivity problems tend to play video games more and, in turn, this increased play seems to exacerbate their attention and impulsivity problems.[7]

Signs of Serious Problems

In 2013, the *New York Times* profiled a young man who spent a lot of time playing a popular game called *Clash of Clans*.[8] According to the article, George Yao left his apartment only to go to work, and managed to play *Clash of Clans* on five iPads simultaneously while not at work, even taking the iPads into the bathroom to ensure continuous play. As he became increasingly involved, he lost 20 pounds and had spent about $3,000 on virtual gems that helped him advance in the game. Though he initially had started playing as a way of entertaining himself and connecting with others online, he found himself so burdened by the pressures to maintain his lead that it began to feel more like work than fun. While Mr. Yao's circumstances are extreme, they are not unique.

A number of residential treatment programs for adolescents have been established to treat Internet, gaming, and social media problems.[9] Because these programs are relatively new, there are few studies to assess their effectiveness (compared to drug and alcohol rehabilitation programs). However, psychologist Dr. Alexander Winkler at the University of Marburg and colleagues did look at 16 different studies that collectively assessed the outcomes of 670 individuals who went through Internet addiction treatment programs and found that in general, such programs were effective at reducing time spent online. Moreover, participants in these treatment programs tended to show fewer signs of depression and anxiety.[10]

The Center for Internet Addiction developed a list of questions to help assess the severity of Internet usage problems, ranging from mild to severe. Their Internet Addiction Test aims to help determine when problems may require more serious attention.[11] The test, which is rated on a scale from "rarely" to "always," includes questions about frequency of Internet use, self-reported negative outcomes associated with use, and perceived problems when Internet access isn't available.

Use of questionnaires like these may be helpful in understanding the magnitude of the problem, but they do not offer solutions. Should you use one of these surveys, keep in mind that as screeners, they are not intended for the purpose of making diagnoses. Just as a vision screening directs someone to an optometrist for further assessment, red flags on the Internet Addiction Test and other screeners should be followed up by consulting with a mental health specialist.

Here we provide our own list of questions that may help you determine whether the concerns you have require intensive intervention at the Red Light Level. Note that the questions are not focused exclusively on "addiction," but rather are a way to assess the severity of the problems caused by screen use. If the answer to one or more of these statements is "yes," then it will be important to put some significant time and energy into helping your child or adolescent make some changes.

Regarding your child's use of screen time (including any of the following: social media, video gaming, computer use, Internet activity), which of the following statements are true?

1. Screen time significantly interferes with my child's relationships (with peers and/or adults). (Yes / No)
2. Screen time significantly interferes with my child's success in school. (Yes / No)
3. Screen time significantly interferes with my child's job (if employed). (Yes / No)

4. Screen time significantly interferes with my child's sleep. (Yes / No)
5. My child's screen use could violate laws and/or have legal consequences. (Yes / No)
6. My child's screen use could result in serious health consequences (e.g., texting while driving). (Yes / No)

Essentially, if screen time interferes with relationships, school, work, or sleep, then it's a problem. While we can't draw a firm line, in general, if the interference is at a mild level, then it might be considered the Yellow Light Level. When the interference is more chronic and severe, then we would consider it to be at the Red Light Level, and thus necessitate stronger intervention. Also, if screen use could result in serious legal or health consequences, then this behavior also falls in the Red Light category. Texting while driving is an example of this. The teen might be fine, so long as she doesn't injure herself or someone else. But, like drunk driving, texting while driving significantly increases the risk of accidents. Moreover, in many states, it is against the law.

If you have tried preventive and intervention levels and continue to see the problems listed in the preceding, it's time to look seriously at increasing the use of controlling strategies at the Red Light Level. In essence, we are now turning up the level of control within our authoritative parenting style. We include chronic sleep loss here because a considerable amount of research has been published on the effects of sleep on our health, relationships, learning, and other important life functions.[12] Sleep deprivation might not be getting the attention that it merits given the problems it causes. Indeed, some research suggests that it can even shrink brain size.[13]

When we talk with parents about the technology problems they see at home, they report failing grades, chronic sleep loss, little to no recreational activities or exercise, complaints of boredom when not in front of a screen, very negative mood when denied screen time, and few relationships outside of gaming or online activity. In most cases, these problems have developed over a long period of time and are not resolved quickly. Although there are no simple solutions, with dedication and support, often these serious problems can be successfully addressed.

We think that many families are capable of addressing their children's serious screen-time problems without resorting to placement in a residential treatment center or outpatient therapy, though these may be appropriate options for the most severe cases. In this chapter, we'll focus primarily on things that parents can do in collaboration with their kids after strategies at the Green and Yellow Light Levels have not been successful. We understand that there are no easy answers for the most challenging screen-time situations, so we present these recommendations with an understanding that each family has its unique needs and must develop solutions that are tailored for the children and problems that are being targeted.

Earlier we considered Max at age 6 in Chapter 8 (Green Light Level) and at age 11 in Chapter 9 (Yellow Light Level). He is now 17 and by most accounts has been doing well. He has friends, makes good grades, and holds down a part-time job. Though his parents were aware that he was an avid gamer, they had no idea how serious his gaming problem had become until they discovered that he had been secretly using their credit cards for expensive gaming purchases. When confronted, Max confessed that he had become rather obsessed with a game that required multiple in-app purchases to advance to higher levels. He felt guilty and remorseful, but also relieved that he had been caught, as he recognized that he needed help with this gaming problem that had become so compelling.

Max's parents were understandably upset and concerned, and though they have a long history of approaching challenges with a warm, empathic parenting style, this particular situation stands out. His parents feel angry, confused, and dismayed. Before talking to Max, they spend some time together discussing their feelings and planning how they will talk to Max about the problem. They also know that it is important to mindfully respond to the problem rather than be emotionally reactive. They realize that if they confront Max with an angry tirade, it could be harmful to both Max and their relationship with him. A harsh, anger-filled confrontation is likely to be counter-productive and not in line with an authoritative parenting style. His parents take time to ensure that they have their own emotions in check before they meet with Max. While they plan to be both serious and firm in their meeting with him, they still want to come from a place of warmth and love.

Max's parents come up with the following plan:

1. Max will have to pay them back for the credit card charges.
2. Gaming will be temporarily suspended while the family works together on solutions to the problem.
3. They install and begin using monitoring programs/apps to temporarily prohibit Max from gaming.
4. They prohibit Max from having electronics in his bedroom.
5. Max and his parents will collaboratively explore ways that he can get his underlying needs met without compulsive gaming. This won't be easy, but the family understands that the core needs don't go away magically when the gaming ceases.
6. Psychotherapy is considered as a supportive resource.

Interventions at the Red Light Level

As noted, Green and Yellow Light approaches should be continued even when more severe Red Light Level problems have emerged. For example, even when screen time problems become severe, we should continue to maintain tech-free zones (e.g., dinner), engage our family members in fun outdoor activities free of screens, role-model healthy screen limits, and try to collaboratively negotiate differences of opinion about screen-time usage with our kids. We understand that these approaches may not seem to be effective when dealing with problems that require Red Light Level inter-vention, but they are the foundation of a healthy interaction with technology and need to be maintained. The following example illustrates a challenging situation that gradually moved from Yellow Light to Red Light and raised serious concerns.

Tamara knew that her daughter, Kara, spent too much time on her phone using social media apps, but until recently she was unaware of how serious the problem had become. Two weeks ago she woke in the middle of the night after hearing a noise and feared that an intruder was in the home. Though she was relieved that it was only Kara, she was angry that she was up at 3 a.m. posting to Instagram. This must be why she's been so tired and lethargic lately, she thought to herself. Two days later, she received a call from the school counselor expressing concern about excessive absences and failing grades. Social media had become the center of Kara's life and had become a serious drain on her sleep and education. Tamara had tried multiple times to set limits, but they were always met with resistance. The straw that broke the camel's back was a call from the principal. Kara had thrown a book at a teacher after being reprimanded for using her phone in class repeatedly. When Tamara expressed her concerns to Kara, she lashed out defiantly and turned over the kitchen table, leaving Tamara feeling scared and uncertain about her capacity to address this behavioral challenge effectively.

Tamara had been proactive throughout Kara's childhood by utilizing a lot of Green Light and Yellow Light strategies. She signed her up for soccer, read books to her, put a trampoline in the back yard, and set limits around television and computer time. Even so, as Kara got older, her interest in social media intensified and she slowly became less responsive to the limits Tamara set. Kara also began to find ways around the limits—by getting on her phone after Tamara went to bed and by skipping school while Tamara was at work. Kara really needs some help, but simply cutting off social media wasn't going to work. When Tamara tried that, Kara would explode and then find ways around her limits. While there are no quick and easy fixes to problems like this, Tamara will likely need to pick her battles carefully, consider

Kara's developmental needs, and work with Kara in a way that's respectful. What follows is some additional guidance in this area.

Strategies Come from the Relationship

Parenting around a serious screen-time problem can be extremely challenging, so some general guidelines may be helpful for learning how to deal with harmful screen time. When kids use screen time excessively and to their detriment, trying to intervene can create tension, anger, resentment, and frustration. Parents must be prepared for strong negative reactions when applying limits and should understand that giving in to more screen time to avoid confrontation only perpetuates the problem.

One important guideline is to put things in perspective before deciding to curtail technology. Your relationship with your child is more important than homework, screen time, messy rooms, and household chores. Sometimes our judgment becomes clouded, and we damage our relationships by prioritizing compliance with our requests. This may be particularly true for adolescents who have a relatively short period of time remaining under our roofs. Do we want a good relationship with these teens, or do we simply want them to follow our rules? That may sound like a false choice, but for many adolescents, their worldview really is all or nothing.[14] As adults, we know that our teens are going to have to move on, become independent, and self-regulate. We can support them in doing so by bolstering our relationships with them. Their psychological need for relatedness is partly met with us. We need to be sure that we're picking our battles. Consider the way in which Tommy's parents decided to address some problems that were arising:

Tommy was a bright, hard-working 17-year-old student. He made good grades, and he was also an athlete who competed at a high level in baseball. His mother, Linda, worried about his poor sleep habits. After school and baseball, he napped from about 6 to 9 p.m., ate a late dinner, and then stayed up until around 2 a.m. doing homework. He would close his door and work on the laptop in his room. Linda knew that some of that time in his room was spent gaming, on social media, and watching videos.

Linda and her partner, Jennifer, wondered whether they should really put their foot down regarding Tommy's study habits and nighttime routine. He was often tardy to school, but he drove himself to school. So they decided to let him deal with the tardies. They noticed he was often tired, grumpy, and that his grades and athletics were at least somewhat negatively affected by his habits. Although his sleep routine was unusual, with his daily three-hour nap, he was getting close to the recommended hours of sleep for teens. Linda and Jennifer had already tried unsuccessfully to problem-solve this with Tommy. Tommy seemed uninterested in changing and pointed out that he is doing pretty well overall.

All of these challenges had arisen during Tommy's senior year in high school. After some discussion, Linda and Jennifer decided it wasn't worth imposing limits and consequences on Tommy. They just couldn't think of a way to do it without it backfiring. They asked themselves, "Is there an effective way to get him to change? Do we want to spend our last six months with Tommy fighting about this?" They decided that there was not a way to win this battle, and that it was more important to maintain a strong relationship as he went off to college than to try to impose (ineffective) limits. They felt that Tommy would just have to experience the natural consequences of his habits and trusted that life was going to be the best teacher for him at this point.

Tommy is clearly experiencing some chronic negative effects from his tech use. It isn't "off the charts," but it is understandably concerning to his parents. Given the ongoing nature of the problems, we could say that he's gone from the Yellow to Red Light Level, although we can't claim that there's a clear distinction. Regardless, we can see why Tommy's parents feel strongly motivated to intervene. However, they have already tried numerous times, and their efforts seemed to make things worse. They decided that they could not set limits without creating more problems than they would solve. Instead, they tried talking to him, as they felt it was important to keep an open conversation about balanced technology usage.

When confronting your child or teen whose problems are at the Red Light Level, there are important points to keep in mind. First, it's critical that we're in a calm state of mind and that we choose a good time to talk about it. When's a good time to talk about it? Certainly not in the middle of an argument at midnight over whether your teen should turn off his laptop and go to bed. Bring it up when it's not a point of tension, such as during a tech-free time like dinner. It also helps for all parents and caregivers to be in agreement about appropriate limits so that you don't find yourself in this situation:

> PARENT 1: I'm concerned that you're spending so much time on social media that your grades are starting to slip.
>
> PARENT 2: Aw, it's not any different than the way we used to spend hours talking on the phone when we were young. Give the kid a break!

Parenting is tough, and working together makes it a whole lot easier. Before having difficult conversations with your kids about technology, have some private conversations with your co-parent so that you can work as a team and not undermine each other. Come to an agreement on how you are going to approach your child and on some ways that you plan to intervene.

Imposing Consequences

Given the seriousness of the problems at the Red Light Level, we need to be clear with our kids that we can empathize with them, while also maintaining some rules and limits for health and well-being. For younger kids who are not about to go out on their own, we should probably impose consequences for breaking the screen-time rules, especially when the problem is at the Yellow or Red Light Level. A good rule of thumb is this: *use the smallest consequence that produces the desired result.* It's not helpful to punish the child who tried to sneak in 30 extra minutes of gaming by taking away her game console and grounding her for a week. If this child would change her behavior after losing screen time for one afternoon as a consequence, then that is all that's needed.

Whenever possible, we should try to use natural consequences. As discussed in Chapter 9, a natural consequence is not doled out by a parent, but rather occurs on its own. Stay up late playing video games all night and one may not feel well enough to enjoy other activities the next day. Sometimes kids need some help connecting the dots here, so it may be useful to explain (in a loving rather than shaming way) that there's a connection between the behavior and the natural consequence. In the case of Tommy, his parents decided to allow natural consequences to take place, such as tardies, rather than imposing their own consequences.

Sometimes logical consequences are the preferred option over natural ones. For example, the natural consequences of drinking and driving could be a horrible accident at the worst or possibly a charge of driving under the influence (DUI). As parents, we can't stand by and let such natural consequences occur. Logical consequences are related to the misbehavior in question. For drinking and driving, parents could (and should) take away driving privileges until the teen can show that he or she can be responsible. Also, such a teen might need specific drug or alcohol counseling. In the example in which a child sneaks an extra 30 minutes of game time, a logical consequence would be the loss of access to gaming for a specified period of time.

Successful parenting also requires some consistency, which can be hard for all of us to maintain. However, we can be consistent by applying consequences in a predictable manner. If kids catch on that sometimes they get in trouble for violating screen-time rules and sometimes they don't, they're likely to take a gamble and hope to get away with it. On the other hand, they are more likely to respect our limits when there's an established pattern of parents following through with consequences.

There may be situations in which we need to restrict access to technology to help our kids live more balanced lives. In general, we don't encourage parents to deny all access (the "cold turkey" approach) when it comes to screen use. There are a number of reasons for this. For one, it's impossible to enforce a cold turkey approach given that kids do much of their schoolwork on computers and tablets. So, the issue is whether we can restrict our kids' *recreational* screen use while not affecting their *productivity* screen use. Social, entertainment, and productivity uses are bundled together with our screens. It is practically impossible to restrict access to all recreational screen use because that would mean restricting productivity screen use. However, if the source of the problematic screen use is a gaming console, then there is a greater chance of being able to impose restrictions on the target behavior with minimal consequences for productivity. Also, if your child's school has provided laptops for students, it might be possible to restrict them from their home devices, which provide recreational screen access, while they still are able to use their school laptops for homework.

There is another important issue to consider regarding the cold turkey approach. When kids are getting most of their psychological needs met through their screen use (e.g., relatedness, autonomy, competence), then taking away their screens leaves a huge void of unmet needs. Some of these kids are using screens, at least in part, to keep negative thoughts and feelings about themselves, the world, and the future at bay. So, when screens are taken away, those negative thoughts and feelings may come rushing in to fill this void. Most of us will not be prepared to deal with the strong feelings of anger, resentment, anxiety, and depression that can result from the abrupt loss of screen access. Though the experts at the residential tech rehab programs may have the knowledge and skills to handle this, most families will need additional resources and supports, such as a mental health professional.

Rather than going completely cold turkey, parents can limit kids' screen privileges. This may include the following:

- Limited Wi-Fi access
- Use of phone without Wi-Fi or cellular data
- Smartphone only accessible during specific time periods (e.g., not during homework)
- Video games played only certain days/time
- No access to recreational screen time when using computers for school.

When limits like these are set, they need to be strictly enforced. Although there are some strategies that are more specific to each level, the difference between Yellow and Red Light interventions are often quantitative (i.e., in amount) rather than qualitative (i.e., in type or kind). Thus, within an authoritative parenting framework, as screen problems rise in severity, so does the level of restrictions, limits, and consequences imposed by parents.

Parents may find it helpful to determine ways for their kids to earn back their technology privileges, though in extreme cases, only a reduction in screen use may be appropriate. It may also be helpful to review the collaborative problem-solving described earlier in the Yellow Light chapter, as those skills are helpful in managing the limit-setting process. The involvement of a supportive family therapist can help families adjust to dramatic changes in screen-time use. Finally, parents should work collaboratively with their kids to help "fill the void" left if screen access is rolled back or restricted. If at all possible, we don't want this void to be filled by negative, ruminating thoughts.

The Case of Josh

Josh is a 15-year-old in a family of five. Both parents are working professionals and are seldom home. Josh isn't close to his 12-year-old sister,

Avery, or his 17-year-old sister, Ruby. Their father is a workaholic and a (somewhat) functional alcoholic. When their parents are around, they tend to argue or keep their distance from one another.

Josh has become increasingly detached from his family and his friends at school. Even so, he has an active online and social media life, using Instagram and Snapchat frequently. He is almost constantly on his phone or, when at home, on his laptop upstairs in his room. Josh's parents don't really know what he is up to online.

One day, Josh's mother, Amber, received a call from the mother of Josh's girlfriend. Amber didn't even know that he had a girlfriend! Apparently, Josh's girlfriend left her phone out, and her mother noticed a very sexually explicit text from Josh. When confronted, Josh tried to explain away the text, but his mother confiscated his phone. After unlocking it, she was shocked to see the many texts and social media interactions dealing with sex and drugs. Apparently, Josh had been exchanging nude photos with several teenage girls, had been meeting girls to "hook up," and had been using drugs for some time now. He was even starting to deal drugs and had created a drug dealer persona on social media. Josh's parents took away his phone. Josh begged to have it back, exclaiming, "My whole life is on that phone!" In a fit of tearful rage, he grabbed a kitchen knife and threatened to stab them or himself if they didn't give it back.

Josh's case is extreme and rare, but serious problems such as this do arise that involve exceptionally risky teen behavior. In a situation such as this, we strongly recommend seeking immediate help from a mental health professional. Josh's parents may blame technology for his difficulties, but in his case the problems with the family system may be the underlying cause. Josh's deviance, played out through social media, may be a sign of deeper problems rather than the source, and some of these problems can be amplified by screen use. It is also important to note that there are some kids and teens who start to engage in very risky behaviors (on- and offline) without any apparent underlying cause. Regardless, when problems are as significant as those of Josh, professional help is usually necessary.

Teens have always engaged in a certain level of risk-taking behavior; it comes with the territory. As neuropsychiatrist Dr. Daniel J. Siegel discusses in his book *Brainstorm: The Power and Purpose of the Teenage Brain*, teens are driven to explore, seek novelty, and take risks as part of the process of gaining separation from their caregivers.[15] If teens didn't take risks, they'd never leave the nest. Still, screens provide new and easy ways for teens to take risks that were not available until recently.

As discussed in Chapter 8, we're not proponents of monitoring kids' screen activity, in the sense of surveillance, without probable cause. Please refer to that chapter, as well as our FAQ section (Appendix 3), for a further discussion of this issue. In short, many kids can find ways to avoid surveillance. The mere effort to control their screen activity can be viewed as a breach of trust and thus can cause much friction in the relationship. In general, we believe that our kids should be given the benefit of the doubt. The Green Light strategies discussed in Chapter 8 can also reduce the likelihood of some of the risky behaviors occurring in the first place. However, when a teen has been found to be engaging in significantly risky behaviors, like Josh, then restricted access (e.g., can't use social media for a period of time until he shows that he can use it responsibly) with some degree of surveillance (e.g., apps that provide parental control over their kids' app use, viewing texts) is warranted.

Josh's parents may come to recognize that his screen-time problems are very likely symptoms of more serious underlying concerns. The smartphone provided them a window to Josh's risky behaviors that need to be addressed. If his parents feel that they are capable of intervening, they must do so in a way that is protective of Josh and simultaneously loving. This will not be easy, as they need to act in such a way that limits his freedom and autonomy for his own good. Most parents in this situation will feel ill-equipped to handle the aggression (directed possibly at self and others), substance abuse, and risky sexual behavior. Given the severity and complexity of the presenting problems, his parents should seek help from a psychologist or other qualified professional. When making contact with a clinician, parents should communicate clearly their concerns about the role that technology has played in facilitating Josh's problematic behaviors.

Though many screen-time problems may be signs of an underlying psychological disorder, there may very well be screen-time problems that fall under our Red Light classification that are not linked to such problems. The high volume of screen time among most teens suggests that heavy use is relatively common (whereas severe psychological problems are not). There appears to be a bidirectional relationship between mental health and screen time. Consider a teen who feels sad (though not clinically depressed) and begins to withdraw from family time and immerse herself in social media. One consequence of heavy Internet use for this teen may be increased feelings of sadness, which may promote further withdrawal.

More research is needed to better understand how child and adolescent use of screen time may impact their relationships. Studies have found both positive and negative effects of screen use, but there does seem to be a dose effect such that excessive screen time will cause problems. Some of these problems might be so severe that they are diagnosable disorders, such as depression. In particular, compulsive screen usage has the potential to limit the kind of face-to-face engagement that's so important to their social and emotional development. In terms of self-determination theory, and perhaps going back to our evolutionary heritage, our need for relatedness is likely to require a sufficient level of in-person engagement for our overall well-being.

The Takeaway?

In this chapter we have provided some suggestions for helping your kids when prevention and minor interventions have proven unsuccessful. When screen problems are severe or have the potential to cause great harm, then we are at the Red Light Level. Sometimes the problems are too great for us to solve alone, perhaps because there are deeper issues that have not been addressed. For example, a kid with social anxiety may immerse himself or herself in screen time because it's easier than dealing with the social world outside. Over time, the screen becomes so rewarding that it dominates all social interaction. Screen time may be the problem, but it's also possible that the screen use is a symptom of another problem.

Within an authoritative parenting style framework, parents must turn up the "control" volume and set more restrictive screen-time limits, as well as impose more severe consequences for Red Light Level screen problems. We still maintain our warmth and continue to use relationship-building and preventive strategies. We attempt to collaboratively problem-solve, but fewer choices will be under consideration.

Red Light Level problems, especially at the most severe and chronic intensity, often require professional assistance. When seeking assistance from a mental health professional, it may be beneficial to find someone who has experience working with screen-time issues, but that's an uncommon specialty. What's most important is finding a professional who has expertise in working with kids, teens, and families and who seems to be a good fit. If you can easily build rapport, establish trust, and feel heard, then you've likely found someone who is a good match. Though there's some controversy in the field of psychotherapy about why counseling works, many researchers believe that the most important element for successful outcomes is a strong alliance between the therapist and the client, regardless of the specific treatment methods.[16] Notably, it's through a strong therapeutic alliance (i.e., the relationship) that clients improve their own relationships.

Depending on your needs, the mental health professional may recommend individual, group, or family therapy. In many cases, when parents are seeking help about a child's screen time, a psychotherapist will want to help the family establish better communication, boundaries, and relationships to strengthen the parent-child relationship. A therapist may also be able to address the underlying problems that may be contributing to Internet or gaming addictions. Moreover, consultation with a professional can offer an objective perspective when trying to determine whether efforts to limit screen time may be counterproductive or damaging to relationships within the family system (e.g., should the video game console be taken away entirely?)

We have gone through the elements of our Tech Happy Life model: the foundation of the relationship; the Green Light Level (preventive); Yellow Light Level (address emerging problems); and Red Light Level (intervene when there are serious problems). We will provide a recap of the overall book and the model in Chapter 12. But before we do that, there is one more area that merits a closer examination: schools and technology, which we discuss in Chapter 11. We mentioned that an increasing number of schools require students to do classwork and homework on tablets and laptops. There is a strong push to integrate technology into the classroom with the idea that students will benefit. However, schools are wrestling with some of the same issues that families are regarding screen use. How families and schools address these issues together (or not) is critical to capitalizing on the positives of technology while minimizing the negatives.

11

Parenting, Technology, and Schooling

Patricia has worked hard to limit the amount of screen time for her children by encouraging outdoor play, reading, and family craft activities. When the new school year started, she experienced some frustration around the quantity of online homework assignments and requirements imposed by the school for her children. As the school year progressed, Patricia's boundaries around screen time at home felt harder and harder to maintain. While she understood that there were clear benefits to her children's use of technology, she also felt some resentment toward the school as she saw her efforts to limit technology in the home being undermined. Ultimately, she felt as if she had little to no control over the situation and lacked the resources to adequately address her concerns.

Technology in the Schools (and Home)

It's not surprising that parents like Patricia experience some stress over the increased use of technology in schools. Today's young students are learning with tools that didn't exist when their parents were in school, and the expectations at home and school are frequently discordant. In this chapter, we try to place educational technologies in a context that will be helpful to parents (and teachers), taking into consideration what we know about child development, learning, and family-school partnering. We recognize that there are many kinds of families and schools, so there won't be a specific approach that will meet everyone's needs. However, there are some general principles that will apply to most cases to help families navigate the new terrain of increasingly technological schools. But first, what do we mean when we talk about technology in schools?

Technology and Education

Immersed in his fictional Ali G character, the actor and satirist Sacha Baron Cohen once described a friend, "Rainbow Jeremy," as someone who didn't use any technology and avoided "everything to do with science." The experts on Baron Cohen's panel quickly pointed out that Rainbow Jeremy lives in a house, wears clothes, and eats food—all products of technology. Of course, Ali G would have none of it, maintaining that his friend was completely tech-free ("you can check out his website"). It's a good bit of comedy, but it also underscores our narrow view of technology as innovation that comes from the digital age. When we step back and take a broader perspective, we can clearly see that teachers and students have been using technology in schools as long as there have been schools.

Depending on your age, you may have encountered one or more of these technological innovations in education: the slide rule, filmstrips, overhead projectors, calculators, or Scantron tests. In the late 1980s and early 1990s, televisions broadcasting Channel One in classrooms began delivering educational and news content while generating criticism for exposing captive audiences of students to advertising. New technologies in the schools offer the promise of *better* in the form of improved learning outcomes, increased efficiency, and enhanced experiences. Of course, not all gadgets deliver on these promises, but we ought to place the use of computers, tablets, and other digital technologies in this context. Laptop computers aren't overhead projectors, but they're essentially another way of introducing new technologies to schools in the interest of helping kids learn. Why is your child's school adopting ebooks, iPads, smartphones, and web-based homework assignments? Because some educators believe that this is the next great thing that's going to make school better and enhance learning. But is it?

In recent years, there has been great interest in trying to understand the effects of new technologies in the classroom, but the results are mixed. A 2015 report from the Organisation for Economic Co-operation and Development (OECD) found that in the 70 countries studied, computers did not have a positive effect on academic achievement test scores.[1] At the moment, data supporting the use of computers and other digital devices are limited, and in some cases, research has shown that providing computers or tablets to kids may be counterproductive.[2]

Why would schools go digital given the limited empirical support for enhanced outcomes? Perhaps there's a strong belief that newer is better, or that students need technology to be better prepared for twenty-first-century jobs. But simply putting devices in the hands of kids does not seem to deliver on the promise of better learning outcomes. In fact, some kids decline in math and reading when given greater access to technology (perhaps because they are spending increased time on games, entertainment, and social media).[3] A recent analysis of student data gathered from a large national sample showed that more time spent in front of screens in ninth grade predicted less time spent on homework in eleventh grade.[4] Other studies have shown that students who take written notes by hand may learn better than those who take notes on laptops.[5] Given these findings, one wonders whether digital technology hinders more than it helps.

We don't want to give the impression that there are no educational benefits to digital technologies. Rather, we want to present some cautious optimism about how technology may enhance your kids' learning. A recent review of the research on tablet use in schools and learning outcomes noted that "the fragmented nature of the current knowledge base, and the scarcity of rigorous studies, makes it difficult to draw firm conclusions."[6] What does seem to be clear is that students gain the greatest benefit from technology in educational settings when there is a clear and specific purpose (e.g., using an iPad to view a 3-D rendering of a molecule that can be rotated to better understand its structure). Students also show better learning outcomes when trained teachers are actively involved in the use of technology for teaching and learning.[7]

Sometimes It's Better Without Screens

Edgar Watkins loves teaching ninth-grade biology and connects well with his students. He organized a special field trip for his class that involved the opportunity to take a boat ride with marine biologists. To his dismay, several of the students missed opportunities to observe dolphins and sea turtles because they were looking at their phones during the tour. The following year he banned phones from the tour and found that the students were much more engaged and benefited greatly from the experience. Many students even expressed gratitude that they were not allowed to bring their phones because they recognized that their devices would have interfered with this unique learning experience.

Granted, not all schools have access to field trips with marine life, and technology in the classroom has the potential to provide enriching experiences as well as distractions. A team of scholars interested in learning more about the advantages and disadvantages of technology in education gathered data from school leaders (e.g., principals, vice principals, and department heads) in Canada and found that some clear benefits emerged, including increased student motivation when technology was utilized.[8] The research also found benefits for students with disabilities, and the development of *reverse mentoring,* in which students were able to take on an expert role and instruct the teachers about technology. On the other hand, school leaders expressed concerns about the distractions of texting, the decline of both traditional literacy and social skills, and the increased demands on teachers of electronic communication from parents ("There's a lot more onus on the teacher to contact parents to make sure they know, for better or for worse, that this is where their children are performing. That takes time away from preparing to be a better teacher in the classroom" (p. 180).

While technology can certainly facilitate learning, we still lack a comprehensive understanding of the degree to which the advantages outweigh the disadvantages (or if they do at all). Technology has many educational benefits, but it also has the potential to interfere with learning. Many students, if allowed to have unfettered access to their cell phones, will periodically focus on their phones instead of instruction and classwork. Indeed, a study of high school students in the United Kingdom showed an increase on test scores after a cell phone ban was instituted.[9] The greatest test score gains were made by underachieving and disadvantaged students. So, when it comes to technology in the schools, it might be prudent for schools to limit the use of cell phones.

Despite the lack of conclusive evidence-based support for the effectiveness of digital technology in the schools, we have little reason to believe that it's going away. If anything, we predict a significant increase in the use of computers, tablets, smartphones, and other devices in the years to come. We expect to see kids coming home from school with e-textbooks, assignments that require Internet access, Power-Point presentations, file sharing, and collaboratively produced projects through services like Google Drive. Since it's not going away, parents can be most helpful when they play an active role in understanding, monitoring, and supporting school-based initiatives that rely on digital technologies. In this chapter, we provide some concrete strategies for doing this by starting with a brief detour to introduce an established and research-supported framework of family-school partnering.

Family-School Partnering

There once was a time when parent involvement in schools was limited to bake sales, volunteering, and the occasional parent-teacher conference. While these forms of participation are certainly valuable, they also have some serious limitations. Old models of parent involvement assumed that schools were primarily responsible for student learning and that parents functioned merely as ancillary support. Consistent with this approach was the idea that information flowed primarily in one direction (from the school to the home). As such, it was easy for parents to blame schools when things were not going well, and just as easy for teachers to fault parents for academic and behavioral problems. There had to be a better way.

Family-school partnering (FSP) rejects the idea of schools as the focal point of learning and recognizes that learning occurs in the home as well. By conceptualizing parents as educators and equal partners, the FSP model promotes shared values, shared decision-making, and shared responsibility. Rather than one-way communication flowing from school to home, parents and teachers engage in two-way communication (because it also helps for teachers to know how a child is doing at home). A growing body of research is demonstrating that kids perform better academically, socially, and emotionally when high-quality FSP is implemented.[10] Furthermore, when there's consistency across family and school settings in terms of values and expectations, kids do better. We recognize that not all school systems have adopted this approach, and that transforming from a traditional "parent involvement" model to an FSP paradigm takes time, but with baby steps, good things can happen. This is exactly where technology fits in. If you want your child to gain the advantages of technology and education and minimize some of the pitfalls, applying this FSP approach with your child's teachers may help.

Recall that in our Tech Happy Life model, the foundation is a strong relationship between parents and their children. Similarly, FSP is about forging a strong relationship between parents and the school. It is this partnering that enables both parties to work collaboratively for the educational development of children.

What follows here are some suggestions regarding FSP and technology to help facilitate better collaboration across home and school.

Naturally, these conversations will look different across grade levels and will be more challenging when the values related to screen time at home and school are more discrepant, but these recommendations represent a starting point that can be modified as needed.

Talk About It

Talk to your child's teacher(s) about technology at home and at school. It will be helpful to learn about the use of technology at school, as well as the expectations. Are students allowed to bring phones to school? If so, to what extent are they allowed to use them? What about other devices? Parents should be very clear about school rules and expectations. But remember, communication should be two-way, so be sure to tell your child's teacher(s) about technology use in your home and about your values and expectations.

Some questions you may want to ask:

- Where does the school or classroom fall on a continuum from "low tech" to "high tech?"
- How do you use technology in the classroom?
- What are your expectations regarding my child's devices (e.g., phone, tablet, gaming device) at school?
- Will my child be expected to complete homework assignments using a computer or other digital device?
- When using technology at school or at home, what tools or recommendations do you have for ensuring that students aren't distracted by chatting, social media, games, and so on?

Some information you may want to share with your child's teacher:

- Where your home environment falls on a continuum from "low tech" to "high tech"
- How technology is used in your home
- Limits or boundaries you have established around screen time

- Any challenges or struggles you have experienced with your child and technology.

Some questions you may want to ask your child:

- How do your teachers use technology at school?
- In what ways does technology help you learn?
- In what ways might technology make it harder for you to learn?
- How do you enjoy learning most? From books, PowerPoint presentations, classroom discussions?
- What kinds of technology skills do kids need to be successful at your school?
- How can you best limit digital distractions so that you can focus attentively on the work at hand?
- In what ways can we help you learn better?

Identify Shared Values and Goals

Chances are good that you and your child's teacher(s) want the same outcomes: a child/student who grows academically, socially, and emotionally over the course of the school year. How can you engage in partnering to help achieve those outcomes, and to what extent does technology play a role? How can parents and teachers support each other's learning environments? In such cases where there's a discrepancy (i.e., school is high tech and home is low tech), how can parents and teachers work together around those differences?

Be Proactive and Sustain the Relationship

Family-school partnering is not something that is accomplished in one meeting. It's characterized by a relationship that requires on-going communication. Over the course of a school year, new devices will be acquired, maturation will occur, and values and expectations may shift. The key to success is for parents and teachers to continue talking about how technology may be used at home and school to further the shared values and goals. When appropriate, including kids in collaborative meetings can promote buy-in and help avoid a top-down approach. Thus, working collaboratively with kids and teens is one way of addressing their needs for relatedness, competence, and autonomy. Conflict can be averted by communicating and understanding how technology should be used across home and school settings. Family-school partnering, in essence, forms the foundation that enables the preventive, Green Light, strategies to work more effectively. Some of the problems that can arise from technology use in the schools can be avoided through establishing some boundaries and limits that are agreed upon by both families and schools.

Limitations

We want to acknowledge that FSP isn't easy. Parents who have multiple children with multiple teachers can't realistically carve out the time to have meaningful, sustained, collaborative relationships with each teacher. Likewise, your child's teacher has other students and families that have their own needs, so teacher availability will certainly be limited. Importantly, if we have established some level of FSP, we have the relationships in place to more quickly identify and address (Yellow Light Level) problems. The idea here is that we approach education as a collaborative endeavor and put our energies where they are most needed, while recognizing that we can't be everywhere at once.

Innovative Solutions for Managing Screen Time in Schools

Some schools are utilizing innovative technology to address concerns about technology in the classroom. For example, educational leaders in many states have encouraged students to use an app that rewards students with points for not using their phones during the school day. Accumulated points can be redeemed for rewards at restaurants and retailers popular with students. By incentivizing decreased use of phones during the school day with extrinsic motivation, schools may be able to increase academic engagement and learning. Since this approach is relatively new, the jury is still out on its efficacy. But it is encouraging that innovative strategies can be used to help students stay on task that don't just rely on punitive measures. Such apps hold the promise that sometimes technology can be used to save us from technology.

Managing School Tech at Home

It's very likely that your child will be asked to complete school assignments at home using a computer, smartphone, tablet, or some other digital device. Consider Patricia, the mother in the vignette that opens this chapter. She wants her kids to read print books, play outside, and have opportunities to connect with family members face to face. When school assignments require screen time at home, she sees this as an encroachment on family time. Moreover, the line between screen-time homework and entertainment often becomes blurred. Her casual observations reveal that Josh, her oldest son, easily bounces from working on a PowerPoint presentation for his science class to checking Snapchat and texting his friends. Patricia wants to strike a healthy balance between supporting Josh's academic growth (including that which involves technology) while at the same time encouraging other aspects of his development to flourish (like social skills). Here are some ways that concerns like these can be managed.

Help Kids Separate Work and Play

When your children have homework assignments that require technology use, support them in staying focused by showing them that they can be more productive when they separate their work from entertainment and online socializing. This can be a challenge, given the fact that our computers are used for so many different purposes (we confess that our laptops are used for writing this book and for watching Bad Lip Reading videos on YouTube). Additionally, we may have multiple devices present at any given time (e.g., laptop, phone, tablet). So, to help your kids with this challenge, encourage them to use one device at a time, turn off Wi-Fi or Internet access when it's not needed, and stick with one task at a time. It might be helpful to establish a computer dedicated to productivity in a study area of the house. The idea is that kids would physically be required to move to a different computer or different area of the house for entertainment or social purposes. Laptops or tablets that are checked out to students by schools should only be used for schoolwork. Be sure to read through the school's usage contract and go over this with your child in detail so they know the expectations, restrictions, and consequences of misuse.

Cell phones can prove to be particularly distracting, so strongly encourage (or require) your child to keep his or her cell phone in another room while doing homework. This strategy is particularly helpful given the "brain drain" effect caused by the mere presence of cell phones.[11] "Deep work" that is necessary for cognitively challenging endeavors is best accomplished through sustained attention.[12] Cell phone and social media time can be a way of rewarding oneself after completing an academic task.

Provide Some Structure

Parents can get irritated when they perceive that their children's time is not well spent or when homework procrastination results in frustration. At the end of the weekend, Patricia frequently looks back and regrets that her children spent too much time in front of screens and not enough time climbing trees. We suggest that Patricia shift her focus from looking back to looking at the present and forward.

Without being overly rigid, build in some structure that will ensure that time spent is better aligned with goals and values. This kind of structure will look different for each family and should be tailored to meet the developmental needs of children as they mature (generally speaking, older children are better able to self-regulate and manage their time, whereas younger children require more guidance and structure). What might this look like? It may be as simple as sitting down at the breakfast table with the family and collaboratively generating a simple plan for a Saturday:

9 a.m. Take the dog to the park
10 a.m. Clean our rooms
11 a.m. Go to the pool and bring picnic lunch
1 p.m. Focused homework time (just work, no play)
2 p.m. Free time (may involve entertaining screen time)
4 p.m. Visit Grandma.

Again, this is not intended to be overly rigid. Maybe the time at the pool is so much fun that more time is spent there than planned. The idea is to separate the work from the play and to dedicate some focused time for work. This kind of planning can help families ensure that there's a healthy balance between the screen time necessary for schoolwork and the outdoor, social, and play time that so many parents value. Importantly, if we don't consciously and deliberately make efforts to create some boundaries, it's all too easy for screen time to infiltrate virtually every moment of our time.

Be a Role Model

Technology has become a pervasive part of our lives. Whereas previous generations had greater separation of work life and home life, today we check our work email on our phone 24 hours a day, seven days a week. In the movie *RV*, Robin Williams plays a character who tries to have it both ways by taking his family on vacation while secretly working on his laptop in stolen moments (obvious moral of the story: family comes first, but the pull of work is mighty powerful). Our kids see us looking at screens all the time, but they may not be able to tell the difference between the time we spend playing *Words with Friends* and sending a work email. When we set up clear boundaries between work and leisure, we show our kids that we can be completely present with them when we are not working and that we can set aside time to be completely focused on work when that's required. We also show them that schoolwork has a time and place, as does family time.

Practice Patience and Compassion

It's very easy to make these recommendations and set these intentions, but implementation can be quite challenging. After all, we may develop our own sense of how much technology we want in the home, but find that the expectations of schools push greater levels of technology into our lives than we desire. As we write these words, we struggle with the screen-time balance in our own families and recognize that we frequently fall short of our aspirations. That's why it's critical that we demonstrate patience and compassion as we try to help our families achieve the goals that we have set.

There will be days on which our choices fail to align with our values, where the ratio of screen time to other activities feels skewed. That's normal and expected, and we can certainly learn from these days, but we should keep our focus on the future and have compassion for ourselves. We can't undo the excessive screen time of yesterday, but we can make better plans for tomorrow. Similarly, we practice compassion, instead of technojudgment, with our kids and understand that the screen has a powerful pull that affects us all.

Promote Self-Regulation

We've emphasized the importance of promoting kids' self-regulation, or self-management, rather than parental control to achieve the best outcomes. In essence, when kids are self-regulating, they are meeting their needs for autonomy and competence. The following example helps illustrate the power of self-directed limits on screen time and the potential for greater academic success.

Jack, age 17, was a model student/athlete. He was tall, athletic, and studious, and well-liked by his peers. He took his academics seriously and competed in sports at an elite level. However, he internalized a lot of the stress of trying to excel in both domains. With his psychologist, he identified a goal of trying to improve some of his grades. Improvement over his already good grades would not be easy, given the fact that he already applied himself academically and had little extra time due to his sports commitments. When asked by his psychologist whether he could think of ways to work more efficiently, Jack noted, "You know, I keep my cell phone by me when I do my homework. I think all the phone checking that I do really slows me down. I bet I could work better if I put my cell in another room while I did my homework." "That sounds like a great idea to me!" replied his psychologist. "Why don't you give it a try and let's see what happens?" Jack tried it out and reported back the next session. Just as Jack suspected, putting his cell in another room really cut down on his homework time, relieved some of his stress, and helped his grades improve.

In this vignette, Jack becomes aware of the role that screen time plays in his life and how it affects his academic success. With the support of his psychologist, Jack is able to monitor his own behavior and adjust to meet his needs. This is far superior to a top-down, adult-driven model in which external limits are placed on Jack. Rather, Jack can take ownership for his success and responsibility for his actions.

When it comes to teens, it is particularly important to allow them greater room to make their own decisions given their increasing need for autonomy. A rigid, top-down approach is likely to be met with resistance and resentment. Our role becomes one of trying to help them think things through by asking open-ended questions. We might want to show them the dots, but we don't want to connect all of the dots for them.

In the next section, we turn to some of the problems that intersect home and school and generate a great deal of concern among parents and teachers. The use of technology to facilitate bullying and sexual behavior raises questions about the roles and responsibilities of students, families, and schools. Increasingly, adults are confronting new challenges and seeking solutions.

Cyberbullying, Sexting, Schools, and Families

In 2015, parents and educators in Cañon City, Colorado, became aware that over 100 high school students were involved in an elaborate exchange of nude photos, mostly of high school students, but also of some eighth graders from the local middle school.[13] Students had managed to keep this activity hidden from adults for some time by using "vault apps" that kept some parts of their phone behind a password-protected screen (some of which looked like innocuous calculators). Even parents who examined their kids' phones were unaware of what remained buried in the concealed recesses of the devices, yet it's now clear that hundreds of nude photos were shared.

The incident raises some important questions about sexting, parenting, and schools. For example,

- How prevalent is sexting? Stories like the one from Cañon High School grab headlines, but is this the norm?
- If kids have the capacity to hide illicit content from parents on smartphones and other devices, what can parents do?
- What's the role of schools in addressing these concerns?

We may never know the extent to which adolescents engage in sexting and cyberbullying, as these behaviors may be hidden from adult view and underreported by teens. Such behaviors are alarming, and it is difficult to know exactly how frequently it is occurring. One study of adolescents in the United States found that only 9.6% reported creating or receiving nude images in the past year.[14] In contrast, another study found the incidence of sexting among adolescents to be 54%, with 28% of sexts containing photographic images.[15] That same study also found that most teens (61%) were unaware that sending such texts could be lead to prosecution charges for possession or dissemination of child pornography.

The picture is also unclear when researchers try to estimate the prevalence of cyberbullying. A review of 58 studies of cyberbullying in the United States found the following reported ranges:

- Perpetration: 1%–41%
- Victimization: 3%–72%
- Overlapping perpetration and victimization: 2.3%–16.7%[16]

In Florida, 12-year-old Rebecca Ann Sedwick was reportedly cyberbullied by other girls via phone messages relentlessly. Her mother found that the school was unresponsive when concerns were voiced and the bullying persisted. She was teased and harassed so extensively that she committed suicide by jumping off a platform at a cement plant.[17]

Do the research findings suggest that sexting and cyberbullying are serious problems? If your child is involved, it's certainly a serious concern for you. The data suggest that some kids are indeed engaging in these behaviors, and like any behavioral health concern, digital problems should be addressed by adults in the context of wellness. It's our responsibility as parents to try to prevent negative outcomes and address them as they emerge.

Given the fact that sexting and cyberbullying are often hidden from adults' view, we don't think the solution is for parents and teachers to spy on teens, intrusively manage their digital lives, or try to catch inappropriate behaviors via technological surveillance. You can't win a cat and mouse game, as kids can cover their tracks, push undesirable content behind digital curtains, and ultimately distance their social world from caring adults. Our responsibility is to provide kids with information and decision-making skills to empower healthy choices and responsible behavior.

While some surveillance may be appropriate, particularly when there is reason to believe that there are concerns, parents should focus on building children's decision-making capacity over excessively managng online activity. Moreover, building and maintaining the type of bond with your children such that they feel they can communicate problems when they arise are particularly important. It seems that parental "monitoring" is actually most effective when our teens self-disclose areas of concern to us, rather than us discovering the information through controlling or solicitation efforts.[18]

Should parents or schools try to tackle these problems? The answer must be yes. As kids move between family systems and school systems, they take their devices with them. Just as families and schools both promote physical health and well-being, so should they collaborate to promote wellness in online environments. In fact, the International Society for Technology and Education (ISTE) has published education technology standards for students, teachers, and school administrators that include the concept of digital health and wellness.[19] When families and schools work together to teach kids about Internet safety, digital citizenship, online etiquette, and risk management, we can promote safe and appropriate use of technology.

If your child reports cyberbullying to you, there are specific and concrete steps you can take to address the problem.

- Listen to your child and validate his or her concerns, assuring him or her that you will do everything you can to keep your child safe.
- Report the bullying to your child's school by contacting the principal and school counselor.

- Assist your child by providing him or her with guidance and support (e.g., showing your child how to block bullies on social media, facilitating access to a psychotherapist, and avoiding any language that suggests that your child is at fault or responsible).

Talk to your child's teachers and school administrators about digital wellness and how you can collaborate to provide students with the tools that will enable them to get the benefits of technology and minimize the potential harms. The mission of schools goes well beyond the development of academic competencies and into the important work of building good citizens, responsible adults, and well-adjusted individuals. Given these aims, teaching responsible and healthy use of technology seems to be a logical extension.

The Takeaway?

Though we're still learning about the impact of digital technologies on student learning and well-being, it's clear that classrooms and homework assignments are increasingly utilizing screens and devices. Moreover, the social and emotional worlds of kids are evolving in this digital landscape. Rather than standing by and wringing our hands with worry, parents and educators should actively involve themselves in joint practices to educate and empower students to successfully meet their academic and social tasks in a hyper-connected world.

12

Summary

The Connors are taking their annual summer trip together as a family. Among their many stops along the way, they are finally going to see the Grand Canyon. They've had this on their "to do" list for quite some time, so Kyle and his wife, Sarah, are excited to finally make the trek. Everyone brings their respective smartphones and tablets for the long drive. Kyle and Sarah take turns driving, and they make a number of interesting stops along the way. Their son, John (age 14), and daughter, Cameron (age 16), sit quietly in back of their minivan for most of the ride. Cameron texts and uses social media throughout the drive, while John is typically gaming. They occasionally lose cellular services during the drive, which leads to complaints from both of the kids.

As Kyle and Sarah traverse the awe-inspiring landscape, they begin to notice that only the driver is really appreciating the scenic views. The family doesn't engage in many conversations, nor do they play the family games along the drive that both Kyle and Sarah recall wistfully from their family vacations when they were kids. As they begin to chat about this, they realize that they have generally been on their devices when they were not driving as well. Instead of the entire trip being a shared experience, Kyle and Sarah realize that for much of the trip, family members are "alone together." They wonder whether the treasures of their relationship, like the splendors along the scenic drive, are just being passed by.

Like us, you are most likely old enough to remember "the Before." We remember a time before just about everyone had Internet access. We remember a time before texting, smartphones, social media, and streaming music and movies. We remember a time when there wasn't Internet pornography, ultraviolent realistic video games, cyberbullying, and online predators. We remember a time that we didn't feel the need to chronicle our lives through Facebook or other social media for those experiences to seem like they mattered. We didn't suffer "FoMO." We remember a time when we weren't alone together. When we were with other people, we were just together.

To be fair, in "the Before," we also remember getting lost while driving to a new place and not being able to contact a person in a time of need. We remember limited TV and video game options. We had trouble keeping in touch with grandparents, favorite relatives, and former classmates. We remember not being able to find important information when we needed it or easily finding options for new activities and restaurants. We remember the record store being out of the CD (or LP!) of our favorite artist.

We didn't experience a sense of loss for not having technologies such as smartphones and social media back in "the Before." It's hard to miss something that you have never experienced. Right now, we don't miss vacations to Mars. Perhaps one day we won't be able to imagine life without those visits.

Given some of the formidable challenges that screens can pose, as parents we might feel a little bit like the protagonist of J. D. Salinger's *Catcher in the Rye*, Holden Caulfield. Holden fantasizes about being a "catcher in the rye," in which he symbolically protects children from falling off the cliff of innocence from childhood into adolescence. With our own kids, we often worry that screens, especially smartphones, are going to cause them to fall off this proverbial cliff. What do our kids gain from these technologies? What is lost?

While technology brings us so much promise and potential, it also brings with it a host of concerns. There is some truth that the invention of the "ship" of technology has brought with it the "shipwreck" of negative consequences. Regardless of what we think about those simpler times, we can be certain that we aren't going back to them. We are all aboard this ship sailing into the future.

How Can We Avoid the Shipwreck?

Perhaps when we think of a shipwreck, images of the *Titanic* sinking come to mind. We don't mean to suggest that technology is about to cause a breach in the hull of humanity and that we are all going to descend into a watery grave. Humans are creative and resilient. We can learn ways to capitalize on the positives of technology while minimizing some of the negatives. If the catastrophic shipwreck is unlikely, perhaps the goal should be to avoid rocking the boat too much while on this voyage.

There are no easy solutions to the challenge of raising balanced kids in a technological world. To life's thorniest problems, there generally are not simple solutions. Establish peace in the Middle East? Create a better health-care system because ours is a "disaster?" Grow the economy so that everyone benefits? Although politicians often promise that they have the answers to such thorny problems, history tells us that easy answers don't exist. If they did, we would have found them by now.

We have drawn many parallels between eating a balanced diet and managing our screen use in a balanced way. There are ways to eat healthy foods, but the temptations to do otherwise are all around us on a daily basis. America's struggles with obesity are growing and solutions are elusive. For example, a search on Amazon for books on "weight loss" will yield thousands of titles. We have no shortage of books on weight loss. But in the United States, we do have a shortage on lost weight. We aren't getting any slimmer despite all the books on how to do just that.

In a manner similar to maintaining a healthy diet, we must make a concerted effort to address the inherent challenges that technology poses in our lives and the lives of our children. There isn't an easy solution in either case. One might say that sometimes answers are simple, but not easy. For instance, it's simple to run a marathon. Just put one foot in front of the other for 26.2 miles! It's a simple idea that's difficult to achieve. One must train for many months to be able to run a marathon. Still, it can be done if one works hard at it. One might say that the simple solution to having a balanced life in a technological world is spending more time with each other while keeping our screen time in check. However, as we all know by now, this is easier said than done.

We wrote this book to offer guidance to parents on how to raise kids in a balanced, healthy way with the challenges inherent in this hyper-connected world. We understand that this is difficult. We struggle with using technology responsibly in our own families. Admittedly, our eyes were sometimes on our screens in the process of writing this book rather than engaging with our own family members! We are both psychologists who understand the mechanisms by which screens can lure us in. We present to groups on these challenges, and yet we still sometimes struggle ourselves with balanced screen use. We get it.

We must all remember that we are in this together and that we should refrain from the "technojudgment" of ourselves or others who struggle with this challenge. Harsh judgments create more problems instead of solving them. Unfortunately, as technology evolves, it isn't going to get any easier. Consequently, we must roll up our collective sleeves to take on this challenge.

The good news is that there is definitely hope. By understanding the task before us and the importance of keeping our screen use in check, we can focus on what really makes us, and our kids, happy and healthy. We won't always get it "right." But there is wiggle room. When we get off course, we must become aware of this and make efforts to get back on track.

When it comes to our screen use, we can't address the problem without stepping back from it periodically to assess whether it is in balance. By consciously asking this question on a daily basis, we can direct efforts of keeping it in check. We need to mindfully engage with technology in order to more effectively meet our needs. By doing so, we can right the course of our ship. With these efforts, it's critical that we all remember that our needs were meant to be fulfilled in real life, not in a digital world.

A Twist on "A Fish Out of Water"?

One of the main appeals of our screens is the promise of getting our wants and needs met better within our screens than in real life. We can access our friends, information, and entertainment with a touch of a button or swipe of the finger. In terms of self-determination theory, we can get our intrinsic needs for relatedness, autonomy, and competence met through our screens. But our species evolved to live in a world that was not digital. If we don't get these needs met in a manner relatively consistent with our evolutionary heritage, we will pay a price. *The emergence of technology has not changed basic human needs that evolved over millions of years.*

We have all heard the expression "a fish out of water," meaning that someone is not in an environment that is good or right for him or her. When we become too immersed in our screens, we're like humans trying to live in the water like a fish, with the digital world being the ocean. Sure, we can go in the ocean and swim and play, but ultimately we need to go back on land to get our needs met. No matter how long we stay in the water, we aren't going to grow fins or gills. If we tried to live within the ocean like a fish, we wouldn't last long. Similarly, our brains and bodies were meant to engage in the real world and with each other, face to face. We can't get all of our needs met by our screens any more than we can live in the ocean like a tuna.

When we look at how much time we spend on screens, there is an opportunity cost involved. That time on screens has to come from somewhere else. Too often screens displace physical activity, sleep, and in-person connections. What is the return on investment? No matter what our kids are doing on their screens to enhance their lives, if they aren't getting these basic needs met, they just aren't going to be too happy. *The benefits of our screens cannot offset the cost of not getting our basic needs met.*

Looking Within Ourselves for Some Answers

There is ample evidence that excessive screen time can have negative effects on mood, sleep, physical activity, and relationships. Thus, even though screens tempt us with promises to make our lives better in ways, when used too much, they can have a negative impact on our well-being. However, instead of looking outside ourselves for evidence that our happiness is connected to the real world and each other, we can also look within ourselves to discern this truth.

Things are true or not on their own. Thus, their truth exists apart from whether someone is saying it is true. In this sense, a person points to a truth. As in the Buddhist analogy about the finger pointing to the moon, one shouldn't mistake the person's index finger for the truth. The moon is the truth, and it exists in its own beauty apart from the person pointing to it.

Using this analogy, we might say that technology is the finger. Our relationships with one another are the moon. Ideally, we use the finger of technology to point us to the moon of our relationships. Our collective challenge is to ensure that we don't focus our attention on the technology at the expense of our relationships.

So we ask you to do some searching right now to see some of the truths for yourself. Ask yourself the following questions and notice how you answer them:

- What have been the happiest times of your life?
- How many of these were dependent upon technology?
- How many didn't involve or rely on technology at all?
- How many of your happiest times have involved in-person engagement with other people?
- When you got a new device, such as a smartphone, how much did it increase your happiness?
- How long did this happiness last?

- When you shared something through social media, how much happiness did you get from it?
- How long did this happiness last?
- When you liked someone else's post, how much happiness did you derive from their post?
- How long did this happiness last?
- How much do you think others are thinking about your posts after they view/like them?

When we ask ourselves these questions, we can see that we don't necessarily need to review research results from studies to tell us the answers. Our happiness cannot be found within our technologies. It is primarily found in being physically engaged, and fully present, with each other and the world around us.

While there is truth about what makes us happy in life that we can find through introspection, we must also acknowledge that there are some limitations to this. Our screens have a seductive way of convincing us that we are effectively meeting our needs through them. Like the story of the frog that is unaware of the peril of remaining in gradually heated water, we seem to have great trouble recognizing how screen use diminishes our productivity, sleep, physical activity, the quality of our in-person relationships, and our overall well-being. In our increasingly hyper-connected world, it is a formidable challenge to evaluate how we (and others) are being affected by our technology use objectively.

Vying for Our Attention

The benefits of technology are real. We experience them every day. But each door that opens to its potential benefits opens another door to its potential costs. The same social media that is responsible for the "Ice Bucket Challenge" going viral and helping raise $115 million to fight Lou Gehrig's disease is the same technology that facilitates the cyberbullying that has contributed to a number of suicides. The conundrum is that, when it comes to our screens, many of its negative effects lurk within the benefits. We can't have one without the other. The yin of the positives and the yang of the negatives complete one another in this circle.

Mary and her teenage daughter, Amber, had an argument one hectic school morning. Feelings were hurt on both sides. Mary went to work and Amber went to school. Both were still upset with one another. Mary cooled off and sent her daughter a considerate, apologetic text within the hour. Amber replied likewise, and they were both glad that they were able to use their cell phones to smooth over their hurt feelings. Without their cell phones, they might have been stewing all day long about their argument and would have had to wait until the afternoon to reconcile.

Rodney sent his teenage son, Jackson, a text that was meant to be humorous about his play at his soccer game. Jackson didn't understand that Rodney was making a joke and took the text literally. He was quite upset with his father. After trying to smooth things over through texting, Rodney decided that it was best to call his son. Jackson rarely talked on his phone, but he eventually answered his father's calls. After some time, they were able to reconcile, but some inadvertent damage had been done.

We know that technologies can both enhance relationships *and* lead to disconnection. Some may suggest that we just need to decide to use our technologies carefully to ensure that we are reaping the benefits while reducing the consequences. It's difficult to do this because our screens beckon us as supernormal stimuli and through variable reinforcement schedules. Primitive areas of the brain get activated by our screens so that we just can't seem to help ourselves. Through classical conditioning, we automatically react to the sounds and sights of our smartphones. Mindfulness practices are one way of strengthening our attention and awareness so that we can make more judicious, conscious decisions about our screen use.

However, we face a steep challenge. The tech industry, like the food industry, wants to make a profit. Their goal is to get consumers to use their products. They are all vying for the most valuable commodity: our attention. Industry insiders know all about variable reinforcement schedules, supernormal stimuli, and the mechanisms that get us hooked on their products. Through analytics and algorithms, they track our every digital move and constantly refine their platforms and ads to maximize profits. They know how to gain our attention. It doesn't matter to these companies if our collective happiness takes a hit due to the incessant pull on our attention. Our long-term happiness isn't required for them to make a profit. In fact, for many companies, focusing on our long-term happiness is a sure way to go out of business!

Corporations aren't evil. Like an organism, the people behind them are just trying to survive and thrive. That's their purpose, and this requires them to make a profit. The well-being of a corporation, for the most part, is measured by a profit and loss statement. Earning our business, and our money, requires corporations to get our attention. They are in competition with one another for our attention, so it is in their best interest to find more frequent and cleverer ways to draw us in and get us "hooked." Our kids and teens are especially susceptible, which is why corporations work so hard to get and keep them as consumers. In a manner similar to the tobacco industry, if tech companies can get young users hooked on their platforms, they will have loyal consumers for years to come.

Unlike the tobacco industry, in general, the technologies that corporations are selling provide benefits. It's the aggregate, long-term effect that causes the real problems. Corporations, like humans, did not evolve to think of the possible, distant, vague consequences of the use of their products. They are looking at quarterly earnings and share prices. This way of doing business leads to the "death by a thousand walnuts" that we spoke of in previous chapters. Since corporations are in competition with one another to get our eyes on our screens so they can make a profit, we're enticed, in essence, to keep eating endless walnuts. It's important for us to find ways for our families to eat a healthy portion of walnuts. This is where our Tech Happy Life model can help.

The Tech Happy Life Model

Our children are growing up in a world in which they know of no "Before." Their hyper-connectivity isn't "hyper" at all for them. It's normal. So we are faced with the increasingly difficult challenge of trying to ensure that our kids have their feet firmly planted in the "real world."

The manner in which we parent our children affects them in many ways. We all strive to have a positive impact on our kids through our parenting so that they can grow to be happy, successful, well-adjusted adults. There is no one "recipe" for effective parenting. However, an authoritative parenting style, one characterized by warmth, involvement, and limiting setting, has been found to engender these desired outcomes. This framework for effective parenting includes developmental considerations for children's intrinsic needs for relatedness, competence, and autonomy. Using an authoritative parenting approach, our Tech Happy Life model represents a framework for addressing screen-time challenges based upon their level of severity.

The Relationship as the Foundation

The three levels of our model, Green Light, Yellow Light, and Red Light, rest on the foundation of the relationship. One, if not the main, goal of parenting is to raise children who are healthy and happy. The foundation upon which we can influence our children in a positive way is our relationship with them. The stronger the relationship that we have with them, the more likely it is that we can influence them positively in all aspects of life. This includes technology. Thus, we must invest in the very thing we are trying to preserve. We endeavor to meet, in part, their psychological need for relatedness through our relationship with them.

The scene is a group of parents watching their kids play in a Little League game. Most of the parents are looking at their cell phones throughout the game. Although the parents try to look up from their screens when a batter is up, sometimes they get too caught up in what they are doing and miss some of the action. Tim and Susannah always attend the games to watch their son, Carter, play first base. But they frequently check their cell phones during games, and they have missed especially good plays by Carter and his teammates at times. Carter would even glance at his parents from his first base position during a break in the action and see both parents looking at their phones instead of watching him play.

One day, after a game, Carter confronted his parents. "Did you see me catch that line drive to get that third out at the bottom of the seventh inning? I don't think you did! You guys are looking at your cell phones more than watching the game! Can't you just watch us play?" Both Tim and Susannah were very apologetic and vowed to Carter that they would put their cell phones away throughout the games. Although they had to fight temptation at times, they kept their word. In the most recent game, they were fortunate enough to witness Carter be part of a double play. Carter was beaming with pride and had the satisfaction of knowing that his parents saw the whole thing.

For us to have a strong relationship with our children, it is necessary for us to keep our own technology use in check. If our eyes are on our screens more than our kids, we weaken our relationships and thus our influence on them. We send the message to them that whatever is on our screens is more important than them. In doing so, we inadvertently model this value to them. *We cannot expect from our kids what we cannot deliver ourselves.*

On the other hand, when we prioritize our children and our face-to-face interactions over our screens, we are modeling the values and behaviors that we want to see in them. Spending quality time with our kids engaged in face-to-face interactions is a way to build the foundation of their happiness. Moreover, this secure attachment enables us to have the positive influence on them that we desire. Using the "magic ratio" of about five positive interactions for every negative interaction is another way that we nurture the growth of the relationship. Our interactions with our kids should not merely consist of a laundry list of to-do items. By establishing and maintaining a strong foundation of the relationship with our kids, we are better able to use preventive strategies within the Green Light Level of our Tech Happy Life model.

Green Light Level

The Green Light Level, or preventive level, is where the majority of our efforts should be. We get the best return on investment for these efforts. We try to get our kids involved in need-satisfying activities such as sports, music, and hobbies that naturally limit screen time. As a family, we carve out islands of time and space that are, in a sense, sacred. We put boundaries in place to protect ourselves and our kids from the pull of our screens. For instance, mealtimes should be free of screens. Gaming consoles and televisions should be kept out of bedrooms. We don't want the standard to be that we are always connected to our devices. When this is the case, we will become less connected to one another.

In a sense, our attention is our most precious resource, but it is finite. We need to be mindful about how we allocate this limited resource. It is essential to both our connections with others as well as our productivity. We need to honor our relationships and the present moment by "being here now." There is much benefit to "mono" or "uni" tasking. We are reminded of a Zen quote that is, "If you walk, just walk. If you sit, just sit. But whatever you do, don't wobble." An interpretation of that quote is that we should fully engage in the endeavors that we are undertaking and avoid succumbing to distractions.

Yellow Light Level

Even under the best circumstances, we can be sure that some struggles with screen time will arise. When problems emerge, such as slipping grades, sleep deprivation, moodiness, and social withdrawal, we need to address these by recognizing that they are at the Yellow Light Level of concern. A key here is spotting these problems quickly and addressing them before they develop into severe problems. We maintain our warmth, but we will likely need to impose more limits, rules, and consequences. In effect, we must "turn up the dial" on some of the intervention strategies within an authoritative parenting style. Still, we must remember to take into account developmental differences in our kids' needs for autonomy, relatedness, and competence.

It's always important to remember that our kids want to succeed. They want to have rich friendships, get good grades, stay out of trouble, and be successful in life. This is why we want to use a collaborative approach to address these issues (i.e., Dr. Ross Greene's Collaborative & Proactive Solutions). In essence, we are partnering with our kids to help them achieve their own goals for themselves. Ultimately, our kids need to learn to use freedom in responsible ways. They need to learn to self-manage. But if we manage everything for them, they don't get to practice this essential skill.

We provide opportunities for kids to use freedom responsibly, but this doesn't mean we just stand back and let them do whatever they want. We model, guide, and provide them with opportunities while also setting reasonable limits. When they exercise freedom responsibly and make healthy choices, we can gently ease back on our limits. When they make unhealthy choices, we're there to help pick them up, dust them off, and help them learn from their mistakes. This can mean that they lose some freedoms and privileges, such as screen access. However, we then need to provide opportunities for them to earn their freedoms back so that they can try again.

Red Light Level

No matter how hard we try as parents, it is possible that our kids will start using technology in ways that can cause significant harm to themselves or others. There are many factors that contribute to how we interact with and respond to technology. For instance, as with other addictions, genetically, some kids may be more "wired" (predisposed, possibly due to heredity) to hear the beckoning call of the screen Sirens more than others.[1,2,3] Sometimes, a school or peer culture can strongly influence them to use technology in very unhealthy ways. One thing that psychology has taught us over the years is that our behavior can be strongly influenced by our environment and situational factors. Our environment, particularly the social aspect, can bring out the best, or worst, in us.

Kids who have entered the Red Light Level are those who are suffering from, or have the potential to suffer from, their use of technology in more pervasive or significant ways. They might suffer from chronic sleep deprivation, have failing grades, steal credit card numbers to make in-app purchases, start harassing others on social media, or become the victim of harassment. They might suffer from depression, anxiety, or social isolation. They might routinely text while driving, exchange nude pictures with classmates, or become addicted to gaming or pornography. Also, it could be the case that kids at this level are causing others to suffer severely through cyberbullying or passing along nude photos of peers. This does not mean that they are bad kids. All of us are susceptible to being lured down dark paths. Good kids can get caught up in bad things.

When our kids have entered the Red Light Level, parents need to intervene in a stronger fashion and change the environment. We must work hard, preferably with our children, to right the ship. This might mean restrictions in access to a smartphone or gaming. It might mean strictly managing their time and monitoring their use with various apps. It is important to keep in mind that kids who are getting most of their needs met on screen might suffer tremendously if forced to go "cold turkey" on their screens. So, we should refrain from restricting all screen access unless absolutely necessary. Moreover, we need to have other need-satisfying activities ready for them. Often kids in Red Light territory are using screens to keep negative thoughts and feelings at bay. If we remove screens entirely, they can be overwhelmed by these thoughts and feelings. Thus, it might be important to consult with a psychologist or counselor to help resolve screen-use problems that are at the Red Light Level.

Even when our kids are struggling immensely with screen use, we must remind ourselves that they still want to be successful. So, we have to remain calm, form a united front with our partners, and problem-solve this with our kids. Their level of involvement will depend upon their age, maturity level, and willingness to be involved. In essence, we are always reaching out to them, conveying the message that we love them, are there for them, and want to be in a relationship with them. This doesn't guarantee that they will respond positively. However, the gesture matters, even if they don't acknowledge it at the time.

Closing Thoughts

We hope we have made a convincing case that the challenge of screen time needs to be taken seriously. While there are many positives of technology, it has the potential, like food, to lure us into an unhealthy lifestyle that slowly leaches away our happiness. Every generation of parents is faced with new challenges. Every generation of parents is warned of some new calamity facing their children. Are these concerns about tech any different?

We aren't claiming that the sky is falling. We don't believe that an entire generation will spiral down a drain into depression and disconnection. The majority of kids growing up in our hyper-connected world will turn out fine. Still, this challenge of tech is like the challenge of eating healthy in an environment with constant temptations to do just the opposite. As parents, we often don't see the full damage of unhealthy eating habits until our children are well into their adult years. Unless we take this seriously, our typical screen use can diminish well-being. No alarm bells will ring because we won't even realize it is happening. It will just seem normal. Like breathing polluted air, we just habituate to it and are not even aware what breathing clean, fresh air feels like.

But if we step back and reflect upon our lives more objectively, we can see what makes us truly happy. It is being in the present moment. It is connecting with each other and the world around us. It is having adventures with our kids and each other. You don't need us to tell you that, though. Search within yourself and you know that this is true. Our job as parents is to guide our children to become mindful of this truth as well.

While technology poses a challenge for our generation and generations to come, there is certainly hope. Just as many families are able to develop healthy eating habits, families can learn to keep screen use in check. It won't be perfect. However, if we can develop habits that generally keep our screen use in check, we stand to reap the benefits along with our children.

Just as schools have taken a larger role over time to help instill healthy eating and exercise habits in children, it's critical that a similar approach be developed regarding technology use. Technology presents unique opportunities and challenges, many of which play out in schools. Thus, teaching good digital citizenship and healthy screen habits should become part of the school curriculum. Ideally, this starts in kindergarten and is woven into the curricula each year. A periodic presentation about good digital citizenship is not enough. Families and schools need to partner with one another so that they can work toward a shared goal of helping kids use technology in healthy, productive ways.

It is essential to remember that we don't suffer deprivation from having a tech-balanced life. If we learn a healthy balance, we can embrace the benefits that our screens have to offer while reducing the downsides. We don't have to choose one or the other. With a mindful approach, we can have both. What we need to remember most is this inescapable, hard-wired truth: Our happiness ultimately resides in having deep, meaningful, in-person relationships with one another. With this truth as our guide, we can keep our ship on course.

A Tech Happy Life

Clarena wakes up early and begins to prepare for the family reunion by filling the ice chest, putting toys in the van, and using her phone to map her route to the ranch that her cousins have rented for the weekend. As her children begin to wake up, she encourages them to do their chores while she prepares breakfast for them. The kids understand that there's no screen time in the morning, but the radio is playing as the kids take care of the pets and get themselves ready. Estefania, the oldest of the three kids, puts her phone in her backpack with a book and a journal. Marco, the middle child, puts his gaming device in the van and looks forward to his one hour of gaming, which he plans to do on the way to the ranch. Ruben is only three years old, which is too young for his own device in this family, but he has brought a coloring book and crayons. On the trip to the ranch, the family sings songs, tells stories, and enjoys the scenery out the window. When they arrive, they spend time with the extended family, share food, and explore the ranch. Occasionally a phone comes out to take some pictures, but the focus is on each other, not the devices. After the trip, there will be some sharing of photos on social networks. But the time spent together at the ranch created the memories that they truly "like."

Appendix 1

Family Assessment of Screen Time (FAST)

Please note that for the following rating scales, "screen time" refers to the total time you (or others) spend at work *and* play with all screen types, including smartphones, computers, tablets (like iPads), televisions, and video games.

Please make a mark on each line for your responses to the following questions. Try to answer these questions as accurately as you can, independently of others in your family. There are no right or wrong answers.

1. **For a typical week, the amount of screen time that I have is**

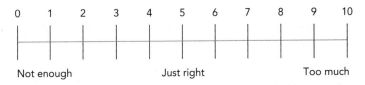

2. **The amount of screen time most people my age use is**

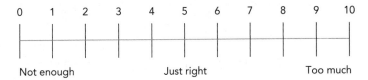

3. **For my family members, the amount of screen time they have is (complete one for each family member)**

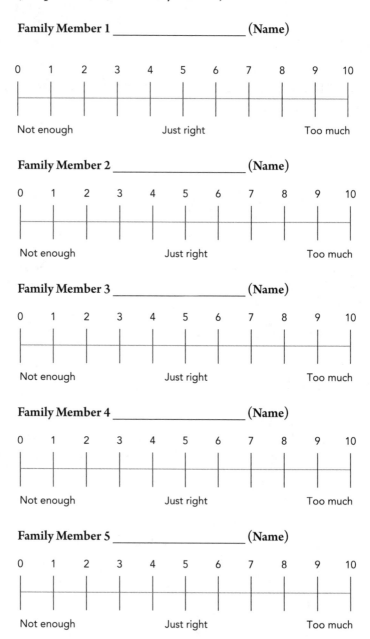

Family Member 1 _____ (Name)

| 0 | 1 | 2 | 3 | 4 | 5 | 6 | 7 | 8 | 9 | 10 |

Not enough   Just right   Too much

Family Member 2 _____ (Name)

| 0 | 1 | 2 | 3 | 4 | 5 | 6 | 7 | 8 | 9 | 10 |

Not enough   Just right   Too much

Family Member 3 _____ (Name)

| 0 | 1 | 2 | 3 | 4 | 5 | 6 | 7 | 8 | 9 | 10 |

Not enough   Just right   Too much

Family Member 4 _____ (Name)

| 0 | 1 | 2 | 3 | 4 | 5 | 6 | 7 | 8 | 9 | 10 |

Not enough   Just right   Too much

Family Member 5 _____ (Name)

| 0 | 1 | 2 | 3 | 4 | 5 | 6 | 7 | 8 | 9 | 10 |

Not enough   Just right   Too much

Family Member 6 _____ **(Name)**

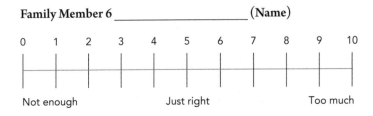

After Completing Your Ratings: Once every family member has completed the scale, take turns sharing your ratings with your family. While one person is sharing his or her ratings, others should focus on listening. Please take into consideration the following points:

- Remember that screen time poses a challenge for everyone. Refrain from harsh criticism or becoming defensive.
- Remember that each person's perspective is valid. Even if you don't agree with others' ratings, each person's ratings reflect his or her own point of view.
- If a person perceives others' screen use as a problem, then it is a problem.

Finding Better Balance: Here are some questions for your family:
- How is the family doing as a whole? Is the family mostly in balance?
- Given what you heard from others and your own reflections, name one change in your screen use that you could make that you think would have a positive impact on your family. Please commit to this change regardless of what other family members do or don't do.
- Try meeting in a month to complete this scale again. How have things changed?

Appendix 2

Quick-Reference Guide to Strategies for a Tech Happy Life

Tech Happy Life strategies are based upon research, our clinical and personal experiences, and suggestions from parents. This is not meant to be an exhaustive list. What's presented here is a condensed set of the strategies that we have already discussed in the book, provided as a quick-reference guide. We realize that parents have different values, so you might agree with some of these strategies more than others. Regardless, we encourage you to review these, pick out a couple, and try them out. Also, while we have attempted to provide general categories for these strategies, there is some overlap between categories. Finally, we will be updating this list and revising it on our website periodically. Please refer to the "Tech Tips" page at www.techhappylife.com for an updated list. We would love to hear your tips and strategies!

General Strategies

- *Turn off all chimes, ringers, and push notifications.* It's neurologically impossible to avoid turning our attention to these. If you need to have some on, just use the bare minimum. Teach your kids that, whenever they install a new game on their tablet or smartphone, they should decline notifications. This is often asked at installation.

- *Limit text and social media notifications.* Consider, as the "default," turning off notifications for texts and social media. By doing so, we choose when to turn our attention to our phones. These micro-distractions throughout the day can interfere with happiness, in-person relationships, and productivity. We can always turn the notifications back on temporarily when we are expecting something critical.
- *Practice monotasking.* Try to focus on one task at a time. Honor people and tasks with your undivided attention. Thus, put boundaries around your tech use such that it is used mindfully and purposefully. Create islands of time by unplugging.
- *Have only one screen on at a time.* When watching TV or movies, all family members should turn off their phones (or put in airplane "do not disturb" mode), tablets, and laptops. Ideally, they are out of sight, as their mere presence can be distracting.
- *Avoid walking and using the phone.* Walking can be a form of monotasking or unitasking. When you walk, just walk. By keeping our eyes up, we reduce our chance of various types of accidents caused by "distracted walking."[1] Also, this allows us the opportunity to connect with the world around us and with other people (assuming their eyes aren't on their phones).
- *Be wary of wearables.* Although the "quantified life" can be fascinating and motivating, the newer wearables come with apps, chimes, push notifications, and messaging capabilities. These can be quite distracting. If you are considering a wearable for your kids or yourself, consider one that is dedicated to fitness only and turn off the notifications. It's worth noting that recent research has cast doubt on the idea that, at least in the general sense, wearables can help people lose weight.[2] Consistent with this strategy, consider wearing an ordinary watch because checking a smartphone for the time can open the door to using it in other ways (e.g., texting, checking the news).
- *Consider using a dedicated music player rather than a smartphone when running or exercising.* We cannot help ourselves from interacting with our smartphones. A dedicated music player allows us to maintain our focus on the workout. There will be time to text people later. On a related note, for part of the time when exercising or running,

try unplugging completely. Connect with your body and the world around you, or consider having a workout partner.

Home and Family

- *Keep certain screens, such as TVs, computers, and gaming consoles, out of bedrooms altogether.* That way, you can keep an eye on what your kids are doing on the computer *and* when they are doing it. If your house has a study area, then we recommend that the computer be kept there. For older teens who tend to keep their laptops in their rooms, encourage them to leave it outside their room before bedtime.
- *Children and teens should only be allowed to have their portable devices in their bedrooms up to a certain time of night.* While it's virtually impossible to prevent kids/teens from having their screens in the bedrooms altogether, there is too much temptation for them to access their devices past bedtime if left in their rooms. Ideally, devices should be out of the room and off (or at a charging station) at least 30 minutes before bedtime.
- *Dinner and mealtimes are sacred spaces.* There should be no cell phones present during mealtimes at all. They should be silenced *and* put out of sight. Meals are a communal time that can be used for conversations and bonding with the people present. Even when a person is eating by him- or herself, we discourage screen use.
- *No devices are allowed in certain rooms in the house.* For instance, you might have a reading or sitting room in the house in which screens are not allowed. Also, we recommend that devices not be allowed in bathrooms. There are many reasons for this, some of which have to do with hygiene. It may be difficult to restrict teens from doing this, but we want to help them develop the habit when they are young.
- *Avoid allowing your children to become early adopters of new technologies.* Thus, don't allow children to access existing (e.g., a smartphone, Snapchat) or new technologies until they are developmentally ready for them. Once they have accessed a new technology, it's very challenging to take it away. While we don't want our kids

to feel left out technologically, being the first in their peer group to access particular technologies has its drawbacks.

- *Establish a device-charging area.* All devices should be charged in one location at night outside of bedrooms.
- *No screen time at least 30 minutes before bedtime.* Exposure to the blue light spectrum of our devices has been shown to disrupt our sleep cycle.[3]

Travel

- *Cell phones should not be used by the driver at all.* Even Bluetooth phone calls increase the chances of accidents. Cell phones should be put away, perhaps in the glove compartment, center console, or trunk, to avoid the temptation. Consider installing and using an app that disables calling or texting while the car is being driven.
- *Children generally shouldn't be allowed screen time while in the car.* Travel times are great for conversations or enjoying music together. There's also value in quiet and even boredom. We might make exceptions for long trips, but that still shouldn't mean unfettered screen access.
- *No cell phones or devices at restaurants.* We want to create a shared experience with meals, including when we go out to eat. Kids benefit from learning to manage their attention and behavior without a screen to occupy their minds. Cell phones should be put away, as their mere presence is distracting.
- *Set time limits on airplane flights.* Screens can be a great way of making travel more entertaining, but unlimited access to electronic devices can be problematic. We want our kids to learn to enjoy other options. Before embarking on a flight, discuss expectations ahead of time with the whole family. Screen time can be more generous during flights, but provide alternative activities such as books, cards, puzzle books and games, and comics.
- *Utilize device features that block notifications while driving.* You will model safe driving behaviors for your kids by blocking incoming messages while you're driving. Many of us find it hard to resist

looking at our phones when we drive, particularly when we hear or see an incoming message. By disabling those notifications when you drive, you limit distractions and maintain your focus on safe driving.

Gaming

- *Avoid allowing your child to start playing games that are considered to be addictive or tend to require a large time commitment.* It's easier to not start playing these games than to stop them once the hooks are in place.
- *Avoid installing games/apps that require your child (or you) to frequently check the status, take a new action, and so on.* Such games lead to the frequent checking that underlies the subtle but pervasive harm caused by our screens. Also, once back on the game, it can be difficult to get them off it.
- *Check for the appropriateness of games and apps by doing some research at the Entertainment Software Rating Board (www.esrb.org) or Common Sense Media (www.commonsensemedia.org).* You can also watch clips of many games on YouTube or within the app store to get a feel for them.
- *Watch your child play the games and/or play with them.* Watching your child play a game for a while can be a great way to connect with him or her. Ask them questions about the game. Find out what they like about it. Sometimes you might enjoy that game as well! Plus, by interacting with your child around the game, you can see firsthand whether you think it is appropriate for him or her.
- *Don't allow gaming in the morning on school days.* Kids need to prepare their minds and bodies for the school day. It can be difficult transitioning from the stimulation of a video game to a classroom environment. Allowing kids, especially younger ones, to play games or watch videos in the morning can open the door to power struggles over time limits.
- *When multiple kids are gaming, require, or at least strongly encourage, that they play the same game or take turns.* Gaming can certainly be fun, but ideally it's a shared experience when the kids are together.

When kids are "alone together" and play their own games and devices, they miss out on the many benefits of interacting with one another.

- *During summers, weekends, and holidays, establish a morning "start" time for gaming.* Kids often want to start gaming first thing in the morning when they wake up. We don't want to set a precedent in which they are waking up at 5 a.m. and gaming for several hours before we get up. Perhaps starting game time at 9:00 or 10:00 a.m. is reasonable.

- *Have children pay for games and in-app purchases with their own money.* When kids want a new gaming console, game, app, or in-app purchase, require them to pay with their own money (or pitch in). This can help teach kids the value of money and how to delay gratification. They are more likely to appreciate what they get when they have paid for it.

- *Set some reasonable time limits.* Consider around one hour of recreational screen time per day during the week and two hours per day on weekends, holidays, and summer vacations. It's easier to enforce such time limits with younger children. Of course, there can be many exceptions, but it is good to have some reasonable limits in mind.

- *Consider using a timer for younger children.* Timers often come in handy with younger children. Giving kids a warning, such as 5–10 minutes before time is up, can enable them to wrap up a level. When kids go over a time limit because they are at an important part of the game, consider timing how much they go over and deducting that time from their next day's game time. This is a logical consequence of going over their time limit, but it avoids the anger and tears from "pulling the plug" on their game at an important juncture. Be sure to discuss this logical consequence prior to implementing it.

- *Choose slow-paced games over fast-paced, intense games.* This may be especially important for younger kids whose brains are changing rapidly. There are some concerns that the fast-paced action of games might "wire" kids' brains to need high levels of stimulation. Thus, sitting in a classroom or reading a book can seem mind-numbingly boring when compared with such games. There are many slow-paced, problem-solving games that can be quite fun and entertaining for kids. Games such as these include *Cut the Rope, Where's My Water?, Scribblenauts, Bad Piggies, Peggle Classic,* and *World of Goo.*

- *Talk to your neighbors.* If your child frequently visits his or her neighborhood friend and plays video games there, talk to the parents about how they handle screen time. Try to form some agreements about expectations and limits for when they have visits.

School

- *Try to partner with your child's school and teachers.* Find out what their expectations and limits are regarding technology use.
- *Separate work from play.* If possible, have one "work" computer in which games, social media, and other recreational uses are not installed or easily accessed (e.g., not running in the background, no saved passwords). Have the "work" computer separated physically from the "rec" computer, such that kids (and adults) must physically go to a different location to access each. If your child's school issues a laptop or tablet for their schoolwork, be sure to review the terms of use with your child/teen and keep that device dedicated to schoolwork. For those who have one computer at home, consider setting up access for two users, with one user access being totally dedicated to work (e.g., games are not installed within that user account) and one user account for recreation (e.g., social media, gaming).
- *Separate phones from schoolwork.* When kids are old enough to have their own smartphones, encourage them to put their phones in another room while they do homework. They can check their phones during periodic breaks of perhaps every 30 minutes. If your teens are resistant to this idea, see if they are willing to try it just as an experiment.

Appendix 3

FAQs for a Tech Happy Life

1. At what age should I introduce screen time to my child?

Although the temptation to provide screen time to infants and toddlers is strong, our position is that children younger than two years of age should not have screen time. Children's brains are undergoing rapid development during this period. We didn't evolve in a world in which our brains were exposed to the type of stimulation that screens provide. In order for baby/ infant brains to develop in a manner that is more congruent with our evolutionary heritage, they need stimulation that comes from natural sources, such as parents, siblings, caregivers, and the environment that surrounds them. Likewise, as caregivers, it is critical that our attention is on our young ones and not on our screens. Healthy attachments, which have lifelong implications, are based upon warm, attentive, and consistent caregiving.

There is a mountain of research indicating that excessive screen time is related to problems of attention, sleep, academic achievement, mood, vision, and obesity. Now, much of this research is correlational because experimental design studies are unethical to conduct. Still, we recommend no screen time before the age of two. We think it is best to err on the "safe" side. That being said, a little screen time here and there won't cause irreparable harm, assuming the content is developmentally appropriate. Yes, it is a challenge in this day and age, but we must have goals in mind to which we aspire.

2. How much screen time should my child have per day?

When considering how much screen time to allow your child per day, there are a number of factors to consider:

- The age of the child (toddler, school-age, teen)
- The type of technology (e.g., TV, iPad, smartphone, Kindle Paperwhite, gaming console, virtual reality headset)
- The media type (e.g., reading material, social media, texting, recreational games, educational games, videos)
- The content (e.g., violent first-person shooter video games, *Game of Thrones*, kid-friendly educational apps)
- The context (e.g., is it alone, with family, peers, in the car, at the airport?)
- Consuming versus creating (e.g., watching YouTube videos vs. creating videos, playing games vs. programming them, writing an essay for school).

In general, we recommend limiting "recreational" screen time (consuming) to about one to two hours per day for children over two years of age. This limit of less than two hours per day is inclusive, meaning all entertainment time on TVs, smartphones, tablets, video game consoles, and so on. Thus, we think that "screen time" is counted differently depending upon how it is being used. For creative endeavors (e.g., making videos, art) and educational/academic screen time (e.g., programming, doing homework, or reading ebooks on a Kindle Paperwhite), we believe it is OK to allow additional time. This is consistent with the most recent version of the Children's Media Guidelines produced by the American Academy of Pediatricians.[1]

However, we realize it is difficult to enforce limits on recreational screen time, and we advocate a more fluid approach. So, there are many possible exceptions (e.g., sleepovers, family movie nights, holidays). Rigidly imposing screen limits (e.g., a child forced to unplug because time is up just as he is about to finish a level) is a recipe for conflicts. While we don't believe in a rigid approach, there are some obvious limits. For instance, a five-year-old should not be playing the M-rated *Call of Duty: Infinite Warfare*.

As parents, we want to try to ensure that our kids' screen use isn't getting in the way of their basic needs. For instance, if our child isn't getting enough sleep or physical activity, we might need to intervene. Also, we want to ensure that our kids are interacting with others in person. While we might grant some extra time for creative endeavors, we still need to set reasonable screen limits with our kids. This is because our physical and psychological needs don't go away just because we are using our screens for productive or creative purposes. Interestingly, results of a large survey conducted by Common Sense Media found that only 3% of tweens' and teens' screen use was for content creation (e.g., blogging, creating artwork).[2]

Once kids have smartphones, it becomes very difficult to limit their screen use. Imposing strict limits on teens is nearly impossible and can often backfire. This is especially true for older teens. So, we recommend that you review some of the Green Light (preventive) strategies in Chapter 8. Creating family expectations and rules around a healthy balance of screen use, with input from all family members, can be helpful in coming up with screen time limits that reflect compromises.

3. When should my child be allowed to have a smartphone?

There isn't any magic age at which children suddenly become responsible enough to manage a smartphone appropriately. Some 10-year-olds are much more mature and responsible than some 18-year-olds. It is a reality that the age at which children are getting smartphones is going down fairly rapidly. There are a sizable percentage of elementary school kids who have smartphones. It can become a problem when our kids are too far "behind the curve" on getting a smartphone. Kids can be left out in a real sense because their friends can't easily connect with them. Also, as children enter middle school, it becomes difficult for parents to manage logistics and schedules if kids don't have cell phones (e.g., coordinating drop-off/pickup times for extracurricular activities).

That being said, if your child seems responsible in many ways (e.g., grades, sports, chores), then probably a smartphone sometime in middle school is most appropriate. Still, it doesn't need to be an "all or nothing" proposition. Consider some of these options:

- Provide them with a "starter" phone with more limited functionality.
- Try to get your child's input regarding their ideas about responsible/fair use of the phone. If they are allowed to have some input, they are more likely to abide by the rules and limits that they helped to create.
- Develop and agree upon a terms of use contract prior to them getting the phone. Thus, possession of the phone is "conditional" upon their responsible use.
- Let them know that you are "lending" them the phone. It isn't theirs, per se. So, the privilege of using the phone is contingent upon their responsible use of it.
- Let them know that you can access it anytime you decide that you'd like to see what is on their phone. So they should think carefully about how they use their phone. Perhaps a rule of thumb that we want our kids to keep in mind is this: If they'd be mortified or upset if we read/saw what they posted, then they should probably not send/post it.
- As they use the phone responsibly, they can earn greater smartphone access.
- Texting and/or calls while driving are never okay.
- Decide upon some consequences of misuse beforehand, which should involve them losing some phone access/privileges.

Just remember that discussions about the appropriate use of various screens should be ongoing. Technology is quickly advancing and our kids are rapidly developing. Our close relationship with them will always be the foundation for us to positively influence their technology use.

4. Do I require my child/teen to sign a contract before he or she gets a smartphone?

Please see Chapter 8 for more coverage of this topic. Our view is that it might be useful to have a contract regarding cell phone use. Regardless of whether you create a formal contract, we believe it is important to go over expectations and responsibilities regarding screen privileges. Their possession of a phone, like driving, should be considered a privilege and not a right. Thus, if kids use tech responsibly, they can gain more access to privileges. Writing up a contract can be a great way to ensure that kids know what the expectations and consequences (for misuse) are. There are a few points that you might want to keep in mind when creating a contract:

- Work on this collaboratively with your child/teen. Creating a contract shouldn't be just a top-down approach. It's important for our kids and teens to think through this and to have skin in the game. This doesn't mean that they get to dictate the terms of the contract, but we do want to try to give them a voice.
- Focus on the main expectations and consequences. If you create a five-page contract filled with many details, it is unlikely to be useful or followed. Have you ever tried reading one of Apple or Google's Terms of Service before agreeing to them? One of the main reasons that people don't read them is that they're too long and complicated!
- It's a good idea to revisit and revise such a contract periodically, as tech is a moving target, and our kids' needs change as they develop.
- Even if you create a contract with your child, continue to have ongoing conversations about responsible technology use. Listen to what he or she has to say. This shouldn't be a one-way street.
- Consider creating a contract for the whole family so that everyone is agreeing to certain terms. For example, it might be a good idea for Mom and Dad, as well as everyone else, to also commit to abiding by rules such as no tech during meals.

5. At what age should I allow my child/teen access to social media such as Instagram, Facebook, and Snapchat?

Just as there is no specific age at which kids should be allowed to get a smartphone, there is not a specific age at which kids should gain access to social media. As with smartphones, the age at which this is "typical" keeps going down. Our recommendation is that kids not be allowed to access social media until sometime in later middle school or, even better, high school (if you can hold off). Here are a few things to keep in mind:

- Avoid having your child become an "early adopter." When are your child/teen's friends gaining access to social media? If your child is the last to get on to social media, this can cause problems, too.

- Go over some dos and don'ts regarding social media use before giving them access.
- Social media use doesn't have to be an "all or nothing" proposition. Your teen might be given access to only one social media platform initially.
- Consider creating a contract with your child/teen regarding social media use, but this should be nested within a more general contract about screen use.
- Though there are certainly individual differences, you might find that tween and teen girls get more caught up in texting and social media use than boys, whereas boys get more into gaming than girls.
- Social media use is nested within general, healthy tech habits, such as no screens at meal times, all devices off by a certain time of night, and no devices in the bathroom. If we can help our kids develop and maintain healthy tech habits in a general sense, then they will also likely be able to manage their social media use responsibly.
- It might be helpful to have ongoing discussions with your child/teen on how tech companies profit from their screen use. They need to understand that tech companies are using neuroscientists, psychologists, and marketing experts to ensure that they are "hooked" on their tech products, especially social media platforms and games. Teens are often particularly sensitive to the idea that they are being manipulated by someone, and knowing how companies are profiting from them might help them to think more critically about their own tech use.
- Many parents struggle as much or more than their teens regarding balanced social media use. As parents, we must always role model what we want to see in our kids. If we can't manage our own social media use effectively and responsibly, how can we expect our kids to?

6. Should I restrict my child/teen from certain video games?

The short answer to this one is "yes." Here's the long(er) answer. The Entertainment Software Rating Board (www.esrb.org) provides a rating system for video games, and a similar one for mobile games, to help guide parents in their purchasing decisions. We recommend that you use the rating system to guide your decisions regarding what content is appropriate for your child. You can see these ratings in the app store and can often see video clips of the game to help decide whether the game is appropriate developmentally and in terms of the content.

As parents, we don't want our six-year-old child to be watching movies like *Pulp Fiction, The Shining, American Pie, Silence of the Lambs,* or viewing pornography. The Motion Picture Association of America (MPAA) has a movie rating system in place to help inform parents about the kind of content to which they are exposing their children. Similarly, we don't want our young children playing games that are inappropriate for their developmental level. These ratings are in place for a reason: That it is possible that such content could be harmful to younger viewers/players in forms such as increased fear and anxiety, desensitization to violence, and/or the development of unhealthy attitudes toward sex.

As with our other recommendations, we don't think that you should be extremely rigid in your decision-making. Life is not black and white, and you can flexibly make some of these decisions. However, it is critical that you remain informed about what games your kids are playing. It's a good idea to preview games by watching video clips of them on YouTube or within the app store and observing your children play any new game. Perhaps you can even play with them! Getting into our kids' "world" of gaming is a way to better understand them, build connection, and demonstrate respect for their interests.

Of course, many kids still want to play games (or watch shows) that are not appropriate for them. In fact, often kids want to play these games *because* they are inappropriate for them. If allowed to play these inappropriate games, they still might enjoy them at the time. However, this *does not* mean it is appropriate for them to play such games. It is very similar to guiding their eating habits. Sure, kids might prefer sodas and chicken nuggets to healthier options, but this doesn't mean that those choices are good for them. Kids might enjoy these developmentally inappropriate games in the moment, but then may have trouble falling asleep, nightmares, and greater levels of anxiety throughout the day (e.g., more easily frightened of the dark, storms, more emotionally reactive).

One Step Further

Here's another recommendation regarding gaming decisions that is particularly relevant if you are the parent of a young child. Focus on games that are slow and require a lot of problem-solving (e.g., *Cut the Rope, Where's My Water?*). The frenetic action of many games, even if the actual content is not disturbing, might not be good for young, developing brains. It is possible that the high-paced action of some games is "wiring" the brains of young kids such that they need a high level of stimulation to be engaged.[3] So when those kids are sitting with the family at a restaurant or a play, or are sitting in a classroom, they might find themselves easily bored and distracted. They might have grown accustomed to the adrenaline rush or the "twitch" provided by fast-paced games such as *Call of Duty, Temple Run, or Geometry Dash.*

The Bottom Line?

There are so many amazing games available these days. If your child wants a game that is inappropriate for his or her age or developmental level, there are countless wonderful alternative games to steer him or her toward. As parents, we start to lose control over what kinds of games our kids play as they get older. So, it is critical that we guide them well in their younger years. We believe it is better to err on the safe side. By doing so, we lay a solid, healthy foundation that can serve them well as they grow.

7. Should I use parental controls or software to manage my child's screen use?

We cover this topic in greater detail in Chapter 8. Generally, it's a good idea to use parental controls on devices and computers, especially for the younger kids. It's too easy nowadays for kids to inadvertently stumble across highly inappropriate content. Certain images that are seen by young eyes cannot be unseen. There is the potential that such content could be damaging to young, developing minds.

However, we don't want to rely solely on parental controls because the issue at stake is much broader than this. We want our kids to have balanced lives. Having balanced lives will help reduce the chances that they will stumble upon inappropriate content. To this end, we recommend using strategies within the Green Light Level of our Tech Happy Life model to get kids involved in other activities. Also, kids should not be allowed unfettered access to screens (e.g., laptops are not kept in bedrooms, tablets have to be out of bedrooms by a certain time of night). We should preview the content of games (see FAQ #6) to ensure that the game content is appropriate for their developmental level. Common Sense Media has parental control strategies and program/app recommendations on their website (www.commonsensemedia.org).

We still should keep in mind that the goal is self-regulation. Older kids who are motivated to circumvent parental controls will likely find ways of doing so. For teens, it might be best to collaboratively address the issue of appropriate content with them. Express your feelings, concerns, values, and expectations. Listen to your teen's perspective on these as well. Then, come up with a plan for easing off parental controls. Ultimately, we have to trust our parenting and our kids. If we have developed a strong, healthy base and have established our values, then it's unlikely that our kids will be totally consumed by the "Dark Side of the (Tech) Force." We have to be mindful that attempts to control our teens' screen use don't result in greater harm than the content from which we are trying to protect them.

8. Should I monitor my teen's screen activity (e.g., texting, social media use)?

Please see Chapter 8 for further discussion of this topic. Overall, we do believe in monitoring in the sense of being involved in our teens' lives and talking to them about their screen use. We should strive to have at least a general awareness of what games they are playing, social media platforms they are using, and with whom they regularly interact online. However, we generally do not believe in monitoring in the sense of secretive (or flagrant) electronic surveillance of their online activities. We fully acknowledge that there is a lot of trouble they could be getting into these days, including sexting, accessing pornography, and cyberbullying. Still, it can be a tremendous invasion of privacy to look through a teen's smartphone, tablet, or computer. Think back to when you were a teen. Can you remember some jokes or conversations that you would not have wanted your parents to hear? Imagine that your parents had a way of eavesdropping on every conversation that you had during those formative years—yikes! Here is the approach that we prefer:

- Establish and model family values such as respect for others, limiting screen use, and the importance of in-person connection.
- Establish and maintain a strong relationship with your kids so that they feel like they can come to you if they do have a problem.
- Talk to them about problem scenarios in which you would expect them to come to you for help or guidance (e.g., your teen daughter receiving sexually harassing texts).
- Review expectations and rules before giving them access to screens, such as smartphones.
- Review the consequences of misuse, which should involve the use of logical consequences (e.g., loss of or limited smartphone access).
- Whenever possible, work collaboratively with your kids/teens on rules and consequences so it is not just a top-down approach.
- Don't allow unfettered access to screens (e.g., cell phones must be turned off by a certain time of night, no computers in their room). This is easier to enforce when they are younger.
- Have ongoing conversations about balanced tech use. Know that if teens learn to balance their tech use, it will reduce the likelihood of other problems (e.g., sexting).
- Model balanced tech use yourself. This should apply to all adult caregivers.
- Give your teen the benefit of the doubt unless you strongly suspect that there is a problem (or have hard evidence).
- If your teen has broken your trust, then it might be the case that you do explicitly oversee his or her online activity and/or restrict access. Thus, he or she has to earn back the trust. Set expectations for how that can occur.

Realistically, teens will most likely be a few steps ahead of parents in their use of technology. Thus, we assume that most teens will find ways around parents' surveillance if they are sufficiently motivated to do so. If, as parents, we are just playing some elaborate cat-and-mouse game with our teens regarding their use of technology, then we've already lost. Supporting our healthy relationships with teens should be prioritized.

9. Should screen time be a privilege so that my child has to do homework and chores first before he or she is given access?

Many parents treat screen time like a dessert that can't be eaten until all of the vegetables are consumed. The reasoning is that screen time is a special reward for doing that which is unpleasant first. Most psychologists recognize that this can undermine intrinsic motivation. Ideally, we want to cultivate a love of learning so that kids internalize the idea that reading is a reward in and of itself (rather than a plate of boiled okra that must be swallowed in order to get chocolate pudding). Parents should place age-appropriate limits on screen time, but also need to exercise caution about inadvertently devaluing the importance of homework and being a helpful member of the household.

That being said, they are called home*work* and *chores* for a reason. Most children will prefer to *play* video games over answering essay questions, doing math worksheets, or folding laundry. Many children respond well to the "work before play" approach. So, if allowing "play before work" creates problems, it's probably best to try setting a limit and requiring work before play.

It could be the case that your child is having ongoing trouble getting any work done because of an excessive focus on gaming. If so, your child might be in the Yellow Light Level of our Tech Happy Life model. Some changes are in order if these struggles are frequent and/or pervasive. This might involve working with your child collaboratively to address this problem. Your child might really need the requirement of completing homework and chores before having screen time. When problems emerge at the Yellow Light Level, it typically requires us to turn up the "control" dial.

Still, as your child gets older, it will be difficult to enforce this type of arrangement. Ultimately, we want our kids to be able to prioritize and manage work/play time on their own. Thus, our parental involvement should to be sensitive to the needs of each individual child as well as his or her developmental level.

10. We set limits on our children's screen time and what they can play, but our neighbors don't. What can we do when our kids visit their friends' homes?

Each family will have their own rules regarding screen time, so it's not surprising that parents express concern about usage when their kids visit other people's homes. A preventive approach might be to start with talking to other parents before your kids visit to find out what their rules are surrounding screen time. Children may not report the rules accurately, so getting an adult perspective may increase the likelihood that you're getting the facts.

It can be awkward discussing the topic of screen limitations with your neighbors. For instance, if you allow your kids one hour of recreational screen time per day during the week and the parents of your child's friend have no such limitations, what are you to do? It's odd to request that your neighbors limit their own kids' screen time because your child is visiting. It might be useful to first have a general conversation about this topic to see where your neighbors stand. You might also consider gently approaching them with how you set limits with your kids.

Consider saying something like, "Our little Johnny sure loves screen time—maybe too much! We've been telling Johnny how important it is to focus on playing with Nathan when he visits your house, rather than focusing on video games. He shouldn't be choosing video games over his friends. So, please let us know if Johnny seems to only want to play video games when he comes to your house for a visit. We are working with him on that. Oh, feel free to kick them off the games and have them play outside, too. We have been working hard to get him outdoors more. It seems that if we let him play video games as much as he wanted, he'd rarely choose to go outside!" By focusing on your own child and your own family values and expectations, you reduce the chances that your neighbors will feel like they are being technojudged or controlled.

You may also want to discuss the content of screen time and agree on age-appropriate ratings for movies and video games, as well as access to the Internet. If the other family's rules are too lax for you or make you feel uncomfortable, another option is for the kids to spend time together at your house or outside (e.g., the park, the neighborhood pool).

As kids get older, parental supervision will wane and responsibility will gradually transfer from parents to children. The degree to which we can control or monitor screen time will diminish, so it's important to try to build healthy habits from an early age.

11. My child is constantly text messaging (or using social media) while doing homework. What should I do about that?

In Chapter 11, we provide an example of a young man who, with the support of his psychologist, was able to self-monitor his behavior and recognize that his texting was interfering with his learning. Consequently, he was able to try to do his homework without his phone in the room and notice his improved productivity firsthand. While this kind of self-regulation is ideal, it may not be a realistic outcome for all kids. For example, teens who are resistant to self-monitoring or who deny that the phone interferes are less likely to benefit from such an approach. A number of studies indicate that people tend not to be aware of how their performance is negatively affected by screen use.

There's no one-size-fits-all solution, as every child and family have their unique circumstances. However, parents may achieve the greatest success in addressing this problem when they model the desired behavior (e.g., parents should avoid texting while reading), discuss the nature of the challenge with them, encourage their kids to make good choices, and allow children to experience the natural consequences of their behaviors (without parental shaming or judging).

If we have invested a lot of time and energy in building a strong relationship, we might have opportunities to periodically broach this subject with our teens. We might ask some open-ended questions about their thoughts on what might help them work more efficiently. Also, we might ask if they'd be willing to try an experiment, just for a week, to move their phone into a different room while they did their homework. If we can let the experience be the teacher instead of us, they might be more open to changing their study habits.

So, let's say that our teen is at the Yellow Light Level and making Cs when he or she could be making As and Bs. Assume that we have tried talking to our teen a number of times in a non-judgmental, compassionate way about her habit of texting or using social media while doing homework, and she is resistant to changing her "multitasking" approach. We have tried to collaboratively problem-solve the situation but, because she doesn't see it as a problem, she isn't willing to budge. Perhaps she is in denial (or just plain unaware) about the negative effects of multitasking on productivity and performance. This also might represent a situation in which your child is "planting her flag" in their attempt to meet her psychological need for autonomy. What's our next move? Should you take away your child's phone whenever when it's time to get the homework completed?

Before taking action, here are a few things to keep in mind:

- Don't make a decision in anger. Be in a calm state of mind first.
- If you have a partner, discuss the options with him or her. Try to form a united front.
- Your teen will not likely respond well to limits that you impose, but this doesn't mean that you shouldn't set them. However, it does mean that you need to carefully consider the repercussions first.
- A question to ask yourself before taking action is, "Is imposing limits likely to produce the desired result?" Thus, there is a difference between being "right" and being "effective." When we are imposing limits and consequences with our kids, especially our teens, we can often be "right" in what we want for them and why (e.g., eat healthier, have better study habits) but ineffective in getting them to change their behavior. Our efforts to guide our teens toward "right" behavior through limit-setting, restrictions, and consequences can be met with indifference, obstinacy, or outright hostility.
- If you decide that it is worth picking the battle because the consequences are too steep (e.g., failing or barely passing grades), then you might, at least temporarily, restrict your teen from having his or her smartphone present while doing homework. To do this,

you might install an app on your phone that enables you to disable your teen's phone, or particular apps, for periods of time. Still, we continue having ongoing discussions with him or her about how this is working out.

- However, if we decide that we can't impose limits without it backfiring, we often must step back a little and allow experience (i.e., natural consequences) to be the teacher.

- A question to ask ourselves at this point is, "Can I bring this up to my teen in a different way that he or she will be responsive to?" If the answer is "no," then it is probably best not to bring it up again because otherwise it will come across as nagging. If you have already mentioned to your teen 100 times how to work more efficiently and with higher quality by leaving any and all devices in another room, it is highly unlikely that a light bulb will go off on the 101st time.

- If you decide that you can't impose limits effectively, perhaps you have the opportunity to say something like, "Hey, Bryan. I know that you have a lot of challenging classes. I know that getting good grades is very important to you. I'd be happy to talk with you about ways that might help you work more efficiently. You might have some of your own ideas that you'd like to try out as well. Also, you can Google this topic, too. There are a lot of good strategies that you can find on the Internet. My door is always open to you, regardless. You know that, right?" We can let them know that the door is open, but we can't force them to walk through it. As we've stated before, even if our kids aren't receptive to such efforts, the gesture of reaching out still matters.

12. I think my teen is sexting or viewing pornography online. What should I do?

Children and adolescents have a natural curiosity about bodies and sex, so it's quite normal for them to seek out knowledge from peers, books, and the Internet. Unfortunately, this may result in exposure to material they're not developmentally ready for or inappropriate screen time use, including sexting and pornography. We recommend that parents approach these concerns in a way that is supportive of children, rather than shaming or punitive. Simply rebuking a kid for sexting or watching pornography will not be productive, and punishment falls short of helping a child develop an understanding of health and appropriate expressions of sexuality. It's also important that parents educate children about the risks associated with sharing photographs of themselves and others (including social, legal, and psychological risks). When we cultivate loving and trusting relationships with our kids, it's easier to have these difficult conversations. Parents may fold such conversations into broader discussions about puberty, sexuality, and relationships. A recommended resource for parents of boys is *Dating and Sex: A Guide for the 21st Century Teen Boy* by Andrew Smiler. For parents of girls, we recommend *GIRL: Love, Sex, Romance, and Being You* by Karen Rayne.

We understand that talking about sex with kids often feels awkward and uncomfortable. Some parents may outsource this task to a professional sexuality educator with values that align with those of the family. We strongly support communication and education around these issues related to sexuality and technology and recommend that the following be included when talking with kids about sexting and pornography:

- Sexual thoughts and feelings are normal and healthy.
- Sharing sexual images via phones and computers presents real risks (e.g., legal, social).
- It's important to respect others (e.g., don't ask for or share nude images of others).

While there are differing opinions on this delicate issue, we generally recommend using our Green Light, preventive strategies here. If we're too heavy-handed in our restrictions, our teens might not fully develop this critical skill. However, if your teen repeatedly transgresses rules and limits regarding sexting and/or viewing pornography, he or she is falling into our Yellow or Red Light Level. At this point, you will likely need to turn up the "control dial" within an authoritative parenting framework. While still maintaining warmth and compassion, you might:

- Limit where he or she can access a laptop (e.g., in a common area only, instead of in his or her room)

- Use parental controls/apps to limit what your teen accesses (e.g., websites, apps) and when
- More strictly limit what technologies your teen can have in his or her bedroom
- Limit his or her access to Wi-Fi
- Consider temporarily replacing his or her smartphone with a flip-phone.

Again, we are only using such controlling efforts because other, less restrictive interventions have not changed our teen's behavior. We still attempt to collaboratively problem-solve, as we know our teen will ultimately need to regulate his or her own behavior. From a practical standpoint, as young teens become young adults, it is virtually impossible to prevent them from accessing pornography or sexting if they are sufficiently motivated to do so. At some point, such as when he or she goes off to college, we will have very little control over his or her day-to-day actions, in real life or online. While it is scary to let go, we must learn to accept this reality and trust that our relationship building and parenting efforts have instilled positive values that will guide them as they leave the nest.

13. My partner and I are in disagreement about our child's screen use. What do we do?

It's going to be a lot easier to set and maintain boundaries around screen time when the adults are in agreement about family screen-time use. In many cases, one parent feels that the other parent has a screen-time problem. When parents disagree, there may be an opportunity to step back from the problem and redirect the focus to shared values and goals. How do we want to spend our family time? What's important to us? How do we best meet our children's needs? Once these questions are addressed, parents can think about the degree to which screen-time use is compatible with these broader goals. In many families there will be a need to compromise. This may also be an opportunity to model for the children how disagreements can be respectfully resolved.

Certainly, it is best not to get into heated arguments about different values, ideas, and limits in front of children. It's important that these matters are discussed and resolved in a civil manner. If they cannot be, it might be worth looking into some couples counseling or family therapy to help come up with a plan that works for your family.

14. My child throws a fit every time he loses screen time. What can I do about that?

Many parents take away screen time as a consequence for misbehavior. Sometimes this is what we call a *logical consequence*. For example, last night Jimmy stayed up late playing video games and didn't complete his homework, so tonight his video game privilege has been revoked. This is considered a logical consequence because it's directly related to the problem. Not surprisingly, many children get upset when their parents take away cell phones, video games, and Internet access. When this becomes a recurring problem, parents are getting valuable information: the consequence is ineffective. An effective consequence is one that results in the desired outcome (and therefore doesn't have to be applied repeatedly).

A pattern of repeated tantrums from the removal of screen privileges is likely in the Yellow Level of our model. We should ask ourselves how we might approach the problem we're trying to solve from a different angle. Can we prevent the problem from occurring? Can we support better self-regulation in our children? Can we encourage them to make better choices? Whenever possible and when everyone is in a calm state, we believe it is important to have our kids be part of this discussion. Family members have the shared experience that the current system is not working. So, it is time for everyone to work together to find a better way.

When your child has a tantrum because screen time has been taken away, the following steps may help:

- Remain calm. Should your temper flare, it may only exacerbate the situation.
- Remain emotionally present. Your child needs to know that you can maintain warmth and love, even when he or she is losing control.

- Try kneeling down to his or her eye level (or even below his or her eye level). Towering over a child can often raise tensions, while lowering your body position can have the opposite effect.
- Remain firm. Handing the iPad back to the crying child sends a confusing message. Moreover, it can inadvertently reinforce the tantrums.
- Use the ACT model (acknowledge, communicate, target)
  - *Acknowledge* his or her feelings (e.g., "Jack, I can see that you are very upset about losing your screen time.")
  - *Communicate* the limit and expectations (e.g., "I'm really sorry about your loss of screen time, but this is the consequence that we had discussed. These are our rules.")
  - *Target* an alternative activity (e.g., "Remember that you have those books in your backpack that you checked out from the school library yesterday. Why don't you take a look at those?")
- If both the loss of screen time and the tantrums are frequently recurring, that is a sure sign that something different needs to be tried. Outside of when the problem is occurring, brainstorm some other possibilities. If you have a partner, be sure to include him or her. Also, if the child is old enough, try to work collaboratively with him or her as well. Finally, if you have exhausted all of these options, it might be time to seek some professional help.

15. How can I convince my child that he should be spending less time on the screen and more time outdoors with other kids in person?

When we were kids, our parents were incapable of convincing us that too much television was bad for us. Now that we're the parents, why should we think that we're capable of convincing our kids that too much screen time is bad for them? Perhaps the goal should not be to convince them of anything, but rather to give them a variety of experiences. This is where the Foundation and Green Light Levels of our model come into play. Take them camping and swimming. Throw a football with them at the park. Take a cooking class together. These activities will be fun and engaging, will build and strengthen relationships, and will provide opportunities for exercise and skill development. Kids will eventually draw their own conclusions about what they like and what they don't, so as parents we should direct our energy toward creating varied opportunities for them.

We will reiterate the principle that if we aren't keeping our own screen time in check, we can forget about convincing our kids that they should be spending less time on the screen. We have to be role models. We must be the change that we want to see in our kids. We also have to accept the fact that we can do things "right" as parents, and our children might still strongly prefer screen time to the outdoors. But, by establishing a strong relationship with them and by role-modeling, we have to trust that our parenting will help them make balanced choices in the long run.

Appendix 4

Tech Happy Life: Resources

The following books and websites do not represent an exhaustive list, but we have found them to inspiring and/or informative. A more extensive and detailed list can be found on the Tech Happy Life website under the "Resources" page.

Books

- *Alone Together: Why We Expect More from Technology and Less from Each Other* by Sherry Turkle
- *Reclaiming Conversation: The Power of Talk in a Digital Age* by Sherry Turkle
- *Moral Combat: Why the War on Violent Video Games Is Wrong* by Patrick M. Markey and Christopher J. Ferguson
- *The Shallows: What the Internet Is Doing to Our Brains* by Nicholas Carr
- *Utopia Is Creepy and Other Provocations* by Nicholas Carr
- *Reality Is Broken: Why Games Make Us Better and How They Can Change the World* by Jane McGonigal
- *The Cyber Effect: A Pioneering Cyberpsychologist Explains How Human Behavior Changes Online* by Mary Aiken
- *Supernormal Stimuli: How Primal Urges Overran Their Evolutionary Purpose* by Deidre Barrett

- *The Big Disconnect: Protecting Childhood and Family Relationships in the Digital Age* by Catherine Steiner-Adair and Teresa H. Barker
- *It's Complicated: The Social Lives of Networked Teens* by Danah Boyd
- *The Distracted Mind: Ancient Brains in a High-Tech World* by Adam Gazzaley and Larry D. Rosen
- *Hooked: How to Build Habit-Forming Products* by Nir Eyal
- *Irresistible: The Rise of Addictive Technology and the Business of Keeping Us Hooked* by Adam Alter
- *The Whole Brain Child: 12 Revolutionary Strategies to Nurture Your Child's Developing Mind* by Daniel J. Siegel and Tina Payne Bryson
- *No Drama Discipline: The Whole Brain Way to Calm the Chaos and Nurture Your Child's Developing Mind* by Daniel J. Siegel and Tina Payne Bryson
- *For Parents and Teenagers: Dissolving the Barrier Between You and Your Teen* by William Glasser
- *How Children Succeed: Grit, Curiosity, and the Hidden Power of Character* by Paul Tough

Online

- Common Sense Media: www.commonsensemedia.org
- Entertainment Software Rating Board: www.esrb.org
- American Psychological Association: http://www.apa.org/helpcenter/digital-guidelines.aspx
- American Academy of Pediatrics: www.healthychildren.org/MediaUsePlan
- National Heart, Lung, and Blood Institute: www.nhlbi.nih.gov/health/educational/wecan/tools-resources/tools-reduce-screen-time.htm
- Screenagers: Growing Up in the Digital Age: http://www.screenagersmovie.com/
- The Campaign for a Commercial-Free Childhood and the Alliance for Childhood: http://www.allianceforchildhood.org/sites/allianceforchildhood.org/files/file/FacingtheScreenDilemma.pdf
- 99u: http://99u.com/articles/6969/10-Online-Tools-for-Better-Attention-Focus

Notes

Chapter 1

1. American Academy of Pediatrics. (2016). Media and young minds. *Pediatrics, 138,* 1–8.

2. Common Sense Media. (2013). Zero to eight: Children's media use in America 2013. San Francisco, CA: Victoria Rideout.

3. Harris Interactive. (2014). Pearson student mobile device survey. National Report: Students in grades 4–12. New York, NY: Pearson.

4. Tandon, P. S., Zhou, C., Lozano, P., & Christakis, D. A. (2011). Preschoolers' total daily screen time at home and by type of child care. *The Journal of Pediatrics, 158*(2), 297–300.

5. Pew Research Center. (2015). Teen, social media and technology overview 2015. Washington, DC: Amanda Lenhart. Retrieved from http://www.pewinternet.org/files/2015/04/PI_TeensandTech_Update2015_0409151.pdf

6. Amanda Lenhart. (2012, March 19). Teens, smartphones & texting. Retrieved from http://www.pewinternet.org/2012/03/19/teens-smartphones-texting/

7. Felt, L. J., & Robb, M. B. (2016). *Technology addiction: Concern, controversy, and finding a balance.* San Francisco, CA: Common Sense Media; 2016.

8. McAfee. (2013). McAfee digital deception study 2013: Exploring the online disconnect between parents and pre-teens, teens, and young adults. Santa Clara, CA. Retrieved from http://boletines.prisadigital.com/rp_digital_deception_survey.pdf

9. Sabina, C., Wolak, J., & Finkelhor, D. (2008). The nature and dynamics of Internet pornography exposure for youth. *CyberPsychology & Behavior, 11*(6), 691–693.

10. Dumoucel, C. (September 2, 2010). Cultural theorist Paul Virilio has been repeating essentially the same thing over and over again for nearly 30 years. Maybe it's time for everybody to start listening to him. *Vice.* Retrieved from https://www.vice.com/en_us/article/qbzbn5/paul-virilio-506-v17n9

11. Felt, L. J., & Robb, M. B. (2016). *Technology addiction: Concern, controversy, and finding a balance.* San Francisco, CA: Common Sense Media; 2016.

12. Shoeppe, S., Vandelanotte, C., Bere, E., Lien, N., Verlonigne, M., Kovács, E., . . . & Van Lippevelde, W. (2017). The influence of parental modelling on children's physical activity and screen time: Does it differ by gender? *European Journal of Public Health, 27,* 152–157.

13. Vaala, S. E., & Bleakley, A. (2015). Monitoring, mediating, and modeling: Parental influence on adolescent computer and Internet use in the United States. *Journal of Children and Media, 9*(1), 40–57.

14. Boileau, I., Payer, D., Chugani, B., Lobo, D., Behzadi, A., Rusjan, P. M., . . . Zack, M. (2013). The D2/3 dopamine receptor in pathological gambling: A positron emission tomography study with [11C]-(+)-propyl-hexahydro-naphtho-oxazin and [11C] raclopride. *Addiction, 108*(5), 953–963.

15. Sigman, A. (2012) Time for a view on screen time. *Archives of Disease in Childhood, 97,* 935–942.

16. Love, T., Laier, C., Brand, M., Hatch, L., & Hajela, R. (2015). Neuroscience of Internet pornography addiction: A review and update. *Behavioral Sciences, 5*(3), 388–433. doi: 10.3390/bs5030388

17. Banz, B. C., Yip, S. W., Yau, Y. H., & Potenza, M. N. (2016). Behavioral addictions in addiction medicine: from mechanisms to practical considerations. *Progress in Brain Research, 223,* 311–328.

18. Caunt, B. S., Franklin, J., Brodaty, N. E., & Brodaty, H. (2013). Exploring the causes of subjective well-being: A content analysis of peoples' recipes for long-term happiness. *Journal of Happiness Studies, 14*(2), 475–499.

19. Stone, L. (2005). Linda Stone's blog. Retrieved from http://www.lindastone.net/

20. Mojtabai, R., Olfson, M., & Han, B. (2016). National trends in the prevalence and treatment of depression in adolescents and young adults. *Pediatrics, 138* (6), 1–10.

21. Child Mind Institute. (2015). Children's Mental Health Report. Retrieved from https://childmind.org/2015-childrens-mental-health-report/

22. Przybylski, A. K., & Weinstein, N. (2013). Can you connect with me now? How the presence of mobile communication technology influences face-to-face conversation quality. *Journal of Social and Personal Relationships, 30*(3), 237–246. https://doi.org/10.1177/0265407512453827

23. Misra, S., Cheng, L., Genevie, J., & Yuan, M. (2016). The iPhone effect: The quality of in-person social interactions in the presence of mobile devices. *Environment and Behavior, 48*(2), 275–298.

24. Schrobsdorff, S. (October 27, 2016). Teen depression and anxiety: Why the kids are not alright. *Time Magazine,* 188(19). Retrieved from http://time.com/magazine/us/4547305/november-7th-2016-vol-188-no-19-u-s/

25. DeVore, E. R., & Ginsburg, K. R. (2005). The protective effects of good parenting on adolescents. *Current Opinion in Pediatrics, 17*(4), 460–465.

26. Leung, J. P., & Leung, K. (1992). Life satisfaction, self-concept, and relationship with parents in adolescence. *Journal of Youth and Adolescence, 21*(6), 653–665.

27. Lin, C. H., Lin, S. L., & Wu, C. P. (2009). The effects of parental monitoring and leisure boredom on adolescents' Internet addiction. *Adolescence,* 44(176), 993.

28. Vaala, S. E., & Bleakley, A. (2015). Monitoring, mediating, and modeling: Parental influence on adolescent computer and Internet use in the United States. *Journal of Children and Media, 9*(1), 40–57.

29. Joussemet, M., Landry, R., & Koestner, R. (2008). A self-determination theory perspective on parenting. *Canadian Psychology/Psychologie canadienne,* 49(3), 194.

30. Turnock, B. J. (2015). *Public health: What it is and why it works.* Burlington, MA: Jones & Bartlett Learning.

Chapter 2

1. Experts Exchange. Processing power compared: Visualizing a 1 trillion-fold increase in computing performance. Retrieved from http://pages.experts-exchange.com/processing-power-compared/

2. Marr, R. (2014). To the moon and back on 4K of memory. *Metro Weekly,* Washington, DC. Retrieved from http://www.metroweekly.com/2014/07/to-the-moon-and-back-on-4kb-of-memory/

3. iPhone X benchmarks. Retrieved from https://browser.geekbench.com/ios_devices/52

4. Richter, D., Grün, R., Joannes-Boyau, R., Steele, T. E., Amani, F., Rué, M., . . . Hublin, J. J. (2017). The age of the hominin fossils from Jebel Irhoud, Morocco, and the origins of the Middle Stone Age. *Nature, 546*(7657), 293–296.

5. Computer History Museum (2017). Timeline of computer history. Retrieved from http://www.computerhistory.org/timeline/computers/

6. Reagan, R. (1989, June 14). *The Guardian*.

7. Domonoske, C. (2017, July 17). Elon Musk warns governors: Artificial intelligence poses "existential risk." *National Public Radio*. Retrieved from http://www.npr.org/sections/thetwo-way/2017/07/17/537686649/elon-musk-warns-governors-artificial-intelligence-poses-existential-risk

8. Carrington, D. (2016). Three-quarters of UK children spend less time outdoors than prison inmates: Survey. Retrieved from https://www.theguardian.com/environment/2016/mar/25/three-quarters-of-uk-children-spend-less-time-outdoors-than-prison-inmates-survey

9. Bragg, R., Wood, C., Barton, J., & Pretty, J. (2013). Measuring connection to nature in children aged 8–12: A robust methodology for the RSPB [Epublication]. Retrieved from https://www. rspb. org. uk/Images/methodology-report_tcm9-354606. pdf

10. Lovely, S. (2016). People spend more than twice as much time on Netflix as with friends. CordCutting. Retrieved from https://cordcutting.com/people-spend-more-than-twice-as-much-time-on-netflix-as-with-friends/

11. Berger, A. (2011). *Self-regulation: Brain, cognition, and development.* Washington, DC: American Psychological Association.

12. Vohs, K. D., & Baumeister, R. F. (2004). Understanding self-regulation. In R. F. Baumeister & K. D. Vohs (Eds.), *Handbook of self-regulation: Research, theory, and applications* (p. 3). New York, NY: Guilford Press.

13. Spiegel, A. (2008, February 21). Old fashioned play builds serious skill. *National Public Radio* [Podcast]. Retrieved from http://www.npr.org/templates/story/story.php?storyId=19212514

14. Ivanova, E. F. (2000). The development of voluntary behavior in preschoolers: Repetition of Z. V. Manuiolenko's experiments. *Journal of Russian & East European Psychology, 38*(2), 6–21. doi: 10.2753/RPO1061-040538026

15. Berk, L. & Meyers, A. (2013). The role of make-believe play in the development of executive function: status of research and future directions. *American Journal of Play*, 6(1), 98–110.

16. Gray, P. (2011). The decline of play and the rise of psychopathology in children and adolescents. *American Journal of Play*, 3(4), 443–463.

17. Granic, I., Lobel, A., Engs, R. C. M. E. (2014). The benefits of playing video games. *American Psychologist*, 69(1), 66–78.

18. Neff, K. (2003). Self-compassion: An alternative conceptualization of a healthy attitude toward oneself. *Self and Identity*, 2(2), 85–101.

19. McGonigal, K. (2012). *The willpower instinct: How self-control works, why it matters, and what you can do to get more of it.* New York: Avery.

20. Marvin, C. (1990). *When old technologies were new: Thinking about electric communication in the late nineteenth century.* Oxford: Oxford University Press.

21. Prater, D., & Miller, S. (2002). We shall soon be nothing but transparent heaps of jelly to each other. *A Journal of Media and Culture*, 5(2). Retrieved from http://www.media-culture.org.au/0205/transparent.php

22. Kardaras, N. (2016, August 27). It's "digital heroin": How screens turn kids into psychotic junkies. *New York Post*, 27. Retrieved from http://blog.wsd.net/aharris/files/2016/08/0.2.4-Digital-Cocaine-Article.docx

23. Waldinger, R., & Schulz, M. (2010). What's love got to do with it? Social functioning, perceived health, and daily happiness in married octogenarians. *Psychology of Aging*, 25(2), 422–431.

Chapter 3

1. Sustainable Development Solutions Network. (2015). World happiness report: 2015. New York, NY: Helliwell, J., Layard, R., & Sachs, J.

2. Mojtabai, R., Olfson, M., & Han, B. (2016). National trends in the prevalence and treatment of depression in adolescents and young adults. *Pediatrics*, 138(6), e20161878.

3. Kantor, E. D., Rehm, C. D., Haas, J. S., Chan, A. T., & Giovannucci, E. L. (2015). Trends in prescription drug use among adults in the United States from 1999–2012. *JAMA*, 314(17), 1818.

4. Curtin, S. C., Warner, M., & Hedegaard, H. (2016). Increase in suicide in the United States, 1999–2014. *NCHS Data Brief*, 241, 1–8.

5. Rothman, L. (2016, July 1). Exclusive: New "Happiness Index" number reveals how Americans feel right now. *Time*. Retrieved from http://time.com/4389726/harris-poll-happiness-index-2016/

6. Sachs, J. (2017). Restoring American happiness. In J. Helliwell, R. Layard, & J. Sachs (Eds.), *World happiness report 2017*. New York: Sustainable Development Solutions Network.

7. Curtin, S. C., Warner, M., & Hedegaard, H. (2016). Increase in suicide in the United States, 1999–2014. *NCHS Data Brief, 241*, 1–8.

8. San Diego State University. (2015, November 5). Adults' happiness on the decline in US: Researchers found adults over age 30 are not as happy as they used to be, but teens and young adults are happier than ever. *Science Daily*. Retrieved from https://www.sciencedaily.com/releases/2015/11/151105143547.htm

9. Bottan, N. L., & Truglia, R. P. (2011). Deconstructing the hedonic treadmill: Is happiness autoregressive? *The Journal of Socio-Economics, 40*(3), 224–236.

10. Ying, Y. U., & Fengjie, J. I. N. G. (2016). Development and application of the hedonic adaptation theory. *Advances in Psychological Science, 24*(10), 1663–1669.

11. Gergen, K. J. (2002). The challenge of absent presence. In J. E. Katz & M. Aakhus (Eds), *Perpetual contact: Mobile communication, Private talk, Public Performance* (pp. 227–214). Cambridge: Cambridge University Press.

12. Turkle, S. (2012). *Alone together: Why we expect more from technology and less from each other*. New York: Basic Books.

13. National Sleep Foundation recommends new sleep times. (2015). Retrieved from https://sleepfoundation.org/press-release/national-sleep-foundation-recommends-new-sleep-times

14. Emsellem, H. A., Knutson, K. L., Hillygus, D. S., Buxton, O. M., Montgomery-Downs, H., LeBourgeois, M. K., & Spilsbury, J. (2014). 2014 sleep in America poll: Sleep in the modern family. *Sleep Health, 1*(2), 13e.

15. Hale, L., & Guan, S. (2015). Screen time and sleep among school-aged children and adolescents: A systematic literature review. *Sleep Medicine Reviews, 21*, 50–58.

16. Thomas, M., Sing, H., Belenky, G., Holcomb, H., Mayberg, H., Dannals, R., . . . Welsh, A. (2000). Neural basis of alertness and cognitive performance

impairments during sleepiness. I. Effects of 24 h of sleep deprivation on waking human regional brain activity. *Journal of Sleep Research, 9*(4), 335–352.

17. Chang, A. M., Aeschbach, D., Duffy, J. F., & Czeisler, C. A. (2015). Evening use of light-emitting eReaders negatively affects sleep, circadian timing, and next-morning alertness. *Proceedings of the National Academy of Sciences, 112*(4), 1232–1237.

18. Wood, B., Rea, M. S., Plitnick, B., & Figueiro, M. G. (2013). Light level and duration of exposure determine the impact of self-luminous tablets on melatonin suppression. *Applied Ergonomics, 44*(2), 237–240.

19. Dworak, M., Schierl, T., Bruns, T., & Strüder, H. K. (2007) Impact of singular excessive computer game and television exposure on sleep patterns and memory performance of school-aged children. *Pediatrics, 120,* 978–985.

20. King, D. L., Gradisar, M., Drummond, A., Lovato, N., Wessel, J., Micic, G., . . . Delfabbro, P. (2013). The impact of prolonged violent video-gaming on adolescent sleep: An experimental study. *Journal of Sleep Research, 22*(2), 137–143.

21. White, R. L., Babic, M. J., Parker, P. D., Lubans, D. R., Astell-Burt, T., & Lonsdale, C. (2017). Domain-specific physical activity and mental health: A meta-analysis. *American Journal of Preventive Medicine, 52,* 653-666. doi: 10.1016/j.amepre.2016.12.008

22. Mischel, W., Shoda, Y., & Rodriguez, M. L. (1989). Delay of gratification in children. *Science, 244*(4907), 933–938. doi: 10.1126/science.2658056

23. Duckworth, A. L., Tsukayama, E., & Kirby, T. A. (2013). Is it really self-control? Examining the predictive power of the delay of gratification task. *Personality and Social Psychology Bulletin, 39*(7), 843–855. doi: 10.1177/0146167213482589

24. Story, G. W., Vlaev, I., Seymour, B., Darzi, A., & Dolan, R. J. (2014). Does temporal discounting explain unhealthy behavior? A systematic review and reinforcement learning perspective. *Frontiers in Behavioral Neuroscience, 8,* 76. doi: 10.3389/fnbeh.2014.00076

25. Rosen, L. D., Whaling, K., Rab, S., Carrier, L. M., & Cheever, N. A. (2013). Is Facebook creating "iDisorders"? The link between clinical symptoms of psychiatric disorders and technology use, attitudes and anxiety. *Computers in Human Behavior, 29*(3), 1243–1254.

26. Rosen, L. D., Lim, A. F., Felt, J., Carrier, L. M., Cheever, N. A., Lara-Ruiz, J. M., . . . Rokkum, J. (2014). Media and technology use predicts ill-being among

children, preteens and teenagers independent of the negative health impacts of exercise and eating habits. *Computers in Human Behavior, 35,* 364–375.

27. Schwartz, B. (2004, January). *The paradox of choice: Why more is less.* New York: Ecco.

28. Schwartz, B. (2005). *The paradox of choice.* Retrieved from https://www.ted.com/talks/barry_schwartz_on_the_paradox_of_choice

29. Iyengar, S., & Lepper, M. (2000). When choice is demotivating: Can one desire too much of a good thing? *Journal of Personality and Social Psychology, 79,* 995–1006.

30. Przybylski, A. K., Murayama, K., DeHaan, C. R., & Gladwell, V. (2013). Motivational, emotional, and behavioral correlates of fear of missing out. *Computers in Human Behavior, 29*(4), 1841–1848.

31. Przybylski, A. K., Murayama, K., DeHaan, C. R., & Gladwell, V. (2013). Motivational, emotional, and behavioral correlates of fear of missing out. *Computers in Human Behavior, 29*(4), 1841–1848.

32. Martin, T. L., Yu, C. T., Martin, G. L., & Fazzio, D. (2006). On choice, preference, and preference for choice. *The Behavior Analyst Today, 7*(2), 234–241. doi: 10.1037/h0100083

33. Gilbert, D. T., & Wilson, T.D. (2000). Miswanting: Some problems in the forecasting of future affective states. In J.P. Forgas (Ed.), The role of affect in social cognition (178-197). Cambridge: Cambridge University Press.

34. Vohs, K. D., Baumeister, R. F., Schmeichel, B. J., Twenge, J. M., Nelson, N. M., & Tice, D. M. (2008). Making choices impairs subsequent self-control: A limited resource account of decision making, self-regulation, and active initiative. *Motivation Science, 1*(S), 19–42. http://dx.doi.org/10.1037/2333-8113.1.S.19

35. Vohs, K. D., Baumeister, R. F., Schmeichel, B. J., Twenge, J. M., Nelson, N. M., & Tice, D. M. (2014). Making choices impairs subsequent self-control: A limited-resource account of decision making, self-regulation, and active initiative. *Motivation Science, 1*(S), 19–42. http://dx.doi.org/10.1037/2333-8113.1.S.19

36. Vohs, K. D., Baumeister, R. F., Schmeichel, B. J., Twenge, J. M., Nelson, N. M., & Tice, D. M. (2014). Making choices impairs subsequent self-control: A limited-resource account of decision making, self-regulation, and active initiative. *Motivation Science, 1*(S), 19–42. http://dx.doi.org/10.1037/2333-8113.1.S.19

37. Lyubomirsky, S., & Ross, L. (1997). Hedonic consequences of social comparison: A contrast of happy and unhappy people. *Journal of Personality and Social Psychology, 73*(6), 1141.

38. Tandoc, E. C., Ferrucci, P., & Duffy, M. (2015). Facebook use, envy, and depression among college students: Is facebooking depressing? *Computers in Human Behavior, 43*, 139–146.

39. Keng, S. L., Smoski, M. J., & Robins, C. J. (2011). Effects of mindfulness on psychological health: A review of empirical studies. *Clinical Psychology Review, 31*(6), 1041–1056.

40. Morelli, S. A., & Lieberman, M. D. (2013). The role of automaticity and attention in neural processes underlying empathy for happiness, sadness, and anxiety. *Frontiers in Human Neuroscience, 7*, 160. doi: 10.3389/fnhum.2013.00160

41. Weinstein, N., Brown, K. W., & Ryan, R. M. (2009). A multi-method examination of the effects of mindfulness on stress attribution, coping, and emotional well-being. *Journal of Research in Personality, 43*(3), 374–385.

42. Buser, T., & Peter, N. (2012). Multitasking. *Experimental Economics, 15*(4), 641–655.

43. Pea, R., Nass, C., Meheula, L., Rance, M., Kumar, A., Bamford, H., . . . Zhou, M. (2012). Media use, face-to-face communication, media multitasking, and social well-being among 8-to 12-year-old girls. *Developmental Psychology, 48*(2), 327.

44. Rosen, L., Whaling, K., Rab, S., Carrier, L., & Cheever, N. (2013). Is Facebook creating "iDisorders"? The link between clinical symptoms of psychiatric disorders and technology use, attitudes and anxiety. *Computers in Human Behavior, 29*, 1243–1254. doi: 10.1016/j.chb.2012.11.012

45. Isikman, E., MacInnis, D. J., Ülkümen, G., & Cavanaugh, L. A. (2016). The effects of curiosity-evoking events on activity enjoyment. *Journal of Experimental Psychology: Applied, 22*(3), 319.

46. Sanbonmatsu, D. M., Strayer, D. L., Medeiros-Ward, N., & Watson, J. M. (2013). Who multi-tasks and why? Multi-tasking ability, perceived multitasking ability, impulsivity, and sensation seeking. *PloS One, 8*(1), e54402.

47. Ward, A. F., Duke, K., Gneezy, A., & Bos, M. W. (2017). Brain drain: The mere presence of one's own smartphone reduces available cognitive capacity. *Journal of the Association for Consumer Research, 2*, n.p. Published online. Retrieved from http://dx.doi.org/10.1086/691462

48. Sanbonmatsu, D. M., Strayer, D. L., Medeiros-Ward, N., & Watson, J. M. (2013). Who multi-tasks and why? Multi-tasking ability, perceived multi-tasking ability, impulsivity, and sensation seeking. *PloS One, 8*(1), e54402.

49. Csikszentmihalyi, M. (2014). *Flow and the foundations of positive psychology* (pp. 209–226). Dordrecht: Springer.

50. Duke, É., & Montag, C. (2017). Smartphone addiction and beyond: Initial insights on an emerging research topic and its relationship to Internet addiction. In C. Montag & M. Reuter (Eds.), *Internet Addiction* (pp. 359–372). Dordrecht: Springer International Publishing.

51. Holder, M. D., & Coleman, B. (2009). The contribution of social relationships to children's happiness. *Journal of Happiness Studies, 10*(3), 329–349.

52. Turkle, S. (2012). *Alone together: Why we expect more from technology and less from each other.* New York: Basic Books.

53. Harlow, H. F., & Zimmermann, R. R. (1959). Affectional response in the infant monkey. *Science, 130*(3373), 421–432.

54. Fox, N. A., Almas, A. N., Degnan, K. A., Nelson, C. A., & Zeanah, C. H. (2011). The effects of severe psychosocial deprivation and foster care intervention on cognitive development at 8 years of age: Findings from the Bucharest Early Intervention Project. *Journal of Child Psychology and Psychiatry, 52*(9), 919–928.

55. Robson, K. S. (1967). The role of eye-to-eye contact in maternal-infant attachment. *Journal of Child Psychology and Psychiatry, 8*(1), 13–25.

56. Else-Quest, N. M., Hyde, J. S., & Clark, R. (2003). Breastfeeding, bonding, and the mother-infant relationship. *Merrill-Palmer Quarterly, 49*(4), 495–517.

57. Field, T. (2010). Touch for socioemotional and physical well-being: A review. *Developmental Review, 30*(4), 367–383.

58. Roelofs, J., Meesters, C., ter Huurne, M., Bamelis, L., & Muris, P. (2006). On the links between attachment style, parental rearing behaviors, and internalizing and externalizing problems in non-clinical children. *Journal of Child and family Studies, 15*(3), 319.

59. Denworth, L. (2016, May 1). The biological blessings of friendship. Retrieved from https://www.scientificamerican.com/article/the-biological-blessings-of-friendship/

60. Tough, P. (2013). *How children succeed.* New York: Random House.

61. Kross, E., Berman, M. G., Mischel, W., Smith, E. E., & Wager, T. D. (2011). Social rejection shares somatosensory representations with physical pain. *Proceedings of the National Academy of Sciences, 108*(15), 6270–6275.

62. Turkle, S. (2015). *Reclaiming conversation: The power of talk in a digital age.* New York: Penguin.

63. Morelli, S. A., & Lieberman, M. D. (2013). The role of automaticity and attention in neural processes underlying empathy for happiness, sadness, and anxiety. *Frontiers in Human Neuroscience, 7,* 160. doi: 10.3389/ fnhum.2013.00160

64. Pea, R., Nass, C., Meheula, L., Rance, M., Kumar, A., Bamford, H., . . . Zhou, M. (2012). Media use, face-to-face communication, media multitasking, and social well-being among 8-to 12-year-old girls. *Developmental Psychology, 48*(2), 327.

65. Neuman, S. B. (1988). The displacement effect: Assessing the relation between television viewing and reading performance. *Reading Research Quarterly, 23,* 414–440.

66. Kayany, J. M., & Yelsma, P. (2000). Displacement effects of online media in the socio-technical contexts of households. *Journal of Broadcasting & Electronic Media, 44*(2), 215–229.

67. Denworth, L. (2016, May 1). The biological blessings of friendship. Retrieved from https://www.scientificamerican.com/article/the-biological-blessings-of-friendship/

68. Dunbar, R. I. (1992). Neocortex size as a constraint on group size in primates. *Journal of Human Evolution, 22*(6), 469–493.

69. Vitousek, P. M., Mooney, H. A., Lubchenco, J., & Melillo, J. M. (1997). Human domination of Earth's ecosystems. *Science, 277*(5325), 494–499.

70. McCright, A. M., & Dunlap, R. E. (2011). The politicization of climate change and polarization in the American public's views of global warming, 2001–2010. *The Sociological Quarterly, 52*(2), 155–194.

71. Why our brains weren't made to deal with climate change. (2016, April 19). Retrieved from http://www.npr.org/2016/04/18/474685770/why-our-brains-werent-made-to-deal-with-climate-change

72. Moser, S. C. (2010). Communicating climate change: History, challenges, process and future directions. *Wiley Interdisciplinary Reviews: Climate Change, 1*(1), 31–53.

73. Tudor-Locke, C., & Bassett, D. R. (2004). How many steps/day are enough?. *Sports Medicine, 34*(1), 1–8.

74. Raichlen, D. A., Pontzer, H., Harris, J. A., Mabulla, A. Z., Marlowe, F. W., Josh Snodgrass, J., . . . Wood, B. M. (2016). Physical activity patterns and biomarkers of cardiovascular disease risk in hunter-gatherers. *American Journal of Human Biology, 29,* 1–13.

75. O'Keefe, J. H., Vogel, R., Lavie, C. J., & Cordain, L. (2011). Exercise like a hunter-gatherer: A prescription for organic physical fitness. *Progress in Cardiovascular Diseases, 53*(6), 471–479.

76. Ergotron, Inc. (2013). JustStand Survey and Index Report. St. Paul, MN. Retrieved from http://www.juststand.org/wp-content/uploads/2017/05/SurveyIndexReport.pdf

77. Diaz, K. M., Howard, V. J., Hutto, B., Colabianchi, N., Vena, J. E., Safford, M. M., . . . Hooker, S. P. (2017). Patterns of sedentary behavior and mortality in US middle-aged and older adults: A national cohort study. *Annals of Internal Medicine, 167,* 465–475.

78. Kim, I. Y., Park, S., Chou, T. H., Trombold, J. R., & Coyle, E. F. (2016). Prolonged sitting negatively affects the postprandial plasma triglyceride-lowering effect of acute exercise. *American Journal of Physiology-Endocrinology and Metabolism, 311*(5), E891–E898.

79. O'Keefe, J. H., Vogel, R., Lavie, C. J., & Cordain, L. (2011). Exercise like a hunter-gatherer: A prescription for organic physical fitness. *Progress in Cardiovascular Diseases, 53*(6), 471–479.

80. O'Keefe, J. H., Vogel, R., Lavie, C. J., & Cordain, L. (2010). Achieving hunter-gatherer fitness in the 21(st) century: Back to the future. *The American Journal of Medicine, 123*(12), 1082–1086. https://doi.org/10.1016/j.amjmed.2010.04.026

81. Lieberman, D. (2014). *The story of the human body: Evolution, health, and disease.* New York: Vintage Books.

82. Shaw, C., & Ryan, T. (2014). *Hunter-gatherer past shows our fragile bones result from physical inactivity since the invention of farming.* Cambridge: Cambridge University Press.

83. O'Keefe, J. H., Vogel, R., Lavie, C. J., & Cordain, L. (2010). Achieving hunter-gatherer fitness in the 21st century: Back to the future. *The American Journal of Medicine, 123*(12), 1082–1086.

84. Gazzaley, A., & Rosen, L. D. (2016). *The distracted mind: Ancient brains in a high-tech world*. Cambridge, MA: MIT Press.

Chapter 4

1. Yildirim, C., & Correia, A. P. (2015, August). Understanding nomophobia: A modern age phobia among college students. In: Zaphiris P., Ioannou A. (Eds.), *International Conference on Learning and Collaboration Technologies* (pp. 724–735). Cham: Springer.

2. Ryan, R. M., & Deci, E. L. (2017). *Self-determination theory: Basic psychological needs in motivation, development, and wellness*. New York: Guilford Press.

3. Di Domenico, S. I., & Ryan, R. M. (2017). The emerging neuroscience of intrinsic motivation: A new frontier in self-determination research. *Frontiers in Human Neuroscience, 11*, 145. http://doi.org/10.3389/fnhum.2017.00145

4. Ardiel, E. L., & Rankin, C. H. (2010). The importance of touch in development. *Paediatrics & Child Health, 15*(3), 153–156.

5. Gallace, A., & Spence, C. (2010). The science of interpersonal touch: An overview. *Neuroscience & Biobehavioral Reviews, 34*(2), 246–259.

6. Haughton, C., Aiken, M., & Cheevers, C. (2015). Cyber babies: The impact of emerging technology on the developing child. *Psychology Research, 5*(9), 504–518. Retrieved from https://www.researchgate.net/publication/284028810_Cyber_babies_The_impact_of_emerging_technology_on_the_developing_childPsychology_Research

7. McDaniel, B. T., & Coyne, S. M. (2016). "Technoference": The interference of technology in couple relationships and implications for women's personal and relational well-being. *Psychology of Popular Media Culture, 5*(1), 85.

8. Przybylski, A. K., Weinstein, N., Ryan, R. M., & Rigby, C. S. (2009). Having to versus wanting to play: Background and consequences of harmonious versus obsessive engagement in video games. *CyberPsychology & Behavior, 12*(5), 485–492.

9. McDaniel, B. T., & Coyne, S. M. (2016). "Technoference": The interference of technology in couple relationships and implications for women's personal and relational well-being. *Psychology of Popular Media Culture, 5*(1), 85.

10. Vandewater, E. A., Bickham, D. S., & Lee, J. H. (2006). Time well spent? Relating television use to children's free-time activities. *Pediatrics, 117*(2), e181–e191.

11. Barrett, D. (2010). *Supernormal stimuli: How primal urges overran their evolutionary purpose*. New York: W. W. Norton.

12. Goodwin, B. C., Browne, M., & Rockloff, M. (2015). Measuring preference for supernormal over natural rewards: A two-dimensional anticipatory pleasure scale. *Evolutionary Psychology, 13*(4), 1–11.

13. Barrett, D. (2010). Supernormal *stimuli: How primal urges overran their evolutionary purpose*. New York: W. W. Norton.

14. Barrett, D. (2010). *Supernormal stimuli: How primal urges overran their evolutionary purpose*. New York: W. W. Norton.

15. Lenoir, M., Serre, F., Cantin, L., & Ahmed, S. H. (2007). Intense sweetness surpasses cocaine reward. *PloS One, 2*(8), e698.

16. Hilton, D. L., Jr. (2013). Pornography addiction: A supranormal stimulus considered in the context of neuroplasticity. *Socioaffective Neuroscience & Psychology, 3*(1), 20767. doi: 10.3402/snp.v3i0.20767

17. Goodwin, B. C., Browne, M., & Rockloff, M. (2015). Measuring preference for supernormal over natural rewards: A two-dimensional anticipatory pleasure scale. *Evolutionary Psychology, 13*(4), 1–11. doi: 10.1177/1474704915613914

18. Cawley, J., & Meyerhoefer, C. (2012). The medical care costs of obesity: An Ergotron, Inc. JustStand Survey and Index Report. Instrumental variables approach. *Journal of Health Economics, 31*(1), 219–230. doi:10.1016/j.jhealeco.2011.10.003

19. West Virginia Health Statistic Center. (n.d.). Obesity: Facts, figures, guidelines. Retrieved from http://www.wvdhhr.org/bph/oehp/obesity/mortality.htm

20. DeBruyne, N., & Leland, A. (2015, January). *Congressional Research Service: American War and Military Operations Casualties Lists and Statistics*. Retrieved from https://fas.org/sgp/crs/natsec/RL32492.pdf

21. Love, T., Laier, C., Brand, M., Hatch, L., & Hajela, R. (2015). Neuroscience of Internet pornography addiction: A review and update. *Behavioral Sciences, 5*(3), 388–433.

22. Ward, A. F. (2013). Supernormal: How the Internet is changing our memories and our minds. *Psychological Inquiry, 24*(4), 341–348.

23. Umberson, D., & Karas Montez, J. (2010). Social relationships and health: A flashpoint for health policy. *Journal of Health and Social Behavior, 51*(1 Suppl), S54–S66.

24. Deci, E. L., & Ryan, R. M. (1985). *Intrinsic motivation and self-determination in human behavior*. New York: Plenum.

25. Steinberg, L. (2008). A social neuroscience perspective on adolescent risk-taking. *Developmental Review, 28*(1), 78–106.

26. Galvan, A. (2010). Adolescent development of the reward system. *Frontiers in Human Neuroscience, 4*, 1–9.

27. Hilton, D. L., Jr. (2013). Pornography addiction: A supranormal stimulus considered in the context of neuroplasticity. *Socioaffective Neuroscience & Psychology, 3*(1), 20767.

28. Di Domenico, S. I., & Ryan, R. M. (2017). The emerging neuroscience of intrinsic motivation: A new frontier in self-determination research. *Frontiers in Human Neuroscience, 11*, 145.

29. Steinberg, L. (2008). A social neuroscience perspective on adolescent risk-taking. *Developmental Review, 28*(1), 78–106.

30. Wohlwill, J. F. (1984). What are sensation seekers seeking? *Behavioral and Brain Sciences, 7*(3), 453–453.

31. Wittmann, B. C., Bunzeck, N., Dolan, R. J., & Düzel, E. (2007). Anticipation of novelty recruits reward system and hippocampus while promoting recollection. *Neuroimage, 38*(1), 194–202.

32. Wittmann, B. C., Bunzeck, N., Dolan, R. J., & Düzel, E. (2007). Anticipation of novelty recruits reward system and hippocampus while promoting recollection. *Neuroimage, 38*(1), 194–202.

33. Kidd, C., & Hayden, B. Y. (2015). The psychology and neuroscience of curiosity. *Neuron, 88*(3), 449–460.

34. Oudeyer, P. Y., Gottlieb, J., & Lopes, M. (2016). Intrinsic motivation, curiosity, and learning: Theory and applications in educational technologies. *Progress in Brain Research, 229*, 257–284.

35. Pirolli, P., & Card, S. (1999). Information foraging. *Psychological Review, 106*(4), 643.

36. Marvin, C. B., & Shohamy, D. (2016). Curiosity and reward: Valence predicts choice and information prediction errors enhance learning. *Journal of Experimental Psychology: General, 145*(3), 266.

37. Bromberg-Martin, E. S., & Hikosaka, O. (2009). Midbrain dopamine neurons signal preference for advance information about upcoming rewards. *Neuron, 63*(1), 119–126.

38. Grabe, M. E., & Kamhawi, R. (2006). Hard wired for negative news? Gender differences in processing broadcast news. *Communication Research, 33*(5), 346–369.

39. Hedger, N., Adams, W. J., & Garner, M. (2015). Autonomic arousal and attentional orienting to visual threat are predicted by awareness. *Journal of Experimental Psychology: Human Perception and Performance, 41*(3), 798.

40. Love, T., Laier, C., Brand, M., Hatch, L., & Hajela, R. (2015). Neuroscience of Internet pornography addiction: A review and update. *Behavioral Sciences, 5*(3), 388–433.

41. Luscombe, B. (2016). Porn and the threat to virility: The first generation of men who grew up with unlimited online porn sound the alarm. *Time, 187*(13), 40.

42. Ryan, R. M., & Deci, E. L. (2017). *Self-determination theory: Basic psychological needs in motivation, development, and wellness.* New York: Guilford Press.

43. Przybylski, A. K., Weinstein, N., Ryan, R. M., & Rigby, C. S. (2009). Having to versus wanting to play: Background and consequences of harmonious versus obsessive engagement in video games. *CyberPsychology & Behavior, 12*(5), 485–492.

44. Masur, P. K., Reinecke, L., Ziegele, M., & Quiring, O. (2014). The interplay of intrinsic need satisfaction and Facebook specific motives in explaining addictive behavior on Facebook. *Computers in Human Behavior, 39*, 376–386.

45. Goodwin, B. C., Browne, M., & Rockloff, M. (2015). Measuring preference for supernormal over natural rewards: A two-dimensional anticipatory pleasure scale. *Evolutionary Psychology, 13*(4), 1–11. doi: 10.1177/1474704915613914

46. Greenfield, D. (2007). The addictive properties of Internet usage. In K. S. Young & C. N. de Abreu (Eds.), *Internet addiction: A handbook and guide to evaluation and treatment.* Hoboken, NJ: John Wiley & Sons. doi: 10.1002/9781118013991.ch8

47. Eyal, N. (2014). *Hooked: How to build habit-forming products.* Penguin.

48. Alter, A. (2017). *Irresistible: The rise of addictive technology and the business of keeping us hooked.* New York Penguin.

49. Ferster, C. B., & Skinner, B. F. (1957). *Schedules of reinforcement.* New York, NY: Appleton-Century-Crofts.

50. Knutson, B., Wimmer, G. E., Kuhnen, C. M., & Winkielman, P. (2008). Nucleus accumbens activation mediates the influence of reward cues on financial risk taking. *NeuroReport, 19*(5), 509–513.

51. Hampton, A. N., & O'Doherty, J. P. (2007). Decoding the neural substrates of reward-related decision making with functional MRI. *Proceedings of the National Academy of Sciences, 104*(4), 1377–1382.

52. Hilton, D. L., Jr. (2013). Pornography addiction: A supranormal stimulus considered in the context of neuroplasticity. *Socioaffective Neuroscience & Psychology, 3*(1), 1–8

53. Schultz, W. (2016). Dopamine reward prediction error coding. *Dialogues in Clinical Neuroscience, 18*(1), 23.

54. Schultz, W., Dayan, P., & Montague, P. R. (1997). A neural substrate of prediction and reward. *Science, 275*, 1593–1599. doi: 0.1126/science.275.5306.1593

55. Saunders, B. T., & Robinson, T. E. (2013). Individual variation in resisting temptation: Implications for addiction. *Neuroscience & Biobehavioral Reviews, 37*(9), 1955–1975.

56. Glimcher, P. W. (2011). Understanding dopamine and reinforcement learning: The dopamine reward prediction error hypothesis. *Proceedings of the National Academy of Sciences, 108*(Suppl 3), 15647–15654.

57. Schultz, W., Dayan, P., & Montague, P. R. (1997). A neural substrate of prediction and reward. *Science, 275*, 1593–1599. doi: 0.1126/science.275.5306.1593

58. Greenfield, D. (2007). The addictive properties of Internet usage. In K. S. Young & C. N. de Abreu (Eds.), *Internet addiction: A handbook and guide to evaluation and treatment*. Hoboken, NJ: John Wiley & Sons. doi: 10.1002/9781118013991.ch8

59. Knutson, B., Adams, C. M., Fong, G. W., & Hommer, D. (2001). Anticipation of increasing monetary reward selectively recruits nucleus accumbens. *Journal of Neuroscience, 21*(16), 1–5.

60. Berridge, K. C. (2007). The debate over dopamine's role in reward: The case for incentive salience. *Psychopharmacology, 191*(3), 391–431.

61. Eyal, N. (2014). *Hooked: How to build habit-forming products*. New York: Penguin.

62. Wittmann, B. C., Bunzeck, N., Dolan, R. J., & Düzel, E. (2007). Anticipation of novelty recruits reward system and hippocampus while promoting recollection. *Neuroimage, 38*(1), 194–202.

63. Bromberg-Martin, E. S., & Hikosaka, O. (2009). Midbrain dopamine neurons signal preference for advance information about upcoming rewards. *Neuron, 63*(1), 119–126.

64. Alter, A. (2017). *Irresistible: The rise of addictive technology and the business of keeping us hooked.* New York: Penguin.

65. Przybylski, A. K., Murayama, K., DeHaan, C. R., & Gladwell, V. (2013). Motivational, emotional, and behavioral correlates of fear of missing out. *Computers in Human Behavior, 29*(4), 1841–1848.

66. Pavlov, I. P. (1941). *Lectures on conditioned reflexes.* Vol. II: *Conditioned reflexes and psychiatry.* New York: International.

67. Schultz, W., Dayan, P., & Montague, P. R. (1997). A neural substrate of prediction and reward. *Science, 275,* 1593–1599. doi: 0.1126/science.275.5306.1593

68. Saunders, B. T., & Robinson, T. E. (2013). Individual variation in resisting temptation: Implications for addiction. *Neuroscience & Biobehavioral Reviews, 37*(9), 1955–1975.

69. Pan, W. X., Schmidt, R., Wickens, J. R., & Hyland, B. I. (2005). Dopamine cells respond to predicted events during classical conditioning: Evidence for eligibility traces in the reward-learning network. *Journal of Neuroscience, 25*(26), 6235–6242.

70. Rescorla, R. A. (1988). Pavlovian conditioning: It's not what you think it is. *American Psychologist, 43*(March), 151–160.

71. Saunders, B. T., & Robinson, T. E. (2013). Individual variation in resisting temptation: Implications for addiction. *Neuroscience & Biobehavioral Reviews, 37*(9), 1955–1975.

72. Tiffany, S. T. (1995). Potential functions of classical conditioning in drug addiction. In D. C. Drummond, S. T. Tiffany, S. Glautier, & B. Remington (Eds.), *The Wiley series in clinical psychology. Addictive behaviour: Cue exposure theory and practice* (pp. 47–71). Oxford: John Wiley & Sons.

73. Kim, J., Lim, J. S., & Bhargava, M. (1998). The role of affect in attitude formation: A classical conditioning approach. *Journal of the Academy of Marketing Science, 26*(2), 143–152.

74. Ward, A. F., Duke, K., Gneezy, A., & Bos, M. W. (2017). Brain drain: The mere presence of one's own smartphone reduces available cognitive capacity.

Journal of the Association for Consumer Research, 2, n.p. Published online. Retrieved from http://dx.doi.org/10.1086/691462

75. Przybylski, A. K., & Weinstein, N. (2013). Can you connect with me now? How the presence of mobile communication technology influences face-to-face conversation quality. *Journal of Social and Personal Relationships, 30*(3), 237–246. doi: 10.1177/0265407512453827

76. McDaniel, B. T., & Coyne, S. M. (2016). "Technoference": The interference of technology in couple relationships and implications for women's personal and relational well-being. *Psychology of Popular Media Culture, 5*(1), 85.

77. Junco, R. (2015). Student class standing, Facebook use, and academic performance. *Journal of Applied Developmental Psychology, 36,* 18–29.

78. Błachnio, A., Przepiórka, A., & Pantic, I. (2015). Internet use, Facebook intrusion, and depression: Results of a cross-sectional study. *European Psychiatry, 30*(6), 681–684.

79. Müller, K. W., Dreier, M., Beutel, M. E., Duven, E., Giralt, S., & Wölfling, K. (2016). A hidden type of Internet addiction? Intense and addictive use of social networking sites in adolescents. *Computers in Human Behavior, 55,* 172–177.

80. Przybylski, A. K., & Weinstein, N. (2017). A large-scale test of the Goldilocks Hypothesis: Quantifying the relations between digital-screen use and the mental well-being of adolescents. *Psychological Science, 28*(2), 204–215.

81. Rosenheck, R. (2008). Fast food consumption and increased caloric intake: A systematic review of a trajectory towards weight gain and obesity risk. *Obesity Reviews, 9*(6), 535–547.

82. Gazzaley, A., & Rosen, L. D. (2016). *The distracted mind: Ancient brains in a high-tech world.* Cambridge, MA: MIT Press.

83. Graham, P. (n.d.). The acceleration of addictiveness. Retrieved from http://www.paulgraham.com/addiction.html

Chapter 5

1. Sleeper movie quotes. Retrieved from http://www.explore-science-fiction-movies.com/sleeper-movie-quotes.html#axzz4JVQH0XKk

2. Teicholz, N. (2015). The scientific report guiding the US dietary guidelines: Is it scientific? *British Medical Journal (Clinical Research Ed.), 351,* h4962. doi: 10.1136/bmj.h4962

3. Wartella, E., Richert, R. A., & Robb, M. B. (2010). Babies, television and videos: How did we get here? *Developmental Review, 30*(2), 116–127. doi: 10.1016/j.dr.2010.03.008

4. Media and young minds. (2016). Retrieved from http://pediatrics. aappublications.org/content/early/2016/10/19/peds.2016-2591

5. Christakis, D. (2009). The effects of infant media usage: What do we know and what should we learn? *Acta Paediatrica, 98*(1), 8–16. http://doi.org/10.1111/j.1651-2227.2008.01027.x

6. DeLoache, J.S., Chiong, C., Sherman, K., Islam, N. Vanderborght, M., Troseth, G.L., . . . O'Doherty, K. (2010). Do babies learn from baby media? *Psychological Science, 21*, 1570–1574.

7. Zimmerman, F. J., Christakis, D. A., & Meltzoff, A. N. (2007). Associations between media viewing and language development in children under age 2 years. *The Journal of Pediatrics, 151*, 364–368.

8. Ferguson, C. J., & Donnellan, M. B. (2014). Is the association between children's baby video viewing and poor language development robust? A reanalysis of Zimmerman, Christakis, and Meltzoff (2007). *Developmental Psychology, 50*, 129–137.

9. Courage, M. L., & Setliff, A. E. (2010). When babies watch television: Attention-getting, attention-holding, and the implications for learning from video material. *Developmental Review, 30*, 220–238.

10. Pempek, T. A., Demers, L. B., Hanson, K. G., Kirkorian, H. L., & Anderson, D. R. (2011). The impact of infant-directed videos on parent-child interaction. *Journal of Applied Developmental Psychology, 32*, 10–19.

11. Mayfield, M., Chen, C., Harwood, D., Rennie, T., & Tannock, M. (2009). Community play spaces: Promoting young children's play. *Canadian Children, 34*(1), 4–12.

12. Espinosa, P., & Clemente, M. (2013). Self-transcendence and self-oriented perspective as mediators between video game playing and aggressive behaviour in teenagers. *Journal of Community & Applied Social Psychology, 23*(1), 68–80.

13. Neuman, S. B. (1988). The displacement effect: Assessing the relation between television viewing and reading performance. *Reading Research Quarterly, 23*, 414–440.

14. Mayfield, M. (1982, November 10). Video games only fit for old. *USA Today*, p. A1.

15. Secunda, V. (1983). Pac Man is (a) gobbling or (b) nourishing our kids. *TV Guide, 31*(2), 10.

16. Cooper, J., & Mackie, D. (1986). Video games and aggression in children. *Journal of Applied Social Psychology, 16*(8), 726–744.

17. Breuer, J., Festl, R., & Quandt, T. (2014). Aggression and preference for first-person shooter and action games: Data from a large-scale survey of German gamers aged 14 and above. *Communication Research Reports, 31*(2), 183–196.

18. DeLisi, M., Vaughn, M. G., Gentile, D. A., Anderson, C. A., & Shook, J. J. (2013). Violent video games, delinquency, and youth violence: New evidence. *Youth Violence and Juvenile Justice, 11*(2), 132–142.

19. Adachi, P., Allaire, J. C., Anderson, J., Annetta, L., Arnett, J. J., Arsenault, D., & Zerovnik, G. (2013). Scholars' open statement to the APA task force in violent media. Retrieved from https://osf.io/dpe9a/

20. Szycik, G. R., Mohammadi, B., Münte, T. F., & Te Wildt, B. T. (2017). Lack of evidence that neural empathic responses are blunted in excessive users of violent video games: An fMRI study. *Frontiers in Psychology, 8.* doi: 10.3389/fpsyg.2017.00174

21. Unsworth, G., Devilly, G. J., & Ward, T. (2007). The effect of playing violent video games on adolescents: Should parents be quaking in their boots? *Psychology, Crime & Law, 13*(4), 383–394.

22. Ferguson, C. J., Trigani, B., Pilato, S., Miller, S., Foley, K., & Barr, H. (2016). Violent video games don't increase hostility in teens, but they do stress girls out. *Psychiatric Quarterly, 87*(1), 49–56.

23. Ferguson, C. J. (2015). Do angry birds make for angry children? A meta-analysis of video game influences on children's and adolescents' aggression, mental health, prosocial behavior, and academic performance. *Perspectives on Psychological Science, 10*(5), 646–666.

24. Schwartz, J. A., & Beaver, K. M. (2016). Revisiting the association between television viewing in adolescence and contact with the criminal justice system in adulthood. *Journal of Interpersonal Violence, 31*(14), 2387–2411.

25. Adachi, P. J., & Willoughby, T. (2013). Demolishing the competition: The longitudinal link between competitive video games, competitive gambling, and aggression. *Journal of Youth and Adolescence, 42*(7), 1090–1104.

26. Bajovic, M. (2013). Violent video gaming and moral reasoning in adolescents: Is there an association? *Educational Media International, 50*(3), 177–191.

27. Gentile, D. A., & Gentile, J. R. (2008). Violent video games as exemplary teachers: A conceptual analysis. *Journal of Youth and Adolescence, 37*(2), 127–141.

28. Ferguson, C. J. (2015). Do angry birds make for angry children? A meta-analysis of video game influences on children's and adolescents' aggression, mental health, prosocial behavior, and academic performance. *Perspectives on Psychological Science, 10*(5), 646–666.

29. Bureau of Justice Statistics, US Department of Justice. (2015). Criminal victimization. Retrieved from https://www.bjs.gov/content/pub/pdf/cv15.pdf

30. Sickmund, M., & Puzzanchera, C. (2014). Juvenile offenders and victims: 2014 national report. Retrieved from https://www.ojjdp.gov/ojstatbb/nr2014/

31. Pinker, S. (2012). *The better angels of our nature: Why violence has declined.* New York: Penguin Books.

32. Adachi, P., Allaire, J. C., Anderson, J., Annetta, L., Arnett, J. J., Arsenault, D., & Zerovnik, G. (2013). Scholars' open statement to the APA task force in violent media. Retrieved from https://osf.io/dpe9a/

33. Statistia. (2017). All time unit sales of selected games in Call of Duty franchise worldwide as of June 2017. Retrieved from https://www.statista.com/statistics/321374/global-all-time-unit-sales-call-of-duty-games/

34. Olson, C. K., Kutner, L. A., Warner, D. E., Almerigi, J. B., Baer, L., Nicholi, A. M., & Beresin, E. V. (2007). Factors correlated with violent video game use by adolescent boys and girls. *Journal of Adolescent Health, 41*(1), 77–83.

35. McVey, C. G., Jr. (1997). The child's experience of video game play. Unpublished doctoral dissertation, The University of Texas at Austin.

36. Brooks, M. C. (2000, June). Press start: Exploring the effects of violent video games on boys. *Dissertation Abstracts International, 60,* 6419.

37. Ferguson, C. J. (2015). Do angry birds make for angry children? A meta-analysis of video game influences on children's and adolescents' aggression, mental health, prosocial behavior, and academic performance. *Perspectives on Psychological Science, 10*(5), 646–666.

38. Przybylski, A. K., Deci, E. L., Rigby, C. S., & Ryan, R. M. (2014). Competence-impeding electronic games and players' aggressive feelings, thoughts, and behaviors. *Journal of Personality and Social Psychology, 106*(3), 441.

39. Caunt, B. S., Franklin, J., Brodaty, N. E., & Brodaty, H. (2013). Exploring the causes of subjective well-being: A content analysis of peoples' recipes for long-term happiness. *Journal of Happiness Studies, 14*(2), 475–499.

40. Bedford, R., Pickles, A., Sharp, H., Wright, N., & Hill, J. (2015). Reduced face preference in infancy: A developmental precursor to callous-unemotional traits? *Biological Psychiatry, 78,* 144–150.

41. Uhls, Y. T., Michikyan, M., Morris, J., Garcia, D., Small, G. W., Zgourou, E., & Greenfield, P. M. (2014). Five days at outdoor education camp without screens improves preteen skills with nonverbal emotional cues. *Computers in Human Behavior, 39,* 387–392.

42. Ryan, R. M., & Deci, E. L. (2000). Self-determination theory and the facilitation of intrinsic motivation, social development, and well-being. *American Psychologist, 55,* 68–78.

43. Tokuna, R. S., & Rains, S. A. (2016). A review and meta-analysis examining conceptual and operational definitions of problematic Internet use. *Human Communication Research, 42,* 165–199.

44. Zelenski, J. M., & Nisbet, E. K. (2014). Happiness and feeling connected: The distinct role of nature relatedness. *Environment and Behavior, 46*(1), 3–23.

45. Nelson, L. J., Coyne, S. M., Howard, E., & Clifford, B. N. (2016). Withdrawing to a virtual world: Associations between subtypes of withdrawal, media use, and maladjustment in emerging adults. *Developmental Psychology, 52,* 933–942.

46. Steers, M.-L. N., Wickham, R. E., & Acitelli, L. K. (2014). Seeing everyone else's highlight reels: How Facebook usage is linked to depressive symptoms. *Journal of Social and Clinical Psychology, 33*(8), 701–731. https://doi.org/10.1521/jscp.2014.33.8.701

47. Sagioglou, C., & Greitemeyer, T. (2014). Facebook's emotional consequences: Why Facebook causes a decrease in mood and why people still use it. *ResearchGate.* https://doi.org/http://dx.doi.org/10.1016/j.chb.2014.03.003

48. Przybylski, A. K., Murayama, K., DeHaan, C. R., & Gladwell, V. (2013). Motivational, emotional, and behavioral correlates of fear of missing out. *Computers in Human Behavior, 29*(4), 1841–1848.

49. Miller, E., & Almon, J. (2009). Crisis in the kindergarten: Why children need to play in school. College Park, MD: Alliance for Childhood.

50. Haughton, C., Aiken, M., & Cheevers, C. (2015). Cyber babies. *Psychology Research, 5,* 504–518.

51. Kardaras, N. (2016, September 1). Generation Z: Online and at risk? Retrieved from https://www.scientificamerican.com/article/generation-z-online-and-at-risk/

52. Peslak, A. R. (2003). A firm level study of information technology productivity using financial and market based measures. *Journal of Computer Information Systems, 43*(4), 72–80.

53. Christakis, D. A., Ramirez, J. S. B., & Ramirez, J. M. (2012). Overstimulation of newborn mice leads to behavioral differences and deficits in cognitive performance. *Scientific Reports, 2,* 546. http://doi.org/10.1038/srep00546

54. Swing, E. L., Gentile, D. A., Anderson, C. A., & Walsh, D. A. (2010). Television and video game exposure and the development of attention problems. *Pediatrics, 126,* 214–221.

55. Schmidt, M. E., & Vandewater, E. A. (2008). Media and attention, cognition, and school achievement. *The Future of Children, 18*(1), 63–85.

56. Gentile, D. A., Swing, E. L., Lim, C. G., & Khoo, A. (2012). Video game playing, attention problems, and impulsiveness: Evidence of bidirectional causality. *Psychology of Popular Media Culture, 1*(1), 62.

57. Ward, A. F., Duke, K., Gneezy, A., & Bos, M. W. (2017). Brain drain: The mere presence of one's own smartphone reduces available cognitive capacity. *Journal of the Association for Consumer Research, 2,* n.p. Published online. Retrieved from http://dx.doi.org/10.1086/691462

58. Becker, M. W., Alzahabi, R., & Hopwood, C. J. (2013). Media multitasking is associated with symptoms of depression and social anxiety. *Cyberpsychology, Behavior, and Social Networking, 16*(2), 132–135.

59. Gazzaley, A., & Rosen, L. D. (2016). *The distracted mind: Ancient brains in a high-tech world.* Cambridge, MA: MIT Press.

60. Carrier, L. M., Cheever, N. A., Rosen, L. D., Benitez, S., & Chang, J. (2009). Multitasking across generations: Multitasking choices and difficulty ratings in three generations of Americans. *Computers in Human Behavior, 25*(2), 483–489.

61. Dux, P. E., & Marois, R. (2009). The attentional blink: A review of data and theory. *Attention, Perception, & Psychophysics, 71*(8), 1683–1700.

62. Gazzaley, A., & Rosen, L. D. (2016). *The distracted mind: Ancient brains in a high-tech world.* Cambridge, MA: MIT Press.

63. Carrier, L. M., Cheever, N. A., Rosen, L. D., Benitez, S., & Chang, J. (2009). Multitasking across generations: Multitasking choices and difficulty ratings in three generations of Americans. *Computers in Human Behavior, 25*(2), 483–489.

64. Turkle, S. (2015). *Reclaiming conversation: The power of talk in a digital age.* New York: Penguin.

65. Andrews, S., Ellis, D. A., Shaw, H., & Piwek, L. (2015). Beyond self-report: Tools to compare estimated and real-world smartphone use. *PloS One, 10*(10), e0139004.

66. Ward, A. F., Duke, K., Gneezy, A., & Bos, M. W. (2017). Brain drain: The mere presence of one's own smartphone reduces available cognitive capacity. *Journal of the Association for Consumer Research, 2,* n.p. Published online. Retrieved from http://dx.doi.org/10.1086/691462

67. Carrier, L. M., Cheever, N. A., Rosen, L. D., Benitez, S., & Chang, J. (2009). Multitasking across generations: Multitasking choices and difficulty ratings in three generations of Americans. *Computers in Human Behavior, 25*(2), 483–489.

68. Sanbonmatsu, D. M., Strayer, D. L., Medeiros-Ward, N., & Watson, J. M. (2013). Who multi-tasks and why? Multi-tasking ability, perceived multitasking ability, impulsivity, and sensation seeking. *PloS One, 8*(1), e54402.

69. Denworth, L. (2015, July/August). The social power of touch. *Scientific American Mind, 26,* 30–38.

Chapter 6

1. Strathearn, L. (2011). Maternal neglect: Oxytocin, dopamine and the neurobiology of attachment. *Journal of Neuroendocrinology, 23*(11), 1054–1065.

2. Burkett, J. P., & Young, L. J. (2012). The behavioral, anatomical and pharmacological parallels between social attachment, love and addiction. *Psychopharmacology, 224*(1), 1–26.

3. Kross, E., Berman, M. G., Mischel, W., Smith, E. E., & Wager, T. D. (2011). Social rejection shares somatosensory representations with physical pain. *Proceedings of the National Academy of Sciences, 108*(15), 6270–6275.

4. Kaminski, J. W., Valle, L. A., Filene, J. H., & Boyle, C. L. (2008). A meta-analytic review of components associated with parent training program effectiveness. *Journal of Abnormal Child Psychology, 36*(4), 567–589.

5. Karavasilis, L., Doyle, A. B., & Markiewicz, D. (2003). Associations between parenting style and attachment to mother in middle childhood and adolescence. *International Journal of Behavioral Development, 27*(2), 153–164.

6. Lau, R. R., Quadrel, M. J., & Hartman, K. A. (1990). Development and change of young adults' preventive health beliefs and behavior: Influence from parents and peers. *Journal of Health and Social Behavior, 31*(3), 240–259.

7. Deci, E. L., & Ryan, R. M. (2008). Self-determination theory: A macrotheory of human motivation, development, and health. *Canadian Psychology/ Psychologie canadienne, 49*(3), 182.

8. Keltner, D., Gruenfeld, D. H., & Anderson, C. (2003). Power, approach, and inhibition. *Psychological Review, 110*(2), 265.

9. Bowlby, J. (1982). *Attachment and loss*, Vol. I. New York: Basic Books.

10. Ainsworth, M. D. S., Blehar, M. S., Waters, E., & Wall, S. (1978). *Patterns of attachment: A psychological study of the strange situation*. Hillsdale, NJ: Lawrence Erlbaum.

11. Levine, E. (2011). Baumrind's parenting styles. In S. Goldstein & J. A. Naglieri (Eds.), *Encyclopedia of child behavior and development* (pp. 213–215). Boston: Springer.

12. Baumrind, D. (1991). The influence of parenting style on adolescent competence and substance use. *The Journal of Early Adolescence, 11*(1), 56–95.

13. Turner, E. A., Chandler, M., & Heffer, R. W. (2009). The influence of parenting styles, achievement motivation, and self-efficacy on academic performance in college students. *Journal of College Student Development, 50*(3), 337–346.

14. DeVore, E. R., & Ginsburg, K. R. (2005). The protective effects of good parenting on adolescents. *Current Opinion in Pediatrics, 17*(4), 460–465.

15. Joussemet, M., Landry, R., & Koestner, R. (2008). A self-determination theory perspective on parenting. *Canadian Psychology/Psychologie canadienne, 49*(3), 194.

16. Soenens, B., & Vansteenkiste, M. (2010). A theoretical upgrade of the concept of parental psychological control: Proposing new insights on the basis of self-determination theory. *Developmental Review, 30*(1), 74–99.

17. Landreth, G. L. (2012). *Play therapy: The art of the relationship* (3rd ed.). New York: Routledge.

18. Greene, R. (2016). Lives in the balance. Retrieved from http://www.livesinthebalance.org/about-lives-in-the-balance

19. Ryan, R. M., & Deci, E. L. (2017). *Self-determination theory: Basic psychological needs in motivation, development, and wellness*. New York: Guilford Press.

Chapter 7

1. Leung, J. P., & Leung, K. (1992). Life satisfaction, self-concept, and relationship with parents in adolescence. *Journal of Youth and Adolescence, 21*(6), 653–665.

2. Karavasilis, L., Doyle, A. B., & Markiewicz, D. (2003). Associations between parenting style and attachment to mother in middle childhood and adolescence. *International Journal of Behavioral Development, 27*(2), 153–164.

3. Kaminski, J. W., Valle, L. A., Filene, J. H., & Boyle, C. L. (2008). A meta-analytic review of components associated with parent training program effectiveness. *Journal of Abnormal Child Psychology, 36*(4), 567–589.

4. Lin, C. H., Lin, S. L., & Wu, C. P. (2009). The effects of parental monitoring and leisure boredom on adolescents' Internet addiction. *Adolescence, 44*(176), 993.

5. Gottman, J. M., & Levenson, R. W. (1999). What predicts change in marital interaction over time? A study of alternative models. *Family Process, 38*(2), 143–158.

6. Losada, M., & Heaphy, E. (2004). The role of positivity and connectivity in the performance of business teams: A nonlinear dynamics model. *American Behavioral Scientist, 47*(6), 740–765.

7. Kaminski, J. W., Valle, L. A., Filene, J. H., & Boyle, C. L. (2008). A meta-analytic review of components associated with parent training program effectiveness. *Journal of Abnormal Child Psychology, 36*(4), 567–589.

8. Dweck, C. (2016). *Mindset, updated edition: Changing the way you think to fulfil your potential.* New York: Random House.

9. Ryan, R. M., & Deci, E. L. (2000). Self-determination theory and the facilitation of intrinsic motivation, social development, and well-being. *American Psychologist, 55*, 68–78.

10. selfdeterminationtheory.org. (2017). Theory. Retrieved from http:// selfdeterminationtheory.org/theory/

11. Joussemet, M., Landry, R., & Koestner, R. (2008). A self-determination theory perspective on parenting. *Canadian Psychology/Psychologie canadienne, 49*(3), 194.

12. Sanders, W., Parent, J., Forehand, R., Sullivan, A. D., & Jones, D. J. (2016). Parental perceptions of technology and technology-focused parenting: Associations with youth screen time. *Journal of Applied Developmental Psychology, 44*, 28–38.

13. Brehm, J. W. (1989). Psychological reactance: Theory and applications. *Advances in Consumer Research, 16*, 72–75.

14. Bass, B. M. (1985). Leadership: Good, better, best. *Organizational Dynamics, 13*(3), 26–40.

15. Vaala, S. E., & Bleakley, A. (2015). Monitoring, mediating, and modeling: Parental influence on adolescent computer and Internet use in the United States. *Journal of Children and Media, 9*(1), 40–57.

16. Sanders, W., Parent, J., Forehand, R., Sullivan, A. D., & Jones, D. J. (2016). Parental perceptions of technology and technology-focused parenting: Associations with youth screen time. *Journal of Applied Developmental Psychology, 44*, 28–38.

17. Neff, K. D., Kirkpatrick, K. L., & Rude, S. S. (2007). Self-compassion and adaptive psychological functioning. *Journal of Research in Personality, 41*(1), 139–154.

18. Germer, C. K. (2009). *The mindful path to self-compassion: Freeing yourself from destructive thoughts and emotions.* New York: Guilford Press.

Chapter 8

1. Sanders, W., Parent, J., Forehand, R., Sullivan, A. D., & Jones, D. J. (2016). Parental perceptions of technology and technology-focused parenting: Associations with youth screen time. *Journal of Applied Developmental Psychology, 44*, 28–38.

2. Vaala, S. E., & Bleakley, A. (2015). Monitoring, mediating, and modeling: Parental influence on adolescent computer and Internet use in the United States. *Journal of Children and Media, 9*(1), 40–57.

3. Przybylski, A. K., Weinstein, N., Ryan, R. M., & Rigby, C. S. (2009). Having to versus wanting to play: Background and consequences of harmonious versus obsessive engagement in video games. *CyberPsychology & Behavior, 12*(5), 485–492.

4. Ryan, R. M., & Deci, E. L. (2017). *Self-determination theory: Basic psychological needs in motivation, development, and wellness.* New York: Guilford Press.

5. Przybylski, A. K., Murayama, K., DeHaan, C. R., & Gladwell, V. (2013). Motivational, emotional, and behavioral correlates of fear of missing out. *Computers in Human Behavior, 29*(4), 1841–1848.

6. Vaala, S. E., & Bleakley, A. (2015). Monitoring, mediating, and modeling: Parental influence on adolescent computer and Internet use in the United States. *Journal of Children and Media, 9*(1), 40–57.

7. Vaala, S. E., & Bleakley, A. (2015). Monitoring, mediating, and modeling: Parental influence on adolescent computer and Internet use in the United States. *Journal of Children and Media, 9*(1), 40–57.

8. Sanders, W., Parent, J., Forehand, R., Sullivan, A. D., & Jones, D. J. (2016). Parental perceptions of technology and technology-focused parenting:

Associations with youth screen time. *Journal of Applied Developmental Psychology, 44*, 28–38.

9. Young, K., Regan, M., & Hammer, M. (2007). Driver distraction: A review of the literature. *Distracted driving.* Retrieved from https://www.monash.edu/__data/assets/pdf_file/0007/217177/muarc206.pdf

10. Baird, B., Smallwood, J., Mrazek, M. D., Kam, J. W., Franklin, M. S., & Schooler, J. W. (2012). Inspired by distraction: Mind wandering facilitates creative incubation. *Psychological Science, 23*(10), 1117–1122.

11. Aiken, M. (2017). *The cyber effect: A pioneering cyberpsychologist explains how human behavior changes online.* New York: Spiegel & Grau.

12. Ruston, D. (2016). *Screenagers* [Film]. https://www.screenagersmovie.com/

13. Everything you need to know about parental controls. (2016, July 14). Retrieved from https://www.commonsensemedia.org/blog/everything-you-need-to-know-about-parental-controls

14. Ropelato, J. (2006). Internet pornography statistics. Retrieved from http://www.ministryoftruth.me.uk/wp-content/uploads/2014/03/IFR2013.pdf

15. Horvath, M. A. H., Alys, L., Massey, K., Pina, A., Scally, M., & Adler, J. R. (2014). Basically . . . Porn is everywhere: A rapid evidence assessment of the effects that access and exposure to pornography have on children and young people. Middlesex University/Children's Commissioner. Retrieved from http://www.mdx.ac.uk/__data/assets/pdf_file/0026/48545/BasicallyporniseverywhereReport.pdf

16. Schiffrin, H. H., Liss, M., Miles-McLean, H., Geary, K. A., Erchull, M. J., & Tashner, T. (2014). Helping or hovering? The effects of helicopter parenting on college students' well-being. *Journal of Child and Family Studies, 23*(3), 548–557.

17. Kerr, M., Stattin, H., & Burk, W. J. (2010). A reinterpretation of parental monitoring in longitudinal perspective. *Journal of Research on Adolescence, 20*(1), 39–64.

18. Kerr, M., Stattin, H., & Burk, W. J. (2010). A reinterpretation of parental monitoring in longitudinal perspective. *Journal of Research on Adolescence, 20*(1), 39–64.

19. Xu, Z., Turel, O., & Yuan, Y. (2012). Online game addiction among adolescents: Motivation and prevention factors. *European Journal of Information Systems, 21*(3), 321–340.

20. Lin, C. H., Lin, S. L., & Wu, C. P. (2009). The effects of parental monitoring and leisure boredom on adolescents' internet addiction. *Adolescence, 44*(176), 993.

21. Kabat-Zinn, J. (2003). Mindfulness-based interventions in context: Past, present, and future. *Clinical Psychology: Science and Practice, 10*(2), 144–156.

22. McLaughlin, K. A., Borkovec, T. D., & Sibrava, N. J. (2007). The effects of worry and rumination on affect states and cognitive activity. *Behavior Therapy, 38*(1), 23–38.

23. Barden, R. C., Garber, J., Leiman, B., Ford, M. E., & Masters, J. C. (1985). Factors governing the effective remediation of negative affect and its cognitive and behavioral consequences. *Journal of Personality and Social Psychology, 49*(4), 1040.

24. Eberth, J., & Sedlmeier, P. (2012). The effects of mindfulness meditation: A meta-analysis. *Mindfulness, 3*(3), 174–189.

25. Greenberg, M. T., & Harris, A. R. (2012). Nurturing mindfulness in children and youth: Current state of research. *Child Development Perspectives, 6*(2), 161–166.

26. Raes, F., Griffith, J. W., Van der Gucht, K., & Williams, J. M. G. (2014). School-based prevention and reduction of depression in adolescents: A cluster-randomized controlled trial of a mindfulness group program. *Mindfulness, 5*(5), 477–486.

27. Bögels, S. M., Lehtonen, A., & Restifo, K. (2010). Mindful parenting in mental health care. *Mindfulness, 1*(2), 107–120.

28. Duncan, L. G., Coatsworth, J. D., & Greenberg, M. T. (2009). A model of mindful parenting: Implications for parent–child relationships and prevention research. *Clinical Child and Family Psychology Review, 12*(3), 255–270.

29. Shonin, E., Van Gordon, W., & Griffiths, M. D. (2014). Mindfulness as a treatment for behavioural addiction. *Journal of Addiction Research & Therapy, 5*(1). Retrieved from http://irep.ntu.ac.uk/id/eprint/25827/1/221563_PubSub2930_Griffiths.pdf

30. Levy, D. M. (2016). *Mindful tech: How to bring balance to our digital lives.* New Haven, CT: Yale University Press.

31. Tang, Y. Y., Hölzel, B. K., & Posner, M. I. (2015). The neuroscience of mindfulness meditation. *Nature Reviews. Neuroscience, 16*(4), 213.

32. Greenfield, D. (2010). The addictive properties of internet usage. In Young, K. S., & De Abreu, C. N. (Eds.). *Internet addiction: A handbook and guide to evaluation and treatment* (p. 133–153). New York: John Wiley & Sons.

33. Hoorens, V. (1993). Self-enhancement and superiority biases in social comparison. *European Review of Social Psychology, 4*(1), 113–139.

34. Ward, A. F., Duke, K., Gneezy, A., & Bos, M. W. (2017). Brain drain: The mere presence of one's own smartphone reduces available cognitive capacity. *Journal of the Association for Consumer Research, 2*(2), 140–154.

35. Wei, R., & Lo, V. H. (2013). Examining sexting's effect among adolescent mobile phone users. *International Journal of Mobile Communications, 11*(2), 176–193.

Chapter 9

1. Manitoba Public Insurance. (2016). Retrieved from https://www.mpi.mb.ca/en/Rd-Safety/Distracted-Driving/Pages/DDOverview.aspx

2. Greene, R. W., Ablon, J. S., Goring, J. C., Raezer-Blakely, L., Markey, J., Monuteaux, M. C., . . . Rabbitt, S. (2004). Effectiveness of collaborative problem solving in affectively dysregulated children with oppositional-defiant disorder: Initial findings. *Journal of Consulting and Clinical Psychology, 72*(6), 1157.

3. Ollendick, T. H., Greene, R. W., Austin, K. E., Fraire, M. G., Halldorsdottir, T., Allen, K. B., . . . Noguchi, R. J. (2016). Parent management training and collaborative and proactive solutions: A randomized control trial for oppositional youth. *Journal of Clinical Child & Adolescent Psychology, 45*(5), 591–604.

Chapter 10

1. Psycho dad shreds video games. Retrieved from https://www.youtube.com/watch?v=EglOsfErtaE

2. American Psychiatric Association. (2013). *Diagnostic and statistical manual of mental disorders* (5th ed.). Washington, DC: Author.

3. Internet gaming disorder. Retrieved from www.DSM5.org/documents/InternetGamingDisorderFactSheet

4. Pies, R. (2009). Should DSM-V designate "Internet Addiction" a mental disorder? *Psychiatry, 6*, 31–37.

5. Love, T., Laier, C., Brand, M., Hatch, L., & Hajela, R. (2015). Neuroscience of Internet pornography addiction: A review and update. *Behavioral Sciences, 5*(3), 388–433.

6. Andreassen, C. S., Billieux, J., Griffiths, M. D., Kuss, D. J., et al. (2016). The relationship between addictive use of social media and video games

and symptoms of psychiatric disorders: A large-scale cross-sectional study. *Addictive Behaviors, 64,* 297–293.

7. Gentile, D. A., Swing, E. L., Lim, C. G., & Khoo, A. (2012). Video game playing, attention problems, and impulsiveness: Evidence of bidirectional causality. *Psychology of Popular Media Culture, 1*(1), 62.

8. Master of his virtual domain. (2013, December 22). *New York Times.* Retrieved from http://www.nytimes.com/2013/12/22/technology/master-of-his-virtual-domain.html

9. reSTART. Retrieved from https://netaddictionrecovery.com/

10. Winkler, A., Dörsing, B., Rief, W., Shen, Y., et al. (2013). Treatment of Internet addiction: A meta-analysis. *Clinical Psychology Review, 33,* 317–329.

11. Internet Addiction Test. Retrieved from http://netaddiction.com/internet-addiction-test/

12. Perfect, M. M., Levine-Donnerstein, D., Archbold, K., Goodwin, J. L., & Quan, S. F. (2014). The contribution of sleep problems to academic and psychosocial functioning. *Psychology in the Schools, 51*(3), 273–295.

13. Sexton, C. E., Storsve, A. B., Walhovd, K. B., Johansen-Berg, H., & Fjell, A. M. (2014). Poor sleep quality is associated with increased cortical atrophy in community-dwelling adults. *Neurology, 83,* 967–973.

14. Dealing with black and white thinking. Retrieved from http://www.strongbonds.jss.org.au/workers/youngpeople/thinking.html

15. Siegel, D. J. (2015). *Brainstorm: The power and purpose of the teenage brain.* New York: Penguin.

16. Messer, S. B., & Wampold, B.E. (2002). Let's face the facts: Common factors are more potent than specific therapy ingredients. *Clinical Psychology: Science and Practice, 9,* 21–25.

Chapter 11

1. OECD. (2015), *Students, computers and learning: Making the connection.* Paris: OECD Publishing. http://dx.doi.org/10.1787/9789264239555-en

2. Pinker, S. (2015, January 30). Can students have too much tech? *New York Times.* Retrieved from http://www.nytimes.com/2015/01/30/opinion/can-students-have-toomuchtech.html?_r=0

3. http://www.urban.org/research/publication/scaling-digital-divide-home-computer-technology-and-student-achievement

4. Youg, S. R., Maddocks, D. L. S., & Keith, T. Z. (2017, February). *Time well spent: Adolescents' homework, screen time, and math achievement.* Poster presented at the annual conference for the National Association of School Psychologists, San Antonio, TX.

5. Ink on paper: Some notes on notetaking. http://www.psychologicalscience. org/news/were-only-human/ink-on-paper-some-notes-on-note-taking. html#.WHQY1JJWLYE

6. Haßler, B., Major, L., & Hennessy, S. (2016). Tablet use in schools: A critical review of the evidence for learning outcomes. *Journal of Computer Assisted Learning, 32,* 139–156. doi: 10.1111/jcal.12123

7. Pinker, S. (2015, January 30). Can students have too much tech? *New York Times.* Retrieved from http://www.nytimes.com/2015/01/30/opinion/can-students-have-too-much-tech.html?_r=0

8. Preston, J. P, Wiebe, S., Gabriel, M., McAuley, A., Campbell, B., & MacDonald, R. (2015). Benefits and challenges of technology in high schools: A voice from educational leaders with a Freire echo. *Interchange, 46,* 169–185.

9. Beland, L.-P., & Murphy, R. (2015). *Ill communication: Technology, distraction and student performance.* Retrieved from https://timedotcom.files. wordpress.com/2015/05/dp1350.pdf

10. Lines, C., Miller, G. E., & Arthur-Stanley, A. (2011). *The power of Family-School Partnering (FSP): A practical guide for school mental health professionals and educators.* New York: Routledge.

11. Ward, A. F., Duke, K., Gneezy, A., & Bos, M. W. (2017). Brain drain: The mere presence of one's own smartphone reduces available cognitive capacity. *Journal of the Association for Consumer Research, 2*(2), 140–154.

12. Newport, C. (2016). *Deep work: Rules for focused success in a distracted world.* New York: Grand Central Publishing.

13. Cloos, K., & Turkewitz, J. (2015). Hundreds of nude photos jolt Colorado school. *New York Times.* Retrieved from http://www.nytimes.com/2015/11/07/us/colorado-students-caught-trading-nude-photos-by-the-hundreds.html?_r=0

14. Mitchell, K. J., Finkelhor, D., Jones, L. M., & Wolak, J. (2011). Prevalence and characteristics of youth sexting: A national study. *Pediatrics, 129,* 13–20. doi: 10.1542/peds.2011-1730

15. McKenchnie, A. (n.d.). Majority of minors engage in sexting, unaware of harsh legal consequences. Retrieved from http://drexel.edu/now/archive/2014/June/Sexting-Study/

16. Selkie, E. M., Fales, J. L., & Moreno, M. A. (2016). Cyberbullying prevalence among US middle and high school-aged adolescents: A systematic review and quality assessment. *Journal of Adolescent Health, 2,* 125. doi: 10.1016/j.jadohealth.2015.09.026

17. Lush, T. (September 14, 2013). Florida girl Rebecca Ann Sedwick, 12, was bullied for months online before suicide. Retrieved from https://www.nbcmiami.com/news/Florida-Girl-Rebecca-Ann-Sedwick-12-Was-Bullied-for-Months-Before-Suicide-223756111.html

18. Kerr, M., Stattin, H., & Burk, W. J. (2010). A reinterpretation of parental monitoring in longitudinal perspective. *Journal of Research on Adolescence, 20*(1), 39–64.

19. Essential elements of digital citizenship. Retrieved from https://www.iste.org/explore/ArticleDetail?articleid=101

Chapter 12

1. Agrawal, A., & Lynskey, M. T. (2008). Are there genetic influences on addiction: Evidence from family, adoption and twin studies. *Addiction, 103*(7), 1069–1081.

2. Schwartz, J. A., & Beaver, K. M. (2016). Revisiting the association between television viewing in adolescence and contact with the criminal justice system in adulthood. *Journal of Interpersonal Violence, 31*(14), 2387–2411.

3. Grant, J. E., Potenza, M. N., Weinstein, A., & Gorelick, D. A. (2010). Introduction to behavioral addictions. *The American Journal of Drug and Alcohol Abuse, 36*(5), 233–241.

Appendix 2

1. National Safety Council. (n.d.). Pedestrian safety. Retrieved from http://www.nsc.org/learn/safety-knowledge/Pages/news-and-resources-pedestrian-safety.aspx

2. Your wearable won't help you lose weight. (n.d.). Retrieved from http://time.com/4501018/wearable-weight-loss/

3. Harvard Health Publications. (n.d.). Blue light has a dark side. Retrieved from http://www.health.harvard.edu/staying-healthy/blue-light-has-a-dark-side

Appendix 3

1. American Academy of Pediatricians. Retrieved from http://pediatrics.
aappublications.org/content/early/2016/10/19/peds.2016-2591

2. Rideout, V., Pai, S., & Saphir, M. (2015). *The Common Sense census: Media use by tweens and teens*. Common Sense Media. Retrieved from https://www.commonsensemedia.org/research/the-common-sense-census-media-use-by-tweens-and-teens

3. Gentile, D. A., Swing, E. L., Lim, C. G., & Khoo, A. (2012). Video game playing, attention problems, and impulsiveness: Evidence of bidirectional causality. *Psychology of Popular Media Culture, 1*(1), 62.

Index

Tables and figures are indicated by an italic *t* and *f* following the page/paragraph number.

Absent presence, 38
ACT model, 110–11
ADHD, 98–99
Aggression-video game violence
    relationships, 86–91
Aiken, Mary, 145
Airplane flights
    recommendations, 244
Alone together, 38, 219, 246
Antidepressants, 35
Anxiety disorders, 36, 44–46, 182
Apps, parental control,
    149–50, 256–57
Attachment theory, 105–6
Attention
    amounts of, 124–25
    awareness deficits, 100–101
    as caring and validation, 123–24
    diminished, happiness and, 43–44
    eye contact importance, 91–92
    mindfulness practice,
        154–59, 226–27
    multitasking, 43, 99–101, 261–63
    reasoning skills, 50–51
    task-switching, 99–100
    technology effects on,
        10, 43–44
    video games and, 98–99
Attentional blinks, 100
Authoritative parenting, 12
Autonomy, 59

Baby Einstein, 83–84
Baron Cohen, Sacha, 202
Bathrooms, device
    recommendations, 140, 243
Baumrind, Diana, 106, 109
Beaver, Kevin, 88–89
Bedrooms, device recommendations,
    139–40, 243
Bedtime recommendations, 140,
    243, 244
Blind spots, 158–59
Blue light spectrum exposure, 244
Branding, 75
Brooks, Mike, viii–ix

Child-adult interaction, importance of, 4–5
Choice as paradox, 40–41, 49
Clash of Clans, 183
Classical conditioning, 69–70, 74–76
Climate change, 50
Cognitive bias, 158–59
Cognitive capacity, smartphones reduction of, 43–44, 99, 158, 211
Cold turkey approach, 193
Collaborative and Proactive Solutions, 111
Compassion, 213
Competence, 59
Compulsive checking, 72–74, 76
Consequences
  logical, 169, 192, 266
  natural, 169, 192
  Red Light Level, 191–97
  Yellow Light Level, 168–76, 266–67
Contracts, 147–49, 252–53
Cortisol, 45
Cyberbullying, 215–18

Deci, Edward, 58, 67–68, 111, 119
Decision fatigue, 41–42
Dedicated music players, 242–43
Delayed gratification, 39–40
Depression
  emotional neglect in, 44–46
  social media impacts on, 43, 96
  technology impacts on, 10, 35, 36, 101, 182
Developmentally appropriate technology, 3, 84–85, 138, 243–44, 249

Device-charging area, 140, 243, 244
Digital divide, 29–30
Digital immigrants, 28–30, 54
Digital natives, 28–30
Displacement effect/ hypothesis, 47–49
Dopamine, 70, 71
Dose effects, 89, 90, 101, 182–83
Driving
  distracted, 73–74, 77, 164–65, 181, 219, 252
  infractions, consequences for, 192
  recommendations, 244–45, 252
  screen time limits, 142, 158–59
  texting while, 181, 185, 232, 252
Dunbar's number, 50
Dweck, Carol, 117

Educational videos, cognitive development and, 84–85
Emotional bonding importance, 44–46, 84–86, 105–6, 125–26, 217
Empathy development, 45–46
Entertainment Software Rating Board, 86, 130, 245, 254–55
Cline, Ernest, 22
Evolutionary heritage, 50–54, 93–94, 104–6
Eyal, Nir, 72, 73

Facebook, 6, 43, 96, 253–54
Family Assessment of Screen Time (FAST), 13, 97, 125, 237–39
Family-school partnering, 205–10
Ferguson, Christopher, 88
Fixed interval reinforcement, 69–70
FoMO (fear of missing out), 41, 74, 220

Gaming. *See* video games
Gentile, Douglas, 98
Goldilocks hypothesis, 77–78
Gottman, John/Julie, 117
Greene, Ross, 111, 167
Greenfield, David, 157
Green Light Level
  contracts, 147–49, 252–53
  home recommendations,
    139–40, 243–44
  mindfulness practice,
    154–59, 226–27
  monitoring, 151–54
  parental controls, 149–51, 256–57
  parental unity *vs.* division,
    141–43, 265–66
  plugging in activities, 132–35
  power/responsibility
    relationships, 143
  prevention, 129–32, 162, 173
  preventive
    recommendations, 137–39
  principles of, 15–16, 15*f*, 17*t*, 94,
    180, 230–31
  time limits, setting, 140–41,
    144–47, 175–76, 245–46,
    250–51, 260–61
  travel recommendations,
    140–41, 244–45
Growth mindset, 117–18

Happiness
  absent presence, 38
  attention, diminished, 43–44
  choice as paradox, 40–41, 49
  decision fatigue, 41–42
  delayed gratification, 39–40
  displacement effect/
    hypothesis, 47–49

  exercise in, 52–53
  factors affecting, 36–37, 224–25
  flow states disruption, 44
  hedonic adaptation/
    treadmill, 37–38
  mood, 95–97, 101
  sedentary lifestyles and, 19,
    38–39, 52–54
  sleep in, 38–39, 48
  social comparison effects
    on, 42–43
  social connectedness and, 33,
    44–46, 59–60
  societal, trends in, 35–36, 54–55
  technology as threat to, 9–11, 33,
    36, 49–51, 101–2
Harlow, Harry, 44–45
Hedonic adaptation/
  treadmill, 37–38
Home recommendations,
  139–40, 243–44
Hook Model, 72, 73

Infinite Warfare, 87
Information, 66
Instagram, 6, 253–54
Internet Addiction Test, 184
Internet addiction treatment
  programs, 183–84
Internet Gaming Disorder, 181–83

Kabat-Zinn, Jon, 154
Kilburn, John, 88

Lasser, Jon, ix
League of Legends, 47–48
Learning outcomes, 84–86
Logical consequences,
  169, 192, 266

Magic ratio, 117–19, 146–47
Marshmallow Test studies, 39–40
Mealtimes, device
    recommendations, 140,
    141, 243
Media violence effects, 86–91
Melatonin, 39
Mental health, technology impacts
    on, 10–11
MET (Mindful Engagement with
    Technology), 156–59
Mindfulness practice,
    154–59, 226–27
Minecraft, 20–21
Miswanting, 41
Monitoring, 151–54, 196, 257–59
Monotasking (unitasking), 139, 242
Mood effects, 95–97, 101. *See also*
    anxiety disorders; depression
Moore's Law, 21
Motivation, fostering, 119–21
Multitasking, 43, 99–101, 261–63

Natural consequences, 169, 192
Need density hypothesis, 68
Negativity bias, 66
Notifications, turning off,
    138–39, 241–42
Novelty, 65
Nucleus accumbens, 70

Obesity, 63–64, 78
O'Keefe, James, 52–53
Opportunity cost, 49, 223
Outdoors time, technology *vs.*, 23
Oxytocin, 45

The Paradox of Choice, 40
Parental controls, 149–51, 256–57

Parent-child collaboration, 167–76
Parenting styles
    adaptability in, 110–12
    authoritarian, 107t, 108, 110–11
    authoritative, 107t, 109–11, 113–
    14, 135, 145–47, 173–76
    coercion in behavior
    management, 119–21
    conflict, approaches to, 107–8
    flexibility in, 109
    intervening *vs.* not intervening,
    165, 189–91
    overview, 106, 112
    parental unity *vs.* division,
    141–43, 265–66
    permissive indulgent, 107t, 108–9
    permissive neglectful, 107t, 108
    role modelling, 12, 121–27,
    212–13, 229–30
    warmth continuum, 106–7, 107t
Patience, 213
Pavlov, Ivan, 74–75
Personal information, posting, 5
Pies, Ronald, 182
Pinker, Steven, 89
Plugging in activities, 132–35
Pokémon Go, 19–20
Pornography, 67, 149, 216, 263–65
Problematic Internet use, 95
Problematic media, 96
Productivity, screen time and,
    98–100, 182–83,
    210–11, 261–63
Przybylski, Andrew, 77–78
Psychological disorders,
    180–81, 194–97
Psychological needs, 58–59, 65,
    67–68, 72–74, 223
Psychological reactance, 120

Quality time, 114–15, 146–47

Ram Dass, 156
Red Light Level
    consequences, 191–97
    Internet addiction, 181–83
    monitoring, 152, 196
    parent-child collaboration, 194
    preventive strategies, 173
    principles of, 15f, 16, 17t, 232–33
    recreational vs. productive screen
        time, 193
    relationship, strategies
        from, 189–91
    screen privileges limitations, 194
    serious problems,
        180–81, 197–99
    serious problems, signs of,
        183–87, 194–96
    sleep deprivation, 185
    strong interventions, 173,
        179–80, 187–97
Relatedness, 59, 65, 105, 110
Relationships
    activities for building, 116
    building, 94, 228–30, 267–68
    classical conditioning effects on,
        69–70, 74–76
    cognitive load in maintenance
        of, 49–51
    conflicting research on, 81–82
    conflicts in, 103–4
    emotional bonding importance,
        44–46, 84–86, 105–6,
        125–26, 217
    evolutionary heritage, 50–54,
        93–94, 104–6
    eye contact importance, 91–92
    healthy, skill development, 91–95

magic ratio, 117–19, 146–47
    mistakes, handling, 126–27
    motivation, fostering, 119–21
    parental influences, 12, 27, 104–6,
        113–14, 137–38
    parenting styles, 106–12, 107t
    parents as successful, 32–33
    positive interactions, 117–18
    positive outcome predictors, 117
    praise for good behaviors, 118
    pre-technology, 22–23
    quality time, 114–15, 146–47
    role modelling, 12, 121–27,
        212–13, 229–30
    self-worth, 92–93, 111
    social cue recognition, 92
    social rejection, 104
    support vs. control, 12
    technojudgment, 25–28, 222
    technology impacts on,
        7–8, 10, 82
    trust in, 151–53
Restaurants, device
    recommendations, 141, 244
Return on investment (ROI), 46–49
Reverse mentoring, 204
Reward prediction errors, 70–71
Reward system (brain), 9, 63, 65, 66,
    68, 70–73, 79, 156–57
Rhesus monkey studies, 44–45
Role modelling, 12, 121–27,
    212–13, 229–30
Ruston, Delaney, 148
Ryan, Richard, 58, 67–68, 111, 119

Schools
    cell phone bans, 205
    cyberbullying, 215–18
    educational technologies in, 202–4

Schools (*cont.*)
   family-school partnering, 205–10
   home, technology management
      in, 210–15
   parent-teacher
      communication, 207–8
   recommendations, 247
   relationships, sustaining, 208–9
   role modelling, 12, 121–27,
      212–13, 229–30
   screen time management, 209–10
   sexting, 215–16, 263–65
   shared values, goals, 208, 211–12
   technology advantages *vs.*
      disadvantages, 204–5
   test scores, technology effects on,
      203, 205
   work/play separation, 210–11,
      247, 259–60
Schwartz, Joseph, 88–89
Screen time
   AAP guidelines, 83, 145
   average *vs.* healthy, 78
   checklist, 2, 13
   children's usage of, 19–25
   classical conditioning,
      69–70, 74–76
   compulsive checking, 72–74, 76
   digital *vs.* real world
      interactions, 59–61
   family evaluation of, 13–14,
      93–97, 124–25
   information, 66
   learning outcomes, 84–86
   likes, 67
   mismatch diseases and, 53–54
   mood effects, 95–97, 101
   nomophobia, 57–58
   novelty, 65

   opportunity cost, 49, 223
   pornography, 67, 149,
      216, 263–65
   productivity and, 98–100,
      182–83, 210–11, 261–63
   psychological needs, 58–59, 65,
      67–68, 72–74, 223
   return on investment
      (ROI), 46–49
   sleep-wake cycle, effects on, 39
   supernormal stimuli (*see*
      supernormal stimuli)
   time limits, setting, 140–41,
      144–47, 175–76, 194, 245–46,
      250–51, 260–61
   variable reinforcement
      schedules, 69–72
   video-game violence effects,
      86–91, 96
   videos, gaming, 66–67
Second-order conditioning, 75
Sedentary lifestyles, happiness and,
   19, 38–39, 52–54
Sedwick, Rebecca Ann, 216
Self-determination theory, 58–59,
   65, 67–68, 110, 119–21, 169
Self-regulation
   decision fatigue, 41–42
   delayed gratification and, 39–40
   development of, 11–13, 24
   motivation, fostering, 119–21
   play and, 24–25
   promotion of, 213–17, 257
Sexting, 215–16, 263–65
Shared values, goals, 208, 211–12
Skinner, B. F., 69–70
Sleep, technology's effects on, 38–39
Smartphones
   as addiction, 4, 61, 73–74

age appropriate, 251–53
benefits of, 196–97
cognitive capacity reduction by,
  43–44, 99–100, 158, 211
contracts, 147–49, 252–53
human attachment effects, 92–95
as learning tool, 85–86, 210
mindfulness practice,
  154–59, 226–27
monitoring, 151–54, 196, 257–59
mood effects of, 98–99
Pokémon Go, 19–20
recommendations, 16, 137–43,
  194, 233, 242–43, 247, 250
research on effects of, 82
self-regulation effects of, 24, 40
sleep effects of, 39
as source of conflict, 19–20, 48
as supernormal stimuli, 66,
  68, 75, 76
usage statistics, 4
work/play separation, 210–11,
  247, 259–60
Snapchat, 253–54
Social connectedness, happiness
  and, 33, 44–46, 59–60
Social media
  benefits, limitations of, 6–7
  likes, 67
  recommendations, 253–54
  relationship building, 94–95
  relationships, impacts on, 7,
    29–30, 44–46
Societal violence, 89–90
Structure, provision of, 211–12
Suicide rates, 36
Supernormal stimuli
  described, 61–62
  human attraction to, 63–64

information, 66
likes, 67
novelty, 65
pornography, 67, 149,
  216, 263–65
role modelling and, 122–23
smartphones as, 66, 68, 75, 76
stimuli hardwired as, 62–63
technology as, 64–68
videos, gaming, 66–67
Surveillance, monitoring *vs.*, 151

Tech Happy Life model
  authoritative parenting, 107*t*, 109
  described, 14–18, 15*f*,
    17*t*, 228–33
  FAQs, 249–68
  Green Light Level (*see* Green
    Light Level)
  parent-child relationships, 17
  principles of, 11–13, 94
  Quick Reference guide, 241–47
  Red Light Level (*see* Red
    Light Level)
  relationship building, 94,
    228–30, 267–68
  video game recommendations, 91
  Yellow Light Level (*see* Yellow
    Light Level)
Technojudgment, 25–28, 222
Technology
  addiction to, 5, 8–9, 57–58, 68,
    73, 78–80, 181–83, 272n10
  adult usage statistics, 8
  balanced approach to, 5–7, 11–13,
    221–22, 235
  developmentally appropriate, 3,
    84–85, 138, 243–44, 249
  development of, 21–22

Technology (*cont.*)
  notifications, turning off,
    138–39, 241–42
  out-of-balance use of, 3–8,
    53–54, 76–78
  pre-technology, 219–20
  pros, cons of, 6–8, 30–34, 225–28
  teens usage statistics, 5
  toddlers/kids usage statistics, 4
  unitasking (monotasking),
    139, 242
Temporal discounting, 40
Time limits, setting, 140–41,
    144–47, 175–76, 194, 245–46,
    250–51, 260–61
Tinbergen, Nikolass, 62
Travel recommendations,
    140–41, 244–45

Unitasking (monotasking), 139, 242

Values/goals, shared, 208, 211–12
Variable ratio reinforcement, 70
Variable reinforcement
    schedules, 69–72
Vegas effect, 70–72, 76
Ventral tegmental area (VTA), 70
Video games
  ADHD and, 98–99
  ESRB rating system, 86, 130,
    245, 254–55
  free play *vs.*, 25

parent-child
    collaboration, 167–68
  recommendations, 91,
    245–47, 254–56
  as supernormal stimuli, 66–67
  violence effects, 86–91, 96
Virilio, Paul, 6, 272n10

Wall-E, 53
Walnut consumption model, 76–78
Ward, Adrian, 100–101, 158
Wearables, 242
Weinstein, Netta, 77–78
Winkler, Alexander, 183
Work/play separation, 210–11,
    247, 259–60

Yellow Light Level
  consequences, 168–76, 266–67
  emerging concerns, 161–64
  parent-child
    collaboration, 167–76
  preventive strategies, 173
  principles of, 15*f*, 16, 17*t*,
    180, 231–32
  recommendations, 164–68
  recreational screen time as
    privilege, 166
  surveillance, 152
  tech-free areas/times, 165–66
  warning signs, 163
  work *vs.* leisure devices, 166